P9-DEC-946

WITHDRAWAL

Modern Historians
on British History, 1485–1945

A critical bibliography, 1945–1969

Modern Historians on British History, 1485-1945

A critical bibliography, 1945-1969

Geoffrey Rudolph

G. R. ELTON

CORNELL UNIVERSITY PRESS
ITHACA, NEW YORK

Copyright © 1970 G. R. Elton

All rights reserved. Except for brief quotations in a review, this book, or parts thereof, must not be reproduced in any form without permission in writing from the publisher. For information address Cornell University Press, 124 Roberts Place, Ithaca, New York 14850.

First published 1970

International Standard Book Number 0-8014-0611-0
Library of Congress Catalog Card Number 77-137676

Printed in Great Britain

Reference
Z
2016
E44
1970a

Contents

Abbreviations	*page*	viii
1 Introduction		1
2 Works of Reference		5
3 Sources		8
a. Collections		8
b. Official Records		9
c. Letters		11
d. Autobiography		13
c. Economic history		15
f. Texts		15
4 General		17
a. Longer periods		17
b. Collections		23
5 The Sixteenth Century (1485 – 1603)		26
a. General		26
b. Political history		28
c. Administration and Constitution		33
d. The Church		37
e. Social and economic history		43
f. Culture and civilization		48
6 The Seventeenth Century (1603 – 1714)		51
a. General		51
b. 1603 – 1640		53

v

c. 1640 – 1660   *page* 57
d. The puritans   62
e. 1660–1714   64
f. Economic history   72
g. Culture and civilization   75

7 The Eighteenth Century (1714 – 1815)   77
a. General   77
b. Political history   78
c. Parliament and parties   82
d. Foreign affairs and war   86
e. Empire   89
f. Administration and Government   90
g. The Church   92
h. Economic history   93

8 The Nineteenth Century (1815 – 1914)   103
a. General   103
b. Political history   105
c. Parliament and parties   113
d. Government   120
e. Foreign affairs   124
f. The Empire   130
g. Economic history   134
h. The Church   141

9 The Twentieth Century (1914 – 1945)   145
a. General   145
b. Political history   146
c. Government   151
d. Foreign affairs   153
e. The Two Wars   155
f. Economic history   161

10 Social History   *page* 163
   a. Welfare   163
   b. Education   166
   c. Printing   170
   d. Law   172

11 History of Ideas   176
   a. Political thought   176
   b. Social thought   185
   c. Historiography   187
   d. Science   191
   e. Religious thought   195

12 Scotland   198
   a. General   198
   b. The sixteenth century   200
   c. The seventeenth century   201
   d. Since 1707   202

13 Ireland   206
   a. Before the Union   206
   b. After the Union   210

  Indexes   217
   a. Authors and editors   217
   b. Subjects   232

Abbreviations

AHR	*American Historical Review*
BIHR	*Bulletin of the Institute of Historical Research*
C	Cambridge
CHJ	*Cambridge Historical Journal*
EcHR¹ *EcHR²*	*Economic History Review*, 1st and 2nd Series
EHR	*English Historical Review*
Ft	*Festschrift*
Hist	*History*
HMSO	Her Majesty's Stationery Office
IHS	*Irish Historical Studies*
JMH	*Journal of Modern History*
L	London
LQR	*Law Quarterly Review*
O	Oxford
PP	*Past and Present*
Rev	Review
RHS	Royal Historical Society
SPCK	Society for the Promotion of Christian Knowledge
TRHS	*Transactions of the Royal Historical Society*
UP	University Press
VS	*Victorian Studies*

I

Introduction

This book grew out of an invitation from the editors of the *Historische Zeitschrift* to produce an article reviewing the writings on modern English history that had appeared since the end of the Second World War; the resulting *Literaturbericht*, running down to May 1967, appeared in *Sonderheft 3* (1969). I am grateful to the *Historische Zeitschrift*, and especially to its now retired editor, Professer W. Kienast, for allowing me to treat that article as my own property. The suggestion made by Mr Peter Wait, of Methuen & Co., that an English version might be useful, found support here and there: hence this book. It differs from the German version in several respects. In the first place, I have continued the story down to the end of 1969. Secondly, the fact that I now have rather more space, and the disquieting discovery of too many omissions, have enabled me to add quite a few items that should have been there before. And lastly, I soon found that it would not be advisable to produce a straight translation. The earlier version was addressed to a German audience unfamiliar with developments in English historiography; the present one thus needs to speak differently and in a different tone. Instead of translating, I have rewritten.

The twenty-five years which have passed since peace restored English scholars to their more normal employment have seen some remarkable transformations in our understanding of English history since the accession of the Tudors. Even though pre-war books and pre-war scholars have not vanished from the field, one may with justice speak of a major renewal and – so far as parts of the story are concerned – of a total reconstitution. There are areas of this history in which nothing written before 1945 can usefully be consulted, and for the whole period it is fair to say that no synthesis – no textbook or general account – of that vintage is any longer at all reliable. There are reasons for this nearly universal replacement of one set of books by another. In the first place, the number of historians working in the field has increased enormously, a fact which may be well measured by a look at the increased size and number of historical journals trying to serve the needs of active writers – and in spite of all the additional pages, it takes longer than ever to get an article into print. But numbers alone prove little: what has increased more significantly is professionalism – a sharper, more precise, more searching attitude to the task of historical study which before the war was distinctly more familiar among medievalists. Add to this the fact that the materials of study have vastly increased, are constantly increasing and cannot, without disaster, be usefully diminished, and the violently active state of affairs in this particular corner of the field will be readily comprehended. Many more historians, many more archives, many new questions, a constant search for new methods of enquiry, and – naturally, in the wake of such things – live and vigorous and often acrimonious debates: English history since 1485 is a seething, heaving territory which it takes unconquerable rashness to review at length. One often feels like a pathfinder, more often like an intruder upon private affairs, and most often like that horseman who galloped across Lake Constance always inches ahead of the breaking ice.

At the same time, this situation offers some justification for an attempt which, in measure, is bound to fail. After a quarter century, the time does seem ripe for some sort of appraisal. Therefore, while in the main I was naturally concerned to provide as full and careful a bibliographical coverage as I could, I also thought it my duty to discuss the historiographical developments as such – to see whether I could discern lines of development, purposes pursued, questions left unanswered or at least open. An essay of this sort needs to be organized, and as anyone who has ever tried his hand at such things will know no scheme can be really satisfactory, let alone perfect. I have tried to minimize the disadvantages which result from dividing historical writings under chronological and topical heads by a good deal of cross-referencing and by providing two indexes, a complete one of authors and a necessarily idiosyncratic one of subjects; both cross-referencing and indexing have been made possible by numbering the bibliographical footnotes through. That some books will still inexplicably occur in what will seem to others the wrong section is something that I accept, not contentedly but regretfully.

Of course, however complete one tries to be, selection is inescapable and in part has been very severe. In particular, I have not been able to include more than a minority of articles and notes, and I am well aware that my judgment of what may be important in that category will differ, sometimes widely, from that of others. I have naturally left out articles that have since become incorporated or absorbed in published books. With respect to books, I have tried to be very much more comprehensive, but even here the mass required sifting. In principle I have tried to confine myself to serious works which contribute either new knowledge, new interpretation or new understanding, but these terms themselves involve constant personal judgments. Some books are not here because I do not think them good enough, others because they have inexcusably escaped my attention; and I propose to offer this double-edged explanation to any author who feels slighted. Judgments and assessments are my own, but I have tried to modify the one-sidedness of this by noting reviews. So far as possible, I have mentioned all reviews and short notices that have appeared in the *English Historical Review* but have drawn on other journals only for reasonably substantial reviews. I have seen no reason to refer to the anonymous and unassessable reviews in the *Times Literary Supplement*.

Apart from accidental or deliberate omissions, three classes of writings have been specifically left out. The enormous production of local historical studies can find accommodation only if the work in question has something of significance to say beyond the strictly local. The history of British expansion and possessions overseas is noted only insofar as the books contribute seriously to the history of the mother-country; the historiography of empire and commonwealth requires a separate volume. And the history of English literature, very relevant though it is for the historian, has also had to be left out, at least as a general rule; some works touching on bibliographical studies or the history of ideas, which their authors may have thought of as belonging to this genre, are here, but in the main this, too, was too mountainous a territory to be managed in the compass.

I am grateful to all those whose bibliographies and footnotes have led me to works I should have been very remiss in not noticing, but the only personal debt I wish to record is to Dr J. Jean Hecht who most kindly drew my attention to some errors in the German version. For this work, I deliberately avoided consulting others; the responsibility for what is in, what is out, and what is said must be mine alone. I have seen virtually all the writings listed; the few which became known to me only indirectly are put in square brackets. Bibliographies ought always to be absolutely accurate but never are. For the mistakes of this one, I would ask not so much forbearance as the sort of annoyance which results in sharp corrective letters to the compiler.

II

Works of Reference

A collection of useful bibliographical articles has been published as a single, somewhat uneven, volume.[1] Read's well-known Tudor bibliography has appeared in a second edition, twice the length of the first and covering down to 1956;[2] a further ten years' yield is added in the first of a handier and more concise bibliographical series.[3] No one has served the seventeenth century since the war; for the eighteenth, we possess the comprehensive work of Pargellis and Medley (fundamental but already sadly out of date),[4] an exhaustive volume for less than thirty years of domestic and imperial history,[5] and a massive list of contemporary writings on economic matters.[6] The supposedly annual volumes in which Milne means to cover current publications for the whole of British history have so far attained only the year 1945.[7] They started in 1933; Mullins provides information on periodical publication down

[1] Elizabeth C. Furber, ed., *Changing Views on British History: essays on historical writing since 1939*. C. (Mass.): Harvard UP: 1966. Pp. xii, 418. *DA 1 F8*

[2] Conyers Read, ed., *Bibliography of British History: Tudor Period*. 2nd ed. O: Clarendon: 1959. Pp. xxviii, 624. Rev: *EHR* 75, 721f. *REF Z 2017.5 R28*

[3] Mortimer Levine, ed., *Bibliographical Handbooks: Tudor England, 1485 – 1603*. CUP: 1968. Pp. xii, 115. *REF Z 2017.5 L4*

[4] Stanley Pargellis and D. J. Medley, eds., *Bibliography of British History: the Eighteenth Century 1714 – 1789*. O: Clarendon: 1951. Pp. xxvi, 642. *REF Z 208 P3*

[5] L. H. Gipson, ed., *Bibliographical Guide to the History of the British Empire, 1748 – 1776*. New York: Knopf: 1969. Pp. xxiii, 478, l. *DA 500 G5*

[6] L. W. Hanson, ed., *Contemporary Printed Sources for British and Irish Economic History, 1701 – 1750*. CUP: 1963. Pp. xxiv, 978. Rev: *EHR* 80, 846f. *REF Z 7165 G8 H35*

[7] A. Taylor Milne, ed., *Writings on British History, 1938; Writings on British History, 1939; Writings on British History, 1940 – 45* (2 vols.). L: Cape: 1951, 1953, 1960. Pp. 333, 310, 1021. *REF Z 2016 R882*

to that date.[8] The same editor has also published a useful guide
list to historical materials published in various series by public
institutions or learned societies; since the book includes only
what is found in the library of the RHS, there are some unexpected gaps.[9] For Wales and Scotland we now possess separate bibliographies, history making its appearance in the
second volume of the Scottish exemplar;[10] as for Ireland, the
periodical *IHS* provides frequent information and especially
an article on sixteenth-century publications.[11] Specialist interests are catered for in Ottley's book on railways and Mrs
Hall's article on the Royal Society.[12]

Many archives are making efforts to bring their collections
to the notice of scholars, though Utopia is still some way off.
In particular, since the war more and more, and ever more
competent, County Record Offices have been set up many of
which publish lists and guides which may be obtained on enquiry. A general list published by HMSO for the Historical
MSS Commission offers the best start for the exploitation of
these useful labours.[13] Among local archives, that of London
must take pride of place from the point of view of general
history; for this there is now a good printed guide.[14] The

REF
Z 5055
G6

REF
Z 2016
M 8

REF
Z 2081
W239

[8] E. L. C. Mullins, ed., *A Guide to the Historical and Archaeological
Publications of Societies in England and Wales, 1901 – 1933*. L: Athlone:
1968. Pp. xiii, 850.

[9] E. L. C. Mullins, ed., *Text and Calendars: an analytical guide to serial
publication*. L: RHS: 1958. Pp. xi, 674. Rev: *EHR* 76, 382.

[10] *A Bibliography of the History of Wales*, prepared by the History and
Law Committee of the Board of Celtic Studies of the University
of Wales. 2nd ed. Cardiff: U of Wales P: 1962. Pp. xviii, 330. –
P. D. Hancock, ed., *Bibliography of Works relating to Scotland, 1916 –
1950* (2 vols.). Edinburgh UP: 1960. Pp. x, 244; viii, 370.

[11] R. Dudley Edwards and David B. Quinn, 'Thirty Years' Work in
Irish History, 1485 – 1603', *IHS* 16 (1968), 15–32.

[12] George Ottley, ed., *A Bibliography of British Railway History*. L:
Allen & Unwin: 1965. Pp. 683. – Marie Boar Hall, 'Sources for the
history of the Royal Society in the seventeenth century', *History of
Science* 5 (1966), 62–76.

[13] *Record Repositories in Great Britain*. L: HMSO: 1964. Pp. xi, 44.

[14] P. E. Jones and R. Smith. *A Guide to the Records in the Corporation of
London Record Office and the Guildhall Library Muniment Room*. L:
English Universities Press: 1951. Pp. 203.

Public Record Office has replaced Giuseppi's well-known *Guide* with a three-volume work; vol. 3 covers effectively the very recent materials.[15] The detailed lists, nearly all until recently available on the spot only, are in process of being published, at the rate of twelve a year, by a new society, able to sell to members only – but very cheaply.[16] The first volume of a specially commissioned series for general sale in this society's publications provides a complete list of all parliamentary materials, 1701 – 50, known to have been printed or now to survive in print.[17]

Deane, Cole and Mitchell have produced two useful collections of statistical tables: the first treats the whole of economic history from the beginning of reliable figures (mostly about 1700), the second (which discusses as well as lists) attends to the problem of economic growth in the last 200 years.[18]

In Colvin's exhaustive general biography of architects, the valuable introduction provides much information especially on the growth of a profession, fact and concept.[19]

Powicke's handbook of chronology has appeared in a second, revised and improved, edition;[20] a second edition of Cheney's handbook of dates is in preparation. A different kind of handbook, in which the materials for historical study are analysed and discussed, covers the sixteenth century.[21]

[15] *Guide to the Contents of the Public Record Office*, 3 vols. L: HMSO: 1963, 1968. Pp. vi, 249, vii, 410; vii, 190.

[16] List and Index Society (address: Swift Ltd., 1–7 Albion Place, St John's Lane, St John's Street, London E.C.1).

[17] Sheila Lambert, ed., *List of House of Commons Sessional Papers, 1701 – 1750*. L: List and Index Society, special series 1: 1968. Pp. xviii, 155.

[18] B. R. Mitchell and Phyllis M. Deane, ed., *Abstract of British Historical Statistics*. CUP: 1962. Pp. xiv, 513. – Phyllis M. Deane and W. A. Cole, *British Economic Growth 1688 – 1959: trends and structure*. 2nd ed., CUP: 1967. Pp. xi, 350.

[19] H. M. Colvin, *Biographical Dictionary of British Architects, 1660 – 1840*. L: Murray: 1954. Pp. xiv, 821. Rev: *EHR* 70, 329f.

[20] F. M. Powicke and E. B. Fryde, ed., *Handbook of British Chronology*. 2nd ed. L: RHS: 1961. Pp. xxxviii, 563.

[21] G. R. Elton, *The Sources of History: England 1200 – 1640*. L: Sources of History Ltd.: 1969. Pp. 255.

III

Sources

(A) COLLECTIONS

The massive series, *English Historical Documents*, edited by D. C. Douglas, has so far yielded five volumes covering the years 1485 – 1558 and 1660 – 1874.[22] The series intends to present a representative selection from every sort of historical source, but this has proved overambitious for the modern period. Nevertheless, there are things of value in these gigantic volumes, and the extended commentaries, though variable in quality (those by Browning and Aspinall stand out), are always worth attention. On the other hand, a two-volume collection of legal and constitutional documents, chosen virtually exclusively from official sources, offers no guidance to the student since its editors were too modest to speak.[23] More useful are four volumes of documents with commentary which, between them, provide the most up-to-date concise analysis of government and constitution between the restoration of strong kingship and the first Ulster crisis.[24]

REF
DA
26
E55

[22] D. C. Douglas (general editor), *English Historical Documents*. L: Eyre & Spottiswoode. Individual volumes: vol. 5, ed. C. H. Williams (1485 – 1558), 1967, pp. xvii, 1087; vol. 8, ed. Andrew Browning (1660 – 1714), 1953, pp. xxxii, 966; vol. 10, ed. D. B. Horn and Mary Ransome (1714 – 83), 1957, pp. xxvii, 972; vol. 11, ed. A. Aspinall and E. A. Smith (1783 – 1832), 1959, pp. xxx, 922; vol. 12, pt. 1, ed. G. M. Young and W. O. Handcock (1833 – 74), 1956, pp. xxiii, 1017. Rev: *EHR*, 69, 487f.; 75, 168ff., 734; 84, 170f.; *HJ* 1, 190ff.

342.42
C824L

[23] W. C. Costin and J. Steven Watson, eds., *The Law and the Constitution: documents 1660 – 1914* (2 vols.). L: Black: 1952. Pp. xviii, 465; xix, 531.

342.4209
E51T

JN 197
K4

[24] G. R. Elton, ed., *The Tudor Constitution, documents and commentary*. CUP: 1960: pp. xvi, 496. Rev: *EHR* 77, 727ff. – John P. Kenyon, ed., *The Stuart Constitution, documents and commentary*. CUP: 1966:

(B) OFFICIAL RECORDS

The Public Record Office's important calendars make snail-like progress, and the cost of these productions has led to a good deal of heart searching. So far, however, no new conclusions have been reached on the best way to render records available, and the series continue, sometimes in modified form.[25] With equal or greater circumspection, the Historical Manuscripts Commission pursues its purpose to make private archives accessible.[26] For the rest (and ignoring the sizable production of such materials in local publications) not a great deal has appeared. Using a roughly chronological order, one may mention a selection of lawsuits heard in the council of Henry VII, with an important and partially correct discussion of the history of the council;[27] a summary edition of the first registers kept in

pp. xvi, 523. Rev: *EHR* 83, 125ff. – E. Neville Williams, ed., *The Eighteenth Century Constitution, documents and commentary 1688 – 1815.* CUP: 1960: pp. xvi, 464. – H. J. Hanham, *The Nineteenth Century Constitution, 1815 – 1914, documents and commentary.* CUP: 1969: pp. xxiv, 486.

[25] (All published L: HMSO). *Calendar of Close Rolls, Henry VII, 1485 – 1500* (1955; pp. vii, 498) and *1500 – 1509* (1963; pp. ix, 517). – *Calendar of Inquisitions Post Mortem, Henry VII*, vol. 3 (1955; pp. vii, 844). – *Calendar of Fine Rolls*, vol. 22, Henry VII (1962; pp. vii, 575). – *Calendar of State Papers Foreign*, vol. 23, 1589 (1950; pp. lxii, 652). – *List and Analysis of State Papers, Foreign Series*, vol. 1, 1589 – 1590 (1964; pp. vii, 562). – *Calendar of State Papers Spanish*, vols. 12 (1949; pp. xxviii, 347) and 13 (1954; pp. xxvii, 482). – *Calendar of State Papers Domestic, James II*, 2 vols. (1960; pp. viii, 578, 554). – *Calendar of Treasury Books*, vols. 20–32, 1705 – 18 (1952 – 57).

[26] (All published L: HMSO). *Manuscripts of the House of Lords*, new series, vols. 9–11 (1949, 1953, 1962; pp. xxxix, 405; lx, 581; xlvii, 566). – *Manuscripts of Lord Polwarth*, vol. 5, 1725 – 80 (1961; pp. xxxvi, 421). – *Manuscripts of A. G. Finch*, vols. 2 and 4, 1691 – 2 (1957, 1965; pp. lviii, 522; xliii, 583). – *Manuscripts of Lord de L'Isle and Dudley*, vols. 5 and 6, 1611 – 98 (1962, 1966; pp. xliii, 488; xix, 169). – *Hastings Manuscripts*, vol. 4, 17th century (1947; pp. li, 463). – *Sackville Manuscripts*, vol. 2: Cranfield Papers 1597 – 1612 (1966; pp. vii, 267). – *Manuscripts of the Marquess of Bath*, vol. 4: Seymour Papers 1532 – 1686 (1968; pp. xx, 457).

[27] C. G. Bayne and W. H. Dunham, eds., *Select Cases in the Council of Henry VII*. L: Quaritch (Selden Soc. vol. 75): 1958. Pp. clxxiv, 197. Rev: *EHR*, 74, 686ff.

the Canterbury office for faculties and licences, created by the Reformation;[28] the remarkable edition (despite some errors quite invaluable) of royal proclamations in the sixteenth century;[29] a calendar which pioneers impressively by making available all the information on the fate of monastic property in one county;[30] the first surviving quarter sessions in Wales, with an excellent discussion of local government;[31] an interesting and, in the main, well edited addition to the materials available for the study of early Stuart parliaments;[32] materials which, though locally found, throw light on the military organization of the king's party in the civil war;[33] an eighteenth-century ambassador's reports from Turkey.[34] Nothing significant thereafter, until one reaches the twentieth century which yields the hefty collection, in three concurrently produced series, of the records of British foreign policy between the two world wars, edited, with the assistance of others, by Woodward and Butler. Only the last series has reached completion, but even so thirty-four volumes have in fact appeared in twenty-five years.[35]

---

[28] D. S. Chambers, ed., *Faculty Office Registers 1534 – 1549*. O: Clarendon: 1966. Pp. lxv, 394.

[29] Paul L. Hughes and James F. Larkin, eds., *Tudor Royal Proclamations*, 3 vols. New Haven: Yale UP: 1964, 1969. Pp. xlvi, 642; xxiii, 548; xiii, 439. Rev: *EHR* 84, 583f.; *HJ* 8, 266ff.

[30] Joyce Youings, ed., *Devon Monastic Lands: calendar of particulars for grants 1536 – 1558*. Torquay: Devon & Cornwall Record Society: 1955. Pp. xxxviii, 154. Rev: *EHR* 71, 669.

[31] W. Ogwen Williams, ed., *Calendar of Caernarvonshire Quarter Session Records*, vol. 1, 1541 – 1558. Caernarvonshire Historical Society: 1956. Pp. cix, 385. Rev: *EHR* 73, 109f.

[32] Elizabeth Read Foster, ed., *Proceedings in Parliament 1610*, 2 vols. New Haven: Yale UP: 1966. Pp. lxix, 366; xxi, 422. Rev: *EHR* 83, 351ff.

[33] Ian Roy, ed., *The Royalist Ordnance Papers 1642 – 1646*. Oxford Record Society Publications 43: 1963/4. Pp. 229. Rev: *EHR* 82, 167.

[34] A. N. Kurat, ed., *The Despatches of Sir Robert Sutton, Ambassador to Constantinople 1710 – 1714*. L: RHS (Camden 3rd Series, vol. 78): 1953. Pp. 220. Rev: *EHR* 69, 338f.

[35] E. L. Woodward, Rohan Butler, J. P. T. Bury, D. Dakin, M. E. Lambert, W. N. Medlicott, eds., *Documents on British Foreign Policy, 1919 – 1939*. L: HMSO. First Series, 1919 – 28, 14 vols. (1947 – 63);

DA
310
67x

J
301
H317

DA
566.7
A18

(C) LETTERS

Rogers has published the letters of Sir Thomas More, illustrating his three characters as humanist, statesman and martyr; a few more have been added by Herbrüggen.[36] The same fate has befallen two Scottish kings whom one may perhaps call the last medieval monarchs of that realm.[37] Lord Mordaunt's letters add to our knowledge of the years in which the puritan Protectorate died the death.[38] The large extant correspondence of Issac Newton is in process of being published; the four volumes to appear so far cover the years of fruitful scientific activity.[39] The War of the Spanish Succession receives thorough attention in the correspondence between the British commander-in-chief and the Dutch grand pensionary.[40] The gigantic new edition of Horace Walpole's letters – admittedly still a leading source for the political and social history of the eighteenth century – has progressed at the most amazing rate; twenty-two volumes have been added to the twelve published before the war, and six more are planned to finish the enterprise.[41] More striking still, in a way, is the edition of Burke's

Second Series, 1929 – 38, 10 vols. (1946 – 69); Third Series, 1930 – 9, 10 vols. (1944 – 61).

[36] Elizabeth F. Rogers, ed., *The Correspondence of Sir Thomas More.* Princeton UP: 1947. Pp. xxiii, 584. Hubertus Schulte Herbrüggen, *Sir Thomas More: Neue Briefe.* Münster: Aschendorff: 1966. Pp. xliv, 131. Rev: *EHR* 82, 832f.

[37] R. K. Hannay, R. L. Mackie, Anne Spilman, eds., *The Letters of James the Fourth, 1505 – 1513.* Edinburgh: Scottish History Soc.: 1953. Pp. lxxii, 338. Rev: *EHR* 69, 439ff. – R. K. Hannay and Denys Hay, eds., *The Letters of James V, 1513 – 1544.* Edinburgh: HMSO: 1954. Pp. xvi, 469. Rev: *EHR* 70, 636ff.

[38] Mary Coate, ed., *The Letter-Book of John Viscount Mordaunt, 1658 – 1660.* L: RHS (Camden 3rd Series, vol. 69): 1945. Pp. xxiv, 196.

[39] H. W. Turnbull and J. F. Scott, eds., *The Correspondence of Isaac Newton,* vols. 1–4, 1661 – 1709. CUP: 1959, 1960, 1961, 1967. Pp. xxxviii, 468; xiii, 551; xviii, 445; xxxii, 578.

[40] B. van 't. Hoff, ed., *The Correspondence 1701 – 1711 of John Churchill, First Duke of Marlborough, and Anthonius Heinsius, Grand Pensionary of Holland.* Utrecht: Kemink en Zoon: 1951. Pp. xix, 640. Rev: *EHR* 68, 613ff.

[41] W. S. Lewis, ed., *Horace Walpole's Correspondence,* vols. 13–34. New Haven: Yale UP: 1948 – 65.

correspondence because this has never been systematically collected before: the enterprise, guided by Copeland, has so far achieved eight volumes and the year 1796.[42] Hoffman has independently produced an edition and discussion of Burke's correspondence with his Irish friend O'Hara and with New York.[43] Aspinall has continued his relentless publication of the letters – all the letters – of George III[44] and George's son, the prince of Wales.[45] Burke is not to be left in undisputed command of the 'projects', and Jeremy Bentham's correspondence comes next: so far two volumes have been published, taking Bentham from three years old to twenty-eight (1780).[46] This work is in the hands of a team; a single-handed devotion to Newman's letters and diaries, which characteristically starts in the first place from his conversion though all is in the end to be in print, has given us nine volumes in nine years.[47] The correspondence, between Gladstone and Granville has much importance for

---

DA
506
I39
A-18

[42] *The Correspondence of Edmund Burke* (CUP): vol. 1, 1744 – 68, ed. T. Copeland (1958; pp. xxvi, 377; Rev: *EHR* 75, 135f.); vol. 2, 1768 – 74, ed. Lucy S. Sutherland (1960; pp. xxiii, 566); vol. 3, 1774 – 8, ed. G. H. Guttridge (1961; pp. xxvi, 479); vol. 4, 1778–82, ed. John A. Woods (1963; pp. xxiv, 475); vol. 5, 1782 – 9, ed. Holden Furber (1965; pp. xxx, 496); vol. 6, 1789 – 91, ed. A. B. Cobban and R. A. Smith (1967; pp. xxvi, 495); vol. 7, 1792 – 4, ed. Peter J. Marshall and J. A. Woods (1968; pp. xxiv, 615); vol. 8, 1794 – 6, ed. R. B. McDowell (1969; pp. xxv, 475).

942.079
B959h

[43] Ross J. S. Hoffman, *Edmund Burke, New York Agent, 1761–1776*. Philadelphia: American Philosophical Society: 1956. Pp. xiii, 632. Rev: *EHR* 73, 313ff.

DA 505
A2 A4

[44] A. Aspinall, ed., *The Later Correspondence of George III*, 4 vols. (out of 5). CUP: 1962, 1963, 1967, 1968. Pp. xlvi, 688; xlii, 676; xxxii, 671; li, 704.

DA 538
A1 A3

[45] A. Aspinall, ed., *The Correspondence of George Prince of Wales*, 6 vols. (out of 7). L: Cassell: 1963 – 9. Pp. xii, 528; xi, 591; x, 519; xii, 590; xii, 561; 565.

B1579
B34 A4

[46] Timothy L. S. Sprigge, ed., *The Correspondence of Jeremy Bentham*, vols. 1 and 2, to 1780. L: Athlone: 1968. Pp. xli, 383; xiv, 542. Rev: *EHR* 85, 129 H.; *JMH* 41, 189ff.

BX 4705
N5 A4

[47] Charles S. Dessain, ed., *The letters and Diaries of John Henry Newman*, vols. 11-19, Oct. 1845–June 1861. L: Nelson: 1961-9. Pp. xxviii, 363; xiv, 441; xiv, 520; xviii, 555; xvi, 568; xvii, 627; xviii, 602; xvi, 624; xvii, 594. Rev: *EHR* 79, 627.

both foreign and domestic history.[48] Conzemius offers new raw
material for the major industry which, perhaps surprisingly,
has grown up around Lord Acton.[49] Drus cites and discusses the papers which prove Joseph Chamberlain's complicity
in the Jameson Raid.[50] Though they have only partial interest
for English history, the four volumes extracted from Jan
Smuts's vast private archive deserve mention.[51] And for historians, at least, Maitland's letters make a welcome book.[52]

(D) AUTOBIOGRAPHY

Osborn discovered and published the fascinating autobiography
of an unusual Elizabethan – pedant, musician and spelling
reformer.[53] Henslowe's well-known diary has at last been
properly edited.[54] Elias Ashmole, multiple man of learning,
emerges from his notes and letters as a rather tedious antiquary
and querulous collector.[55] The Restoration appears in the

---

[48] Agatha Ramm, ed., *The Political Correspondence of Mr Gladstone and
Lord Granville 1868 – 1874*, 2 vols. L: RHS (Camden 3rd Series,
vols. 81–2): 1952. Pp. xix, 518. Rev: *EHR* 68, 289ff. – Idem, *The
Political Correspondence of Mr Gladstone and Lord Granville 1876 – 1886*,
2 vols. O: Clarendon: 1962. Pp. xlviii, 482; 509. Rev: *EHR* 79,
573ff.

[49] Victor Conzemius, *Ignaz v. Döllinger: Briefwechsel mit Lord Acton,
1850 – 1870*, 2 vols. Munich: Beck: 1963, 1965. Pp. xlvii, 580; xi,
468. Rev: *EHR* 81, 190f., and 83, 803ff.; *HJ* 9, 140ff. and 10, 318ff.

[50] Ethel Drus, 'A report on the papers of Joseph Chamberlain relating
to the Jameson Raid and the Inquiry', *BIHR* 25 (1952), 33–64.

[51] W. K. Hancock and Jean Van der Poel, eds., *Selections from the
Smuts Papers, 1886 – 1919*, 4 vols. CUP: 1966. Pp. xiv, 663; v, 638;
v, 688; 461.

[52] C. H. S. Fifoot, ed., *The Letters of F. W. Maitland*. CUP: 1965.
Pp. xxiv, 397. Rev: *EHR* 82, 359ff.

[53] James M. Osborn, ed., *The Autobiography of Thomas Whythorne*. O:
Clarendon: 1961. Pp. lxvi, 328.

[54] R. A. Foakes and R. T. Rickert, eds., *Henslowe's Diary*. CUP:
1961. Pp. lix, 367.

[55] C. H. Josten, ed., *Elias Ashmole (1617 – 1692): his autobiographical
and historical notes, his correspondence and other contemporary sources
relating to his life and work*, 5 vols. O: Clarendon: 1966. Pp. xx, 2065.
Rev: *EHR* 83, 355ff.

diary kept by one Thomas Rugg;[56] seventeenth-century book-trade practices in one kept by two printers;[57] more general trade practices in the memoirs of a Quaker who enriched himself on spices and iron;[58] parliamentary affairs in the age of Walpole in a belated example of a private member's diary.[59] The extensive records kept by Humfrey Wanley greatly illumine the history of historical writing and the fortunes of the Harleian library and collection at the start of the eighteenth century.[60] De Beer's definitive edition of Evelyn's *Diary* contains an important historical introduction in volume 1.[61] The notes etc. of Joseph Spence are in the main of interest to literary history, especially to that of Alexander Pope.[62] Aspinall, indefatigable editor, illustrates the crisis of the Great Reform Bill by means of three separate diaries.[63] The most massive diaries of all are those of Gladstone which Foot is bravely editing; two volumes, covering fourteen years, have appeared, and one can only hope that the future will justify the policy of total printing.[64] For the great man's first admin-

---

[56] William L. Sachse, *The Diurnal of Thomas Rugg, 1659 – 1661*. L: RHS (Camden 3rd Series, vol. 91): 1961. Pp. xxi, 203. Rev: *EHR* 78, 175f.

[57] Norma Hodgson and Cyprian Blagden, eds., *The Notebook of Thomas Bennet and Henry Clements (1686 – 1719) with some aspects of book trade practice*. O: Oxford Bibliographical Soc. Publications, new series, vol. 6: 1956 (for 1953). Pp. viii, 228. Rev: *EHR* 72, 546f.

[58] J. D. Marshall, ed., *The Autobiography of William Stout of Lancaster 1665 – 1752*. Manchester UP: 1967. Pp. viii, 311.

[59] Aubrey N. Newman, *The Parliamentary Diary of Sir Edward Knatchbull, 1722 – 1730*. L: RHS (Camden 3rd Series, vol. 94): 1963. Pp. xiv, 162. Rev: *EHR* 80, 602.

[60] C. E. and Ruth C. Wright, eds., *The Diary of Humfrey Wanley, 1715 – 1726*, 2 vols. L: OUP: 1966. Pp. xcv, 518. Rev: *EHR* 83, 186f.

[61] Esmond S. de Beer, ed., *The Diary of John Evelyn*, 6 vols. O: Clarendon: 1955. Pp. xiv, 171; vii, 579; x, 639; ix, 654; viii, 622; 630.

[62] James M. Osborn, ed., *Joseph Spence: Observations, Anecdotes and Characters*, 2 vols. O: Clarendon: 1966. Pp. civ, 939.

[63] A. Aspinall, ed., *Three Early Nineteenth Century Diaries*. L: Williams and Norgate: 1952. Pp. lxx, 402. Rev: *EHR* 68, 99ff.

[64] M. R. D. Foot, ed., *The Gladstone Diaries*, vols. 1 and 2. O: Clarendon: 1968. Pp. xlix, 596; vii, 699. Rev: *Hist* 55, 142f.

Z 720
W26 A3

992.075
A 841 T

DA 563
A34

istration, the memoirs of the earl of Kimberley contribute some
sombre information.[65] The beginnings of social democracy in
England are given the dimension of personality but also the
butcher's treatment in the diaries of Beatrice Webb, sharp of
mind and sharper of tongue.[66]

(E) ECONOMIC HISTORY

Once again, when local historical publications are removed,
there is little to report. Willan studies the Tudor customs system
through a book of rates.[67] Smit supplies massive and so far
barely exploited source material for the history of a sixteenth-
century trade.[68] Batho enables one to understand the administration of a noble estate.[69] Demography benefits from the
edition (not entirely reliable) of a list of London's inhabitants
in 1695.[70] Minchinton prints important Bristol materials.[71]

(F) TEXTS

Here, too, the sixteenth century predominates. Hay has edited
afresh the last books of Polydore Vergil's history, with an
excellent translation; these cover the years for which Polydore

---

[65] Ethel Drus, ed., *A Journal of Events during the Gladstone Ministry,
1868 – 1874*. L: RHS (Camden 3rd Series, vol. 90): 1958. Pp. xx, 49.

[66] Margaret Cole, ed., *Beatrice Webb: Diaries*, 2 vols. (1912 – 24,
1924 – 32). L: Longmans: 1952, 1956. Pp. xxvi, 272; xxv, 327.
Rev: *EHR* 68, 293ff.

[67] T. S. Willan, ed., *A Tudor Book of Rates*. Manchester UP: 1962.
Pp. lx, 97.

[68] H. J. Smit, ed., *Bronnen tot geschiedenis van den handel met Engeland,
Schotland en Irland 1485 – 1585*, 2 vols. The Hague: Nijhoff: 1942,
1950. Pp. xv, 1571. Rev: *EHR* 65, 392ff; 66, 583ff.

[69] G. R. Batho, ed., *The Household Papers of Henry Percy, ninth earl of
Northumberland, 1564 – 1632*. L: RHS (Camden 3rd Series, vol. 93):
1962. Pp. lvii, 190.

[70] *London Inhabitants within the Walls 1695*, with an introduction by
D. V. Glass. L: London Record Society: 1966. Pp. xliii, 337. Rev:
Hist 53, 428f.

[71] Walter E. Minchinton, ed., *The Trade of Bristol in the Eighteenth
Century*. Bristol Record Soc. Publications, vol. 20: 1957. Pp. xxv,
210.

was a contemporary witness.[72] Yale University's enterprise for
the republication of all Thomas More's works has so far produced *Richard III* and *Utopia*, the latter volume containing an
exceptionally important analytical and philosophical discussion by Hexter.[73] The interesting and somewhat hypocritical
treatise on the state which Edmund Dudley, Henry VII's
fallen minister, wrote in prison, has been handsomely edited.[74]
We now have a new and accurate edition of Cavendish's *Life
of Wolsey*.[75] A new collection of Wyatt papers throws light on
the rebel but not on his father, the poet.[76] Peel, and since Peel's
death his collaborator Carlson on his own, have continued to
bring out the writings of the Elizabethan puritans.[77] And in an
unexpected place one finds the only decent edition of the works
of Halifax, the Trimmer, with an excellent introduction.[78]

[72] Denys Hay, ed., *The Anglica Historia of Polydore Vergil. A.D. 1485 –
1537*. L: RHS (Camden 3rd Series, vol. 74): 1950. Pp. xlii, 373.
[73] *The Complete Works of St. Thomas More*. New Haven: Yale UP.
Vol. 2: *The History of King Richard III*, ed. Richard S. Sylvester;
1963; pp. cvi, 312. – Vol. 4: *Utopia*, ed. Edward Surtz and J. H.
Hexter; 1965; pp. cxciv, 629; Rev: *EHR* 82, 158f.; *PP* 38, 153ff.
[74] Edmund Dudley, *The Tree of Commonwealth*, ed. D. M. Brodie.
CUP: 1948. Pp. viii, 111.
[75] Richard S. Sylvester, ed., *The Life and Death of Cardinal Wolsey*.
L: OUP for Early English Text Soc.: 1959. Pp. xli, 304.
[76] David M. Loades, ed., *The Papers of George Wyatt Esq*. L: RHS
(Camden 4th Series, vol. 5): 1968. Pp. xi, 261.
[77] Albert Peel, ed., *Tracts Ascribed to Richard Bancroft*. CUP: 1953.
Pp. xxix, 169. Rev: *EHR* 70, 150f. – Albert Peel and Leland H.
Carlson, eds., *Elizabethan Nonconformist Tracts*. L: Allen & Unwin:
I. *Cartwrightiana* (1951; pp. xii, 268); II. *The Writings of Robert
Harrison and Robert Browne* (1953; pp. xii, 560); III. *The Writings
of Henry Barrow 1587 – 1590* (1962; pp. xiv, 680); IV. *The Writings of
John Greenwood* (1962; pp. 344); V. *The Writings of Henry Barrow
1590 – 1591* (1966; pp. x, 397).
[78] George Savile, Marquess of Halifax, *Complete Works*, ed. John P.
Kenyon. Harmondsworth: Penguin Books: 1969. Pp. 346.

DA20
R71 3d SERIES
    v.74

PR 2321
A1 1963
PR 3321
A1 1963

74 Edmund Dudley

PR 1119
A2 NO. 243

DA 20
R913
V.5

BX 9339
C3 A3
BX 7117
H3 1753

IV

General

(A) LONGER PERIODS

General histories of Britain have appeared, but they all leave a good deal to be desired. Feiling's book, though already somewhat out of date and not exactly a work of art, at least puts together a usable picture and account;[79] the two volumes in the Michigan 'History of the World' need to be treated with much care.[80] Cantor's remarkable mixture of straight, somewhat old-fashioned, history, and subtle and rather modern historiography contains some new insights.[81] Covering only half the period, Webb does better with a lively, beautifully written treatment of some 200 years which gains greatly from the author's relative distance from conventional accounts.[82]

Betty Kemp's brief survey of the troubles between king and parliament benefits from the choice of an unusual pair of terminal dates.[83] More original, but unhappily not as reliable, exhaustive or lucid as might be wished, are the studies in parliamentary business to which Orlo Williams was inspired by his professional experience as a clerk to the commons; his work enshrines some traditions of the house which might otherwise

---

[79] Keith Feiling, *A History of England from the Coming of the English to 1938*. L: Macmillan: 1950. Pp. xxxiv, 1229. Rev: *AHR* 57, 121ff.

[80] Maurice Ashley, *Great Britain to 1688*. Ann Arbor: U of Michigan P: 1961. Pp. xi, 444, xxii. – K. B. Smellie, *Great Britain since 1688*. *Ibid.*: 1962. Pp. vi, 462, xviii.

[81] Norman F. Cantor, *The English: to 1760*. New York: Simon & Schuster: 1967. Pp. 526.

[82] Robert K. Webb, *Modern England: from the eighteenth century to the present*. L: Allen & Unwin: 1969. Pp. xviii, 652.

[83] Betty Kemp, *King and Parliament 1660 – 1832*. L: Macmillan: 1957. Pp. vii, 168. Rev: *EHR* 73, 354.

have been lost.[84] The most important enterprise in parliamentary history is, no doubt, that undertaken by the 'History of Parliament Trust' with its plan to compose biographies of all known members of the commons and thus to reveal the political structure of the house. Since so far only three volumes, covering part of the eighteenth century, have appeared, judgment must remain reserved about the outcome of all that labour.[85]

Too few general histories have been written about agencies of government, the best – and most courageous – being Roseveare's study of the treasury, which also usefully reveals how much more we need to learn.[86] Craig's study of the London mint is superficial;[87] Robinson does a little better for the post office.[88] From the college of heralds comes a historical compendium on all aspects of genealogy.[89] The lowest administrative division is made accessible to both professional and amateur historians by Tate's study of materials.[90] There has been some swift sailing over the oceans: the first volume of a general (and rather simple) naval history comes down to 1776;[91] a more expert hand offers to paint the navy's por-

---

[84] Orlo C. Williams, *The Historical Development of Private Bill Procedure and Standing Orders in the House of Commons*, 2 vols. L: HMSO: 1948/9.Pp. x, 340; xiii, 283. – Idem, *The Clerical Organisation of the House of Commons 1661 – 1850*. O: Clarendon: 1954. Pp. xv, 366. Rev: *EHR* 71, 104ff.

[85] Lewis B. Namier and John Brooke, *The History of Parliament: the House of Commons 1754 – 1790*, 3 vols. L: HMSO: 1964. Pp. xx, 545; viii, 692; viii, 685. Rev: *EHR* 80, 801ff.

[86] Henry Roseveare, *The Treasury: the evolution of a British institution*. L: Allen Lane The Penguin Press: 1969. Pp. 406.

[87] John Craig, *The Mint: a history of the London Mint from A.D. 287 to 1948*. CUP: 1953. Pp. xviii, 450. See also his *Newton at the Mint*, CUP 1946, pp. 128, for Newton's activity as master of the mint and currency reformer.

[88] Howard Robinson, *The British Post Office: a history*. Princeton UP: 1948. Pp. xvii, 467.

[89] Anthony R. Wagner, *English Genealogy*. O: Clarendon: 1960. Pp. xii, 397.

[90] W. E. Tate, *The Parish Chest: a study of the records of parish administration in England*. CUP: 1951 (2nd ed.). Pp. xi, 346.

[91] G. J. Marcus, *A Naval History of England*, vol. 1: the formative centuries. L: Longmans: 1961. Pp. xii, 494.

HJ 1037
R65

929.10942
W132e

942
M322N

trait;[92] and Richmond produced no less than two highly elegant summaries of the commonplaces touching the role of sea-power.[93]

With respect to economic history, Clapham and Court have tried to do the impossible by summarizing the state of knowledge; however, despite the inevitable shortcomings (especially the fact that in this area knowledge constantly changes and increases), the two books offer a fair start on the problems.[94] There have been three interesting investigations of the history of economic theory: Tucker deals with two centuries of thinking about the connection between the rate of interest and the rate of growth,[95] Schulin reviews writings about trade from Thomas More to Daniel Defoe,[96] and Letwin, choosing a shorter period, thoroughly analyses the first century of really specialized work on economic matters in general.[97] Agriculture is served by Fussell's mildly antiquarian compilations about village life;[98] but also, more searchingly, by Thirsk's study of

[92] Michael A. Lewis, *The Navy of Britain: a historical portrait.* L: Allen & Unwin: 1948. Pp. 660.

[93] Herbert Richmond, *Statesmen and Seapower.* O: Clarendon: 1946. Pp. xi, 369. – Idem, *The Navy as an Instrument of Policy.* CUP: 1963. Pp. 404. Rev: *EHR* 69, 442ff.

[94] John Clapham, *A Concise Economic History of Britain from Earliest Times to 1750.* CUP 1949. Pp. xv, 324. – W. H. B. Court, *A Concise Economic History of Britain from 1750 to Recent Times.* CUP 1954. Pp. viii, 368. Rev: *EcHR*² 8, 452f.

[95] G. S. L. Tucker, *Progress and Profit in British Economic Thought 1650 – 1850.* CUP 1969. Pp. viii, 206. Rev: *EcHR*² 14, 149f.

[96] Ernst Schulin, *Handelsstaat England.* Wiesbaden: Steiner: 1969. Pp. xi, 390.

[97] William Letwin, *The Origins of Scientific Economics: English economic thought, 1660 – 1776.* L: Methuen: 1963. Pp. x, 316.

[98] G. E. Fussell, *The Old English Farming Books from Fitzherbert to Tull, 1523 – 1730.* L: Crosby Longwood: 1947. Pp. 141. – Idem, *The English Rural Labourer.* L: Batchworth: 1949. Pp. 160. – Idem, *The Farmer's Tools 1500 – 1900.* L: Melrose: 1952. Pp. 246. Rev: *EHR* 68, 437f. – Idem, *The English Dairy Farmer, 1500 – 1900.* L: Cass: 1966. Pp. 357. – Idem, with K. R. Fussell, *The English Country Woman 1500 – 1900.* L: Melrose: 1953. Pp. 221. Rev: *EHR* 69, 483. – Idem et eadem, *The English Countryman, his Life and Work, A.D. 1500 – 1900.* Pp. 221. L: Melrose: 1955.

one important region[99] and Kerridge's pugnacious (and convincing) attempt to demonstrate that the most important transformations took place before 1650.[100] Hoskins's essays on agrarian problems in the Midlands have served to define the sort of local history which, by tackling the real questions, contributes substantially to all sorts of general enquiries.[101] Ramsay provides a useful first introduction to the history of trade in the sixteenth and seventeenth centuries.[102] Two German works apply statistical methods to trade and industry since 1700; both no doubt contribute some unusual expertise and some stimulating ideas, but neither seems sufficiently secure in the use of historical materials and method to be trusted without reservation.[103] Two studies concern themselves at length with particular industries: Coleman on paper is excellent, Schubert on iron less satisfactory.[104] An interesting contrast is provided by two leading scholars who each undertook to review the British economy since about 1750: Hobsbawm, impressionistic and literary, mingles brilliance with

---

[99] Joan Thirsk, *English Peasant Farming: the agrarian history of Lincolnshire from Tudor to recent times*. L: Routledge: 1957. Pp. xv, 350. Rev: *EcHR*² 11, 159f.

[100] Eric Kerridge, *The Agrarian Revolution*. L: Allen & Unwin: 1967. Pp. 428.

[101] W. G. Hoskins, *Essays in Leicestershire History*. Liverpool UP: 1950. Pp. viii, 196. – Idem, *Provincial England: essays in social and economic history*. L: Macmillan: 1963. Pp. xii, 236. – Idem, *The Midland Peasant: the economic and social history of a Leicestershire village*. L: Macmillan: 1957. Pp. xii, 322.

[102] G. D. Ramsay, *English Overseas Trade during the Centuries of Emergence*. L: Macmillan: 1957. Pp. x, 279. Rev. *EHR* 73, 346f.

[103] W. Schlote, *British Overseas Trade from 1700 to the 1930s*, trs. W. O. Henderson and W. H. Chaloner. O: Blackwell: 1952. Pp. xv, 181. – W. G. Hoffmann, *British Industry 1700 – 1950*, trs. W. O. Henderson and W. H. Chaloner. *Ibid.*: 1955. Pp. xxvi, 338. Rev: *EHR* 71, 654f.

[104] Donald C. Coleman, *The British Paper Industry 1495 – 1860*. O: Clarendon: 1958. Pp. xvi, 367. Rev: *EHR* 74, 526f.; *EcHR*² 11, 524f. – H. R. Schubert, *History of the British Iron & Steel Industry from c. 450 B.C. to A.D. 1775*. L: Routledge: 1957. Pp. xxi, 445. Rev: *EcHR*² 11, 157f.

some hair-raising scampers,[105] while Mathias, though less readable, provides a very solid foundation of fact and analysis.[106] In economic history, things are so much on the move that the serious results of enquiry are often to be found only in articles, a fact which makes the several collections of such pieces most welcome: three volumes of assorted goods from the *EcHR*,[107] two of specialist stuff about agriculture,[108] and one more specialized still on the vital problem of population (containing in Part II ten pieces on Great Britain, 1700 – 1850).[109]

A few books in which topics of various kinds are treated at greater temporal length may be listed together. Allen reviews, lucidly and sovereignly, the relations between Britain and the United States.[110] Williams's history of Wales since 1484 fills a very noticeable gap.[111] Aveling for once takes the history of persecuted Roman Catholics beyond the reign of James I.[112] At last one of the many remarkable landed families of England has found a serious historian to chronicle its fortunes and pos-

---

[105] Eric J. Hobsbawm, *Industry and Empire: an economic history of Britain since 1750*. L: Weidenfeld: 1968. Pp. xiv, 336. Rev: *EcHR*² 22, 140f.; *Hist* 54, 293f.

[106] Peter Mathias, *The First Industrial Nation*. L: Methuen: 1969. Pp. xiv, 522. Rev: *EcHR*² 22, 563.

[107] E. M. Carus-Wilson, ed., *Essays in Economic History*, 3 vols. L: Arnold: 1954, 1962. Pp. viii, 438; viii, 373; viii, 373.

[108] Walter E. Minchinton, ed., *Essays in Agricultural History*, 2 vols. Newton Abbot: David & Charles: 1968. Pp. 263; 315.

[109] David V. Glass and D. E. C. Eversley, eds., *Population in History: essays in historical demography*. L: Arnold: 1965. Pp. ix, 692. Rev: *EHR* 82, 217f.

[110] Harry C. Allen, *Great Britain and the United States: a history of Anglo-American relations 1783 – 1952*. L: Odham's: 1954. Pp. 1024. Rev: *EHR* 70, 467ff.

[111] David Williams, *A History of Modern Wales*. L: Murray: 1950. Pp. 308. Rev: *AHR* 56, 98ff.

[112] Hugh Aveling, 'The Catholic recusants of the West Riding of Yorkshire', *Proceedings of the Leeds Literary and Philosophical Society*, 10 (1963), 191–306. – Idem, *Northern Catholics: the Catholic recusants of the North Riding of Yorkshire 1558 – 1790*. L: Chapman: 1966. Pp. 477. Rev: *EHR* 83, 601f. – Idem, *Post-Reformation Catholicism in East Yorkshire 1558 – 1790*. East Yorkshire Local History Society: 1960. Pp. 70.

sessions.[113] Transport, still a somewhat neglected field, is surveyed in a volume which apparently (and unexpectedly) has a few gaps in it, but pioneers most worthily.[114] Two volumes, one a collection of essays, attend to the history of the Jews in England.[115] Two towns have received serious attention, although, perhaps, the history of dissent in Exeter, in itself a thorough and competent study,[116] can hardly be regarded as equal to the exceptionally good history that has been written for Birmingham.[117] The early history of a more or less civil maritime organization explains something about the rise of England's naval power.[118] A book on censorship – the effect of printing on government and of government on printing – is welcome, but Siebert's study is both too legalistic and too obviously the outcome of an interest in the American aspect of the problem.[119] The relatively new discipline of scientific demography yields both a general introduction (in a mixed collection of essays)[120] and an informative example in Hollingsworth's tabulated, statistical analysis of the peerage through four centuries (1550 – 1950).[121] It is rather a jump from the pro-

[113] Aubrey N. Newman, *The Stanhopes of Chevening: a family biography*. L: Macmillan: 1969. Pp. 414. Rev: *Hist* 55, 130.

[114] [H. J. Dyos and D. H. Aldcroft, *British Transport: an economic survey from the seventeenth century to the twentieth*. Leicester UP: 1969. Pp. 473.]

[115] Albert M. Hyamson, *The Sephardim of England: a history of the Spanish and Portuguese Jewish community 1492 – 1951*. L: Methuen: 1951. Pp. xii, 468. – V. P. Lipmann, ed., *Three Centuries of Anglo-Jewish History*. C: Heffer: 1961. Pp. xi, 201.

[116] A. Brockett, *Nonconformity in Exeter 1650 – 1875*. Manchester UP: 1962. Pp. vii, 252.

[117] Conrad Gill and Asa Briggs, *History of Birmingham*, 2 vols. L: OUP: 1952. Pp. xv, 454; xi, 384. Rev: *EHR* 68, 270ff.

[118] G. G. Harris, *The Trinity House at Deptford, 1514 – 1660*. L: Athlone: 1969. Pp. xii, 310.

[119] Frederick S. Siebert, *Freedom of the Press in England, 1476 – 1776: the rise and decline of government controls*. Urbana: U of Illinois P: 1952. Pp. xiv, 411.

[120] E. A. Wrigley, ed., *An Introduction to English Historical Demography from the sixteenth to the nineteenth century*. L: Weidenfeld: 1966. Pp. xii, 283. Rev: *EcHR*[2] 20, 140ff.

[121] T. H. Hollingsworth, *The Demography of the British Peerage*. Supplement to *Population Studies*, vol. 18, no. 2, 1965. Pp. iv, 108.

CS439
S84
1969

HE 244
D93

Z657
S58x

HB 3583
W7 1966

mising refinement of such work to the very old-fashioned mud-
dle of what has been done to the Society for the Propagation
of the Gospel.[122] A general history of retailing, amusing but
also informative, may conclude this section.[123]

(B) COLLECTIONS

Hexter's beautifully written essays – sharp, exhilarating, but
also searching – touch both upon some problems of early
modern history and on general historiographical issues: no
undergraduate should fail to read them, while his seniors have
all already done so.[124] For the rest, there is a surprising and
augmenting number of those usually worthy tributes presented
to revered scholars for which there is no English name; particularly important contributions to such *Festschriften* will be
listed in appropriate places later. The volume for Sir John
Neale contains essays on the social and administrative history
of the reign of Elizabeth I.[125] That dedicated to R. H. Tawney
deals with a variety of aspects of 'his' century (1540 – 1640)
without ever discovering a centre of gravity.[126] Diplomatic and
political problems of about the same era predominate in the
posthumous *Festschrift* for Garrett Mattingly.[127] E. Harris
Harbinson also, unhappily, did not live to read the interesting

[122] Henry P. Thompson, *Into All Lands: a history of the Society for the Propagation of the Gospel in Foreign Parts, 1701 – 1950.* L: SPCK: 1951. Pp. xv, 760. Rev: *EHR* 67, 583ff.

[123] Dorothy Davis, *A History of Shopping.* L: Routledge: 1966. Pp. xii, 322. Rev: *JMH* 40, 538f.

[124] J. H. Hexter, *Reappraisals in History.* L: Longmans: 1961. Pp. xxi, 214. Rev: *EHR* 78, 726ff.

[125] S. T. Bindoff, Joel Hurstfield, C. H. Williams, eds., *Elizabethan Government and Society: essays presented to Sir John Neale.* L: Athlone: 1961. Pp. x, 423. Rev: *EHR* 77, 532ff.

[126] F. J. Fisher, ed., *Essays in the Economic and Social History of Tudor and Stuart England in Honour of R. H. Tawney.* CUP: 1961. Pp. 235. Rev: *EHR* 78, 135ff.

[127] Charles H. Carter, ed., *From the Renaissance to the Counter-Reformation: essays in honour of Garrett Mattingly.* New York: Random House: 1965. Pp. vii, 417. Rev: *EHR* 83, 599f.

studies, again in the same period, intended for him.[128] The volumes for David Ogg[129] and Keith Feiling[130] present somewhat mixed menus of mainly seventeenth-century matters. Mark Thomson, yet another honorand who died too soon, received a mixture of his own and other people's work on international affairs late in that century.[131] Church history naturally dominates the volume (again posthumous) for Norman Sykes.[132] Trevelyan was offered a mixture, in part interesting in part strange, of studies in social history.[133] More rigorous economic history makes its appearance in the agrarian studies inspired by David Chambers.[134] Namier earned a volume which did justice to both his chief interest in parliamentary history and his side-interest in nineteenth-century diplomacy.[135] T. S. Ashton had exceptional cause to be proud of the important articles offered up by friends and pupils.[136] Where so much was posthumous, it is gratifying to be able to point out that the important collection of nineteenth-century studies presented to Kitson Clark has in no sense signalled the hono-

---

CB361
A25

9D8.2
B433h
1963

DA26
T7
1965

DA47.1
T418
1968

BR755
B4
1966a

942.004
P739S

HC254.5
L3
1967

904
P228e

338.0942
P935S

[128] Theodore K. Rabb and J. E. Seigel, eds., *Action and Conviction in Early Modern Europe*. Princeton UP: 1969. Pp. xii, 463.

[129] H. E. Bell and Richard L. Ollard, eds., *Historical Essays 1600 – 1750 presented to David Ogg*. L: Black: 1963. Pp. xi, 274. Rev: *EHR* 80, 124f.

[130] Hugh R. Trevor-Roper, ed., *Essays in British History presented to Sir Keith Feiling*. L: Macmillan: 1964. Pp. ix, 305.

[131] Ragnhild Hatton and J. S. Bromley, eds., *William III and Louis XIV: essays 1680 – 1720 by and for Mark A. Thomson*. Liverpool UP: 1968. Pp. ix, 332. Rev: *EHR* 84, 356ff.

[132] G. V. Bennett and J. D. Walsh, eds., *Essays in Modern English Church History in Memory of Norman Sykes*. L: Black: 1966. Pp. x, 227.

[133] J. H. Plumb, ed., *Studies in Social History: tribute to G. M. Trevelyan*. L: Longmans: 1955. Pp. 287.

[134] E. L. Jones and G. E. Mingay, eds., *Land, Labour and Population in the Industrial Revolution*. L: Arnold: 1967. Pp. xvii, 286. Rev: *EHR* 84, 403f.; *EcHR*[2] 22, 353f.

[135] Richard Pares and A. J. P. Taylor, eds., *Essays presented to Sir Lewis Namier*. L: Macmillan: 1956. Pp. viii, 542.

[136] L. S. Presnell, ed., *Studies in the Industrial Revolution presented to T. S. Ashton*. L: Athlone: 1960. Pp. 350. Rev: *EHR* 76, 733f.

rand's withdrawal from the field.[137] Straight diplomatic history (since 1800) quite rightly fills the volume for W. N. Medlicott,[138] and a charming mixture of philosophy and history with equal justice that for Michael Oakeshott.[139]

[137] Robert Robson, ed., *Ideas and Institutions of Victorian Britain*. L: Bell: 1967. Pp. viii, 343. Rev: *EHR* 84, 202f.; *VS* 11, 407f.
[138] Kenneth Bourne and D. C. Watt, eds., *Studies in International History*. L: Longmans: 1967. Pp. xiii, 446. Rev: *EHR* 84, 640.
[139] Preston King and B. C. Parekh, *Politics and Experience*. CUP: 1968. Pp. vii, 424.

V

The Sixteenth Century (1485 – 1603)

Also nn. 1–3, 24–31, 36–7, 53–4, 67–9, 72–7, 1024, 1037, 1041–3, 1055, 1065–6, 1088–9, 1091–2, 1098–1107, 1166–8, 1181–4, 1235–7.

(A) GENERAL

Of all the periods of English history, the Tudor age seemed once the best known and most firmly settled. On the basis of traditions formulated in the nineteenth century, A. F. Pollard (with assistance) had built up a seemingly unshakable orthodoxy according to which the restoration of royal power by Henry VII was completed by his son (Reformation) and then exploited by Elizabeth. The century presented the picture of a coherent age, growingly 'modern', separated precisely from the Middle Ages by the phenomena of humanism and protestantism, and already consciously looking ahead to the distant end of empire. No doubt there were details to be learned and filled in, but the master plan was thought complete and beyond change. Today, little of it survives and debate rules everything. Recognition has grown that the date 1485 really means very little; research on topics of intellectual and economic history, tackling questions of which the previous generation had not even been aware, has done much to dissolve certainties; but it is interesting to note that the revision really started at the point where Pollard seemed best armoured – in the analysis of policy, government and administration. Fortunately, the revisionist interpretation has not ossified into a new orthodoxy; much further work is in the pipe-line, and this can be only an interim report.

However, the older views still found disciples in the years under discussion. The moderately useful conspectus of the problems of the early Reformation put together by Maynard Smith carries after only twenty years a strikingly oldfashioned air,[140] while Mackie's contribution to the *Oxford History of England* handsomely summarizes much that can no longer be accepted.[141] Even Bindoff's often brilliant short account, which does give weight to more recent findings in economic history, still stands under Pollard's powerful influence.[142] And Williamson, who wrote later, could easily have written fifty years earlier.[143]

On the other hand, Elton has made an effort to see the century afresh, believing as he does that the findings of research force a very different interpretative scheme upon the historian.[144] He sees the years 1530 – 40 as the fulcrum of the whole story: in that decade, he claims, a still traditional system of government and ideas was so drastically transformed that the history of England can be said to have thereafter, and only thereafter, developed along genuinely new lines. He emphasizes (no doubt too much so) the part played by Thomas Cromwell and treats the age of Elizabeth, in which the older tradition discovered the makings of a coming revolution, as essentially conservative. This thesis, which in part rests on the author's own research, has some support from other work to be mentioned later. However, the very idea of a revolution where none was mentioned before was bound to evoke protest; in the ensuing debate both sides no doubt believed themselves victorious, but at least the defence of the revolution was left with the last word.[145]

---

[140] H. Maynard Smith, *Henry VIII and the Reformation*. L: Macmillan: 1948. Pp. xv, 480.

[141] J. D. Mackie, *The Earlier Tudors, 1485 – 1558*. O: Clarendon: 1952. Pp. xxii, 669. Rev: *EHR* 68, 276ff.

[142] S. T. Bindoff, *Tudor England*. Harmondsworth: Penguin Books: 1950. Pp. 320.

[143] James A. Williamson, *The Tudor Age*. L: Longmans: 1952. Pp. xxii, 448. Rev: *EHR* 69, 656f.

[144] G. R. Elton, *England under the Tudors*. L: Methuen: 1955 (ed. 1962 with new bibliography). Pp. xi, 504. Rev: *CHJ* 12, 92ff.; *EHR* 71, 668.

[145] Penry H. Williams and G. L. Harriss, 'A revolution in Tudor history?', *PP* 25 (1963), 3–58. – G. R. Elton, 'The Tudor revolution: a reply', *ibid.* 29 (1964), 26–49. Further contributions *ibid.* 31 (1965), 87–96, and 32 (1965), 103–9.

Histories of particular parts of the age do not on the whole help much towards a resolution of these problems of general interpretation. The much-needed new investigation of the reign of Henry VII still waits to be done, despite Storey's brief and myopic study.[146] The first volume of Jordan's enthusiastic history of Edward VI's reign repeats exploded errors and fails to advance knowledge.[147] Rowse's survey of Elizabeth's reign also remains so far incomplete; what we have presents the results of genuine study but uses a highly conventional and oldfashioned framework, helped out only by the too frequent substitution of explosive prejudice for serious thought.[148] Much more interesting is MacCaffrey's history of Elizabeth's early years in which the creation of a solid monarchy after the disturbances of the mid-century is brought out by means of a political narrative.[149]

(B) POLITICAL HISTORY

Elton has attempted brief revaluations of the first two Tudors. He demonstrates that Henry VII's reputation (misery and miserliness) rests on partisan statements and ignorance of the facts of Tudor law;[150] while in the eighth Henry he sees a skilful opportunist dependent on others and not Pollard's great statesman.[151] This view is in small part supported and in great

[146] Robin L. Storey, *The Reign of Henry VII*. L: Blandford: 1968. Pp. xii, 243. Rev: *Hist* 54, 91f.

[147] Wilbur K. Jordan, *Edward VI: the Young King*. L: Allen & Unwin: 1968. Pp. 544. Rev: *HJ* 12, 702ff.

[148] A. Leslie Rowse, *The England of Elizabeth*. L: Macmillan: 1950. Pp. 547. Rev: *EHR* 66, 589ff. – Idem, *The Expansion of Elizabethan England*. L: Macmillan: 1955. Pp. 450. Rev: *EHR* 71, 284ff.; *CHJ* 12, 94ff.

[149] Wallace T. MacCaffrey, *The Shaping of the Elizabethan Regime*. Princeton UP: 1968. Pp. xiv, 501.

[150] G. R. Elton, 'Henry VII: rapacity and remorse', *HJ* 1 (1958), 21–39. – John P. Cooper, 'Henry VII's last years reconsidered', *ibid.* 2 (1959), 103–29. – G. R. Elton, 'Henry VII: a restatement', *ibid.* 4 (1961), 1–29.

[151] G. R. Elton, *Henry VIII: an essay in revision*. L: Routledge: 1962. Pp. 28.

DA 330
S75 1968b
DA 345
J6
DA 356
R65
1951
DA 355
R67
DA 355
M27

part contradicted in Scarisbrick's monumental biography: the king appears here as the maker of his age but as an unstable, wayward, intellectually eclectic character of insufficient political sense.[152] It is not clear that Scarisbrick's king, without Elton's Cromwell, could in face have achieved what was achieved in the reign. The main crisis of that reign has received a little attention. Parmiter once more recounts the familiar story of the Divorce, accurately enough but without surprises.[153] Elton investigates the resistance to the king's policy and finds Thomas More sufficiently involved, despite the legend.[154] The famous northern rising is once again interpreted as basically religious in inspiration.[155] The politics of Edward VI's reign have yielded no fresh work; for that of his successor, Loades argues convincingly that resistance derived more from the politics of patriotism than from religion.[156] Two new attempts to write the life of Elizabeth I add here and there to the portrait long since painted by Neale without dethroning that work of art.[157] Yet things are stirring in Elizabethan studies where relative plenitude of evidence at last enables the historian to chart an underwater course. After Neale showed the way in his discussion of the dubious politics of that golden age,[158] only MacCaffrey has so far, in three important articles, really come to grips with the political importance of social hierarchy and

[152] John J. Scarisbrick, *Henry VIII*. L: Eyre & Spottiswoode: 1968. Pp. xiv, 561. Rev: *HJ* 12, 158ff.; *Hist* 54, 31ff.

[153] G. de C. Parmiter, *The King's Great Matter: a study of Anglo-Papal relations 1527 – 1534*. L: Longmans: 1967. Pp. xiii, 322. Rev: *EHR* 83, 832f.

[154] G. R. Elton, 'Thomas More and the opposition to Henry VIII', *BIHR* 41 (1968), 19–34.

[155] C. S. L. Davies, 'The Pilgrimage of Grace reconsidered', *PP* 41 (1968), 54–76.

[156] David M. Loades, *Two Tudor Conspiracies*. CUP: 1965. Pp. vii, 284. Rev: *EHR* 82, 159f.

[157] Joel Hurstfield, *Elizabeth I and the Unity of England*. L: English Universities Press: 1960. Pp. xiii, 226. Rev: *EHR* 77, 365f. – Neville J. Williams, *Elizabeth, Queen of England*. L: Weidenfeld: 1967. Pp. xii, 388. Rev: *Hist* 54, 100f.

[158] John E. Neale, 'The Elizabethan Political Scene', *Essays in Elizabethan History*. L: Cape: 1958, 59–84.

patronage.[159] Of all political problems, that of the succession had the longest life: Levine tackles the high point at the start of the reign,[160] Hurstfield that at the end.[161]

There have been political biographies of some of the monarchs' good servants. The second duke of Norfolk hardly offered his biographer enough to do.[162] Dickens extensively rehabilitates Thomas Cromwell, whose reputation also acquires a new respectability in a collection of tales derived from cases dealt with in star chamber.[163] Read's vast book on Burghley ought to have been enormously important, but since it ploddingly assembles masses of undigested material its most obvious use will be as a quarry for others.[164] His 1100 pages still leave Burghley incomprehensible; Beckingsale, employing more modest methods and more searching art, at least achieves a sort of picture of this still mysterious man.[165] Hatton, the unexpected lord chancellor, now has a not entirely expected biography.[166] Raleigh continues to attract the historians; among several works, Rowse's family history and Strathmann's

---

[159] Wallace T. MacCaffrey, 'Place and Patronage in Elizabethan Politics', *Neale Ft* (n. 125), 95–126; 'Elizabethan politics: the first decade 1558 – 1568', *PP* 24 (1962), 25–42; 'England: the crown and the new aristocracy 1540 – 1600', *ibid.* 30 (1965), 52–64.

[160] Mortimer Levine, *The Early Elizabethan Succession Question, 1558 – 1568.* Stanford UP: 1966. Pp. ix, 245. Rev: *Hist* 53, 101.

[161] Joel Hurstfield, 'The succession struggle in late Elizabethan England', *Neale Ft* (n. 125), 369–96.

[162] Melvin J. Tucker, *The Life of Thomas Howard, earl of Surrey and second duke of Norfolk, 1443 – 1524.* The Hague: Mouton: 1964. Pp. 170. Rev: *EHR* 81, 824.

[163] A. G. Dickens, *Thomas Cromwell and the English Reformation.* L: English Universities Press: 1959. Pp. 192. Rev: *EHR* 76, 104f. – G. R. Elton, *Star Chamber Stories.* L: Methuen: 1958. Pp. 244. Rev: *EHR* 75, 155f.

[164] Conyers Read, *Mr Secretary Cecil and Queen Elizabeth.* L: Cape: 1955. Pp. 510. Rev: *EHR* 72, 505ff. – Idem, *Lord Burghley and Queen Elizabeth.* L: Cape: 1960. Pp. 603. Rev: *EHR* 76, 501ff.

[165] B. W. Beckingsale, *Burghley: Tudor Statesman.* L: Macmillan: 1967. Pp. x, 340. Rev: *EHR* 84, 176.

[166] E. St John Brooks, *Sir Christopher Hatton, Queen Elizabeth's Favourite.* L: Cape: 1946. Pp. 408.

study of the personality are the best.[167] The opposition is represented by the unhappy fourth duke of Norfolk, victim of his own ambition and the Queen of Scots' irresponsibility,[168] and by the collective biography of some Catholic exiles who settled in Spain.[169] Outside the classifications stands the charming story of a successful adventurer who began his career as a papal agent, continued it as a diplomatist in Elizabeth's service, and finished it upon a gentleman's estate in Cambridgeshire.[170]

There is too little to report on foreign policy. Wernham's survey suffers from the fact that much of it rests on secondary material and thus says too little that is new.[171] A new look at the relations between England and the papacy in the age of Wolsey casts comprehensive doubt upon Pollard's view of Wolsey's purposes and motives; the new look is right.[172] Elizabeth's first decade can be studied from the point of view of Spain's ambassadors; the author is too trusting in the face of his one-sided sources.[173] On the other hand, Wernham's

[167] A. Leslie Rowse, *Raleigh and the Throckmortons.* L: Macmillan: 1962. Pp. xi, 348. Rev: *EHR* 79, 601f. – E. A. Strathmann, *Sir Walter Raleigh: a study in Elizabethan skepticism.* New York: Columbia UP: 1951. Pp. xi, 292. – See also n. 291.

[168] Neville J. Williams, *Thomas Howard, fourth Duke of Norfolk.* L: Barrie & Rockliff: 1964. Pp. xiii, 289. Rev: *EHR* 81, 161f. – Francis Edwards, S. J., *The Marvellous Chance: Thomas Howard, fourth Duke of Norfolk, and the Ridolphi Plot, 1570 – 1572* (L: Hart-Davis: 1968; pp. 416) is a pretentious, overwritten and unreliable attempt to revive the legend that the only plotter of the age was William Cecil.

[169] Albert J. Loomie, *The Spanish Elizabethans.* New York: Fordham UP: 1963. Pp. xii, 280. Rev: *EHR* 80, 831.

[170] Lawrence Stone, *An Elizabethan: Sir Horatio Pallavicino.* O: Clarendon: 1956. Pp. xix, 345.

[171] R. Bruce Wernham, *Before the Armada: the growth of English foreign policy, 1485 – 1588.* L: Cape: 1966. Pp. 447. Rev: *EHR* 83, 122ff.; *Hist* 54, 95f.

[172] D. S. Chambers, *Cardinal Bainbridge in the Court of Rome.* O: Clarendon: 1965. Pp. xii, 178. Rev: *EHR* 81, 826. – Idem, 'Cardinal Wolsey and the papal tiara', *BIHR* 38 (1965), 20–30.

[173] Manuel F. Alvarez, *Tres embajadores de Felipe II en Inglaterra.* Madrid: Consejo Superior de Investigaciones Cientificas: 1951. Pp. 319.

defence of Elizabeth against the charge that her policy in the war with Spain rested on nothing but greed and irresponsible dilatoriness is entirely successful.[174]

Serious work on military history is really new in this period, and Cruickshank's impressive analysis of the forces available in war and the use to which they were put shows how much can be done.[175] He receives some support in depth in studies which tackle both Elizabethan thinking on war (not negligible) and the practical problems of armies (pretty overwhelming).[176] The specialist skill of fortification receives attention in a useful biography.[177] Falls provides a lucid survey of the conquest of Ireland and a lively picture of England's best commander in that age.[178] Miller takes on a less familiar soldier.[179] Most striking of all in this field of studies is Mattingly's brilliant and comprehensive summing up of some forty years' research, by himself and others, around the events of 1588.[180]

Lastly, two pieces of local history. Eagleston disposes of the side issue of the Channel Islands,[181] while MacCaffrey, in his

[174] R. Bruce Wernham, 'Queen Elizabeth and the Portugal expedition of 1589', *EHR* 66 (1951), 1–26, 194–218; 'Elizabethan war aims and strategy', *Neale Ft* (n. 125), 340–68.

[175] Charles G. Cruickshank, *Elizabeth's Army.* O: Clarendon: 1966 (2nd ed., much enlarged). Pp. xii, 316. Rev: *EHR* 83, 167; *HJ* 10, 470ff.

[176] Henry J. Webb, *Elizabethan Military Science: the books and the practice.* Madison: U of Wisconsin P: 1965. Pp. xvi, 240. Rev: *EHR* 82, 383f. – C. S. L. Davies, 'Provision for armies 1509 – 1560, a study of the effectiveness of early Tudor government', *EcHR*² 17 (1964 – 1965), 234–48. – Lindsay Boynton, 'The Tudor provost-marshal', *EHR* 77 (1961), 437–55; *The Elizabethan Militia.* L: Routledge: 1967. Pp. xvii, 334. Rev: *EHR* 83, 603f.; *EcHR*² 20, 389f.

[177] L. R. Shelby, *John Rogers: Tudor military engineer.* O: Clarendon: 1967. Pp. xi, 182. Rev: *EHR* 84, 840f.

[178] Cyril Falls, *Elizabeth's Irish Wars.* L: Methuen: 1950. Pp. 362. – Idem, *Mountjoy, Elizabeth's General.* L: Odham: 1955. Pp. 256. Rev: *EHR* 72, 539f.

[179] Amos C. Miller, *Sir Henry Killigrew, Elizabethan soldier and diplomat.* Leicester UP: 1963. Pp. xi, 279. Rev: *EHR* 80, 161f.

[180] Garrett Mattingly, *The Defeat of the Spanish Armada.* L: Cape: 1959. Pp. 342. Rev: *EHR* 77, 110ff.

[181] A. J. Eagleston, *The Channel Islands under Tudor Government, 1485 – 1642.* CUP: 1949. Pp. xii, 194.

UA649
C75
1966

355.0942
W366e

U6125
R63 S45

DA937
F3
1970

942.055
BX48m

exemplary study of Exeter, approaches somewhat nearer to the centre of affairs.[182]

(c) ADMINISTRATION AND CONSTITUTION

The commentary to Elton's *Tudor Constitution* (n. 24) provides a concise and reasonably up-to-date summary of the state of knowledge. Recent research has in the main attended to two major questions. The details of government have for the first time been subjected to intensive study by means of the massive unprinted sources; and secondly, attempts have been made to discover the ideas behind the events. Controversy has attended both endeavours.

The novel view of the century came into existence first with Elton's investigation of the central machinery of government in Henry VIII's reign.[183] This presented the thesis that until about 1534 government subsisted on the 'medieval' principle of a personal royal administration, while thereafter Cromwell's deliberate reform policy initiated a general reliance on 'modern' national organization. Resistance to the thesis, sporadically found here and there, found fuel in Richardson's study of the financial offices under the early Tudors according to which the reforms of Henry VII, employing private treasuries, remained dominant to the middle of the century.[184] It is of interest to note that in his later book on the short-lived office charged with the administration of the confiscated monastic properties Richardson silently accepted the main lines of the Elton interpretation.[185] A short study of Henry VII's estate management also offered more support than discouragement.[186]

---

[182] Wallace T. MacCaffrey, *Exeter 1540 – 1640*. C (Mass.): Harvard UP: 1958. Pp. 311. Rev: *EHR* 75, 724f.; *EcHR*² 12, 306f.

[183] G. R. Elton, *The Tudor Revolution in Government: administrative changes in the reign of Henry VIII*. CUP: 1953. Pp. xiii, 466. Rev: *EHR* 71, 92ff.

[184] Walter C. Richardson, *Tudor Chamber Administration*. Baton Rouge: Louisiana State UP: 1952. Pp. xiii, 541. Rev: *AHR* 58, 896f.

[185] Walter C. Richardson, *History of the Court of Augmentations 1536 – 1554*. Baton Rouge: Louisiana State UP: 1962. Pp. xvi, 542. Rev: *EHR* 79, 111ff.

[186] Bertram P. Wolffe, 'Henry VII's land revenue and chamber finance', *EHR* 79 (1964), 225–54.

However, of Cromwell's *ad hoc* creations only one survived independently for any length of time – the court of wards, maintained for the sake of the crown's somewhat antiquated feudal claims and in despite of landowners' frequently expressed dissatisfaction. Two scholars have attended to this institution: Bell analysed its history administratively,[187] while Hurstfield, in an interesting series of writings, came to grips with the social consequences of court and claims.[188] The legal background to this method of public financing was well brought out in Thorne's edition of a lecture delivered in 1492.[189] Little has so far been done for the most central organ of all, the king's council, an omission explained in Elton's analysis of the sources and source problems involved.[190] Two subordinate councils, however – the long lived council in the marches of Wales, and the evanescent council of the west – have been newly and properly analysed.[191] Administrative history has scored some further admirable successes. Jones's book on the chancery at last gives us a real discussion of a Tudor court; moreover, he has destroyed just about every conventional legend attending that court and its place in the politics of the day.[192] This is a major work; a short piece on the methods of the Cecils helps

---

187 Harry E. Bell. *An Introduction to the History and Records of the Court of Wards and Liveries.* CUP: 1953. Pp. x, 215. Rev: *EHR* 69, 104ff.

188 Joel Hurstfield, *The Queen's Wards: wardship and marriage under Elizabeth.* L: Longmans: 1958. Pp. xii, 366. Rev: *EHR* 74, 503ff. – Idem, 'The revival of feudalism in early Tudor England', *Hist* 37 (1952), 131–45; 'Corruption and reform under Edward VI and Mary: the example of wardship', *EHR* 68 (1953), 27–36; 'Lord Burghley as master of the Court of Wards 1561 – 1598', *TRHS* (1949), 95–114.

189 Robert Constable, *Prerogativa Regis: Tertia Lectura,* ed. S. E. Thorne. New Haven: Yale UP: 1949. Pp. lix, 165.

190 G. R. Elton, 'Why the history of the early Tudor Council remains unwritten', *Annali della Fondazione Italiana per la Storia Amministrativa,* 1 (1964), 268–94.

191 Penry H. Williams, *The Council in the Marches of Wales under Elizabeth I.* Cardiff: U of Wales P: 1958. Pp. xiv, 385. Rev: *EHR* 75, 160f.; *HJ* 2, 191ff. – Joyce A. Youings, 'The Council of the West', *TRHS* (1960), 19–39.

192 William J. Jones, *The Elizabethan Court of Chancery.* O: Clarendon: 1967. Pp. xvii, 528. Rev: *EHR* 84, 354ff.; *HJ* 11, 376ff.

to advance knowledge, while the only recent attempt to make
sense of local government loses itself in a pointless mass of
personal detail, uninformative classifications, and the solemn
production of well-known generalizations as though they were
new.[193] More hopeful are the signs that scholars at last may be
recognizing the fundamental importance of law and lawyers
in the sixteenth century. Ives has given attention both to the
lawyers' place in society and to one of the lawyers' chief concerns, the disposal of landed property;[194] while Elton has
clarified the political origins and the legal essence of the early-
Tudor treason law.[195] Elton's demonstration that the act of
proclamations embodied no autocratic ambitions has been
well confirmed in Heinze's case study of one set of proclamations.[196] Five Tudor biographies offer very useful contributions
to an understanding of government. Slavin shows neatly what
at the time it meant to make a career;[197] Dewar follows the
fortunes of a scholar who wished to put his brains at the disposal
of the great world but never quite achieved the success he
deemed due to himself;[198] Emmison and Lehmberg, writing
about people, say relevant things about secretaries of state and
chancellors of the exchequer;[199] Cross shows what a nobleman

---

[193] Alan G. R. Smith, 'The secretariats of the Cecils', *EHR* 83 (1968),
481–504. – J. H. Gleason, *The Justices of the Peace in England 1558 –
1640*. O: Clarendon: 1969. Pp. xvi, 285. Rev: *Hist* 54, 422f.

[194] E. W. Ives, 'The common lawyers in pre-Reformation England',
TRHS (1968), 145–73; 'The genesis of the statute of uses', *EHR*
82 (1967), 673–97.

[195] G. R. Elton, 'The law of treason in the early Reformation', *HJ* 11
(1968), 211–36. – *Also* L. M. Hill, 'The two witness rule in English
treason trials', *American Journal of Legal History*, 12 (1968), 95–111.

[196] G. R. Elton, 'Henry VIII's act of proclamations', *EHR* 75 (1960),
208–22. – Rudolph W. Heinze, 'The price of meat: a study in the
use of royal proclamations in the reign of Henry VIII', *HJ* 12
(1969), 583–95.

[197] Arthur J. Slavin, *Power and Profit: a study of Sir Ralph Sadler 1507 –
1547*. CUP: Pp. xvii, 238. Rev: *EHR* 83, 164f.; *HJ* 12, 566ff.

[198] Mary Dewar, *Sir Thomas Smith: a Tudor intellectual in office*. L:
Athlone: 1964. Pp. ix, 222. Rev: *EHR* 81, 160f.

[199] F. E. Emmison, *Tudor Secretary: Sir William Petre*. L: Longmans:
1961. Pp. xx, 364. Rev: *EHR* 78, 168f. – Stanford E. Lehmberg,

active in public life was likely to suffer in labour and financial distress.[200]

However, in any discussion of the constitution, parliament clearly remains of paramount interest, at least to historians. A general summary of the state of knowledge, with some possibly rash suggestions, is offered in Elton's survey of the operational and representative functions of parliament down to 1600.[201] The chief parliamentary historian of the period is unquestionably Neale whose major works use new materials to analyse the lower house and to describe the tense situation there throughout Elizabeth's reign.[202] True, criticisms are beginning to gather (what in truth was the part played by religion? should one ignore finance? were relations between crown and commons really so predominantly marked by conflict?), but it is obvious that Neale not only raised the whole subject to a new level of learning but also destroyed old legends of servile parliaments. Much less is so far known about the first half of the century, though Miller and Elton have made a beginning.[203] All this labour has succeeded in casting grave doubts upon the old concept of a 'Tudor despotism', doubts which are strongly reinforced by work on the content of constitutional ideas in the period. How well the almost painfully exact legalism of the early Tudors was reflected in thinking upon the matter has

---

Sir Walter Mildmay and Tudor Government. Austin: U of Texas P: 1964. Pp. xii, 335. Rev: *EHR* 81, 388f.

[200] Claire Cross, *The Puritan Earl: the life of Henry Hastings, third earl of Huntingdon 1536 – 1595*. L: Macmillan: 1966. Pp. xviii, 372. Rev: *EHR* 83, 602f.

[201] G. R. Elton, *The Body of the Whole Realm*. Charlottesville: U of Virginia P: Jamestown Foundation: 1969. Pp. 57.

[202] John E. Neale, *The Elizabethan House of Commons*. L: Cape: 1949. Pp. 455. Rev: *EHR* 65, 119ff. – Idem, *Elizabeth I and her Parliaments*, 2 vols. L: Cape: 1953, 1957. Pp. 434, 452. Rev: *EHR* 69, 632ff.; 75, 124ff.; *CHJ* 13, 187ff.

[203] Helen Miller, 'London and Parliament in the reign of Henry VIII', *BIHR* 35 (1962), 128–49; 'Attendance in the House of Lords during the reign of Henry VIII', *HJ* 10 (1967), 325–51. – G. R. Elton, 'Evolution of a Reformation statute', *EHR* 64 (1949), 174–97; 'Parliamentary drafts 1529 – 1540', *BIHR* 25 (1952), 117–32. *See also* n. 224.

been made plain by Zeeveld[204] and Elton.[205] However, a sort of counter-attack has been launched by Hurstfield, though it is not apparent that he has either found new matter to advance or convincing arguments for discrediting the views he attacks.[206] A last point worth mentioning touches the 'imperial' pretensions of the monarchy, a problem so far more opened up than solved; in addition to the specific contribution made by Koebner,[207] the thoughtful discussion in Scarisbrick's *Henry VIII* (n. 152) is relevant here.

(D) THE CHURCH

Bowker has called in doubt a great many familiar notions about the declining state of the pre-Reformation clergy.[208] Such novelties have not yet reached the general accounts of the Reformation, of which several have appeared. The weightiest is that by Philip Hughes, in three volumes; the first volume rests on sound labours and is important, but the other two surrender to Roman Catholic prejudices.[209] Parker's short book is plain and a trifle old-fashioned in its reluctance to admit religion and spiritual force among the official promoters of the Reformation.[210] Both these are relegated to the shadows by Dickens

[204] W. Gordon Zeeveld, *Foundations of Tudor Policy*. C (Mass.): Harvard UP: 1948. Pp. vii, 291. Rev: *AHR* 54, 578ff. *See also* nn. 1099, 1101, 1166.

[205] G. R. Elton, 'The political creed of Thomas Cromwell', *TRHS* (1956), 69–92; 'King or minister? The man behind the Henrician Reformation', *Hist* 39 (1956 for 1954), 216–32.

[206] Joel Hurstfield, 'Was there a Tudor despotism after all?' *TRHS* (1967), 83–108.

[207] Richard Koebner, ' "The Imperial Crown of the Realm": Henry VIII, Constantine the Great, and Polydore Vergil', *BIHR* 26 (1953), 29–52.

[208] Margaret Bowker, *The Secular Clergy in the Diocese of Lincoln 1495 – 1520*. CUP: 1968. Pp. xii, 253. Rev: *EHR* 84, 712; *HJ* 12, 367ff.

[209] Philip Hughes, *The Reformation in England*, 3 vols. L: Hollis & Carter: 1950, 1953, 1954. Pp. xxi, 404; xxvi, 366; xxix, 457. Rev: *EHR* 66, 586ff.

[210] Thomas M. Parker, *The English Reformation to 1558*. L: OUP: 1950. Pp. viii, 200. The 2nd ed. of 1966 is almost unchanged.

whose vigorous and searching work, both learned and comprehensible, succeeds in renovating an ancient theme.[211] Contrary to tradition, he stresses the religious roots of the English Reformation and concentrates attention upon the reign of Henry VIII. Davies summarizes the Anglican teaching on episcopacy;[212] Cremeans smells Calvin's influence everywhere;[213] Kressner, in a rather superficial doctoral dissertation, substitutes Zwingli.[214] No one shall be left out: Tjernakel, in a book whose weaknesses of scholarship make assessment of the result difficult, imports Lutherism into England.[215] The first English biography of Martin Bucer also directs attention abroad.[216] The last volume of Knowles's monumental history of the enclosed orders is palpably shadowed by the thunder-clouds of the coming Dissolution; this is a splendid work of art, but also the best history of the end of monasticism.[217] A happy sign of things to come is the increasing number of local studies from which we shall ultimately learn what really happened. Haigh attends to the Dissolution in the north-west,[218] while Hodgett follows the fate of the deprived in the east;[219] Dickens

---

[211] A. G. Dickens, *The English Reformation*. L: Batsford: 1964. Pp. x, 374. Rev: *EHR* 81, 384f.

[212] E. T. Davies, *Episcopacy and the Royal Supremacy in the Church of England in the XVIth Century*. O: Blackwell: 1950. Pp. vi, 137.

[213] C. D. Cremeans, *The Reception of Calvinistic Thought in England*. Urbana: U of Illinois P: 1949. Pp. viii, 127.

[214] Helmut Kressner, *Schweizer Ursprünge des anglikanischen Staatskirchentums*. Gütersloh: Bertelsmann: 1953. Pp. 136.

[215] Neelak S. Tjernakel, *Henry VIII and the Lutherans*. St Louis: Concordia Publishing House: 1965. Pp. xii, 326.

[216] Constantin Hopf, *Martin Bucer and the English Reformation*. O: Blackwell: 1946. Pp. xiv, 290.

[217] David Knowles, *The Religious Orders in England: III, The Tudor Age*. CUP: 1959. Pp. xiv, 522. Rev: *EHR* 76, 98ff.

[218] Christopher Haigh, *The Last Days of the Lancashire Monasteries and the Pilgrimage of Grace*. Manchester: Chetham Society 3rd Series, vol. xvii: 1969. Pp. x, 172.

[219] Gerald A. J. Hodgett, *The State of the Ex-Religious and Former Chantry Priests in the Diocese of Lincoln, 1547 – 1574*. Lincoln Record Society, vol. 53: 1959. Pp. xxii, 181. Rev: *EHR* 76, 142.

BR 375
D5

DA 332
T55

BX 2542
K 553

successfully studies the impact of reform in the north-east,[220] while Oxley demonstrates how not to do it for Essex;[221] Hembry shows what can be done by concentrating on one diocese, though the state of the evidence compels her to deal in the main with matters economic.[222]

Some work has been done on the political aspects of the Reformation. Ogle's study of the Hunne case justifiably attacks Thomas More and makes a reality of the anticlericalism from which so much support for innovation came.[223] The effects of such feelings are at the heart of the discussion which has grown up around the Church's retreat before the king's threats and parliament's eager hostility.[224] Smith's approach to the same problem from the bishops' position, though marred by certain inaccuracies, explains a good deal about the state of the Church.[225] It is clear that resistance proved stronger than used to be believed, a conclusion also supported by Scarisbrick.[226] Smith's attempt to explain Henry VIII's curious shift towards reform in his last years is factually but not psychologically in agreement with Scarisbrick's views (n. 152).[227] Bishop Fisher, whom Smith forgot, makes a full-scale appearance, in

[220] A. G. Dickens, *Lollards and Protestants in the Diocese of York, 1509 – 1558*. L: OUP: 1959. Pp. viii, 272. Rev: *EHR* 76, 357.

[221] J. E. Oxley, *The Reformation in Essex to the Death of Mary*. Manchester UP: 1965. Pp. xii, 320. Rev: *EHR* 82, 382f.; *Journal of Theol. Studies* 17, 512ff.

[222] Phyllis M. Hembry, *The Bishops of Bath and Wells 1540 – 1640*. L: Athlone: 1967. Pp. xi, 287. Rev: *HJ* 11, 187ff.

[223] Arthur Ogle, *The Tragedy of the Lollards' Tower: the case of Richard Hunne and its aftermath in the Reformation Parliament*. O: Pen-in-Hand: 1949. Pp. 393.

[224] G. R. Elton, 'The Commons' Supplication of 1532: parliamentary manœuvres in the reign of Henry VIII', *EHR* 66 (1951), 507–34. – John P. Cooper, 'The Supplication against the Ordinaries reconsidered', *ibid.* 72 (1957), 661–41. – Michael J. Kelly, 'The Submission of the Clergy', *TRHS* (1965), 97–119.

[225] Lacey Baldwin Smith, *Tudor Prelates and Politics*. Princeton UP: 1953. Pp. ix, 333. Rev: *EHR* 69, 663f.

[226] John J. Scarisbrick, 'The pardon of the clergy', *CHJ* 12 (1956), 22–39.

[227] Lacey Baldwin Smith, 'Henry VIII and the Protestant triumph', *AHR* 71 (1966), 1237–64.

canonicals as it were, in Surtz's work of piety.[228] Again, there is
nothing on the religious politics of the mid-Tudor period, but
with Elizabeth's accession interest revives. Neale has shown
how a group of extremists in the Commons forced the Queen to
adopt a more reformed Church than she had intended;[229] and
Haugaard, following the fortunes of convocation through the
first years of the reign, effectively rewrites the history of the new
Church's formative period.[230] As it happens, the north provides
better archiepiscopal materials (especially court records) than
the south, a fact which has produced two administrative
treatises: Marchant's is much the more important.[231] The
general problems of a reign in which an official middle way
encountered attack from both wings (not to mention the needs
of undergraduates) have produced several very useful essays of
which McGrath's (a full, firm outline of the conventional
story)[232] and Cross's (saying new things about both theory and
practice)[233] deserve special mention. New's striking attempt to
find fundamental theological differences between anglicans
and puritans has persuaded few.[234]

As always, there are biographies, of varying value. Two early
reformers receive straightforward treatment,[235] while a whole

[228] Edward Surtz, *The Works and Days of John Fisher, 1469 – 1535.*
C (Mass.): Harvard UP: 1967. Pp. xvii, 572. Rev: *EHR* 84, 841f.;
Hist 54, 94f.

[229] John E. Neale, 'The Elizabethan acts of supremacy and uniform-
ity', *EHR* 65 (1950), 304–32.

[230] William P. Haugaard, *Elizabeth and the English Reformation.* CUP:
1968. Pp. xv, 392. Rev: *Hist* 54, 422. – *See also* A. J. Carlson, 'The
puritans and the convocation of 1563', *Harbison Ft* (n. 128), 133–53.

[231] Ronald A. Marchant, *The Church under the Law: justice, adminis-
tration and discipline in the diocese of York, 1560 – 1640.* CUP: 1969.
Pp. xiii, 272 – C. I. A. Ritchie, *The Ecclesiastical Courts of York.*
Arbroath: Herald Press: 1956. Pp. 215. Rev: *EHR* 73, 525f.

[232] Patrick McGrath, *Papists, and Puritans under Elizabeth I.* L: Blandford: 1967. Pp. x, 434.

[233] Claire Cross, *The Royal Supremacy in the Elizabethan Church.* L: Allen
& Unwin: 1969. Pp. xiv, 239.

[234] John F. H. New, *Anglican and Puritan: the basis of their opposition
1558 – 1640.* Stanford UP: 1964. Pp. 140. Rev: *EHR* 80, 592f.

[235] Allan G. Chester, *Hugh Latimer, Apostle of the English.* Philadelphia:
U of Pennsylvania P: 1954. Pp. x, 261. – C. C. Butterworth and

BX 4700
P3458

BX 5071
H3

DA 356
M25
1967 b
BX 5071
C 75
BR 756
N48

group of them appear in a book which has little new to say, though it ventures rightly to diverge from the conventional estimate of Sir Thomas More.[236] Ridley has produced rather laborious but thorough accounts of his own ancestor and of Cranmer.[237] The latter's theology has become involved in controversy. While Dugmore endeavoured to derive his eucharistic teaching solely from a native tradition, Brooks' critique, which again emphasizes the continental influence, proves more convincing.[238] Two American scholars attend to John Jewel: one thoroughly analyses the writings, while the other offers an interesting but not entirely well-based discussion of Jewel's teaching on authority.[239] The dividing stream of the latter part of the century also receives biographical treatment in books on Whitgift, the calvinist scourge of calvinist puritans, and on Lancelot Andrews, the unwitting ancestor of a sentimental anglo-catholicism.[240] Porter's study of religious quarrels in Cambridge throws a flood of light on the problems of the Church in general.[241]

At one time it seemed as though the lively labours about the

Allan G. Chester, *George Joye: a chapter in the history of the English bible and the English Reformation*. Philadelphia: U of Pennsylvania P: 1962. Pp. 293. Rev: *EHR* 79, 838f.

[236] William A. Clebsch, *England's Earliest Protestants, 1520 – 1535*. New Haven: Yale UP: 1964. Pp. xvi, 358. Rev: *EHR* 81, 585f.

[237] Jasper G. Ridley, *Nicholas Ridley*. L: Longmans: 1957. Pp. 453. – Idem, *Thomas Cranmer*. O: Clarendon: 1962. Pp. 450. Rev: *EHR* 79, 168f.

[238] C. W. Dugmore, *The Mass and the English Reformers*. L: Macmillan: 1958. Pp. xiv, 262. Rev: *EHR* 76, 359f. – Peter Brooks, *Thomas Cranmer's Doctrine of the Eucharist*. L: Macmillan: 1965. Pp. xviii, 134.

[239] John E. Booty, *John Jewel as Apologist of the Church of England*. L: SPCK: 1963. Pp. xi, 244. Rev: *EHR* 80, 591f. – W. M. Southgate, *John Jewel and the Problem of Doctrinal Authority*. C (Mass.): Harvard UP: 1962. Pp. xiv, 236. Rev: *EHR* 79, 841.

[240] Powell Mills Dawley, *John Whitgift and the English Reformation*. New York: Scribner 1954. Pp. xii, 254. Rev: *EHR* 73, 155. – Paul A. Welsby, *Lancelot Andrewes 1555 – 1626*. L: SPCK: 1958. Pp. xiv, 298. Rev: *EHR* 74, 732.

[241] Harry C. Porter, *Reformation and Reaction in Tudor Cambridge*. CUP: 1958. Pp. xi, 461. Rev: *EHR*, 75, 347; *HJ* 2, 83ff.

BH—D

early puritans would concern themselves exclusively with their political activities in parliament, but this is no longer true. Above all, Collinson's outstanding general treatise now provides a really secure foundation of knowledge; in particular he disposes of much of the revolutionary legend.[242] Collinson has also dealt with the revolutionary organizer John Field, while Knox has written a life of the leading theologian of the party.[243] Marchant's investigation of puritanism in the north extends to the Civil War; it demonstrates effectively how little coherence and continuity there was in the movement – though it is not clear whether the author realized this.[244] The three main crises of Elizabethan puritanism have been separately treated. Primus solidly, and heavily, recounts the vestments controversy of the 1560's;[245] McGinn, bemused by literary criteria, tackles the Admonitions of 1571 – 2;[246] the same author also settles the problems of Martin Marprelate, at least to his satisfaction, in favour of Penry's authorship.[247] The opposing party has done less well. Schenk died before his larger study of Cardinal Pole was completed; the book we have is a useful beginning.[248] Two fascinating accounts by leading Jesuits of their troubles in England have been edited with rather dubious introductions.[249] Bossy offers an impressive portrait of the catholic

[242] Patrick Collinson, *The Elizabethan Puritan Movement*. L: Cape: 1967. Pp. 582. Rev: *EHR* 83, 833f.; *HJ* 11, 586ff.

[243] Patrick Collinson, 'John Field and Elizabethan Puritanism', *Neale Ft* (n. 125), 127–62. – S. J. Knox, *Walter Travers: paragon of English puritanism*. L: Methuen: 1962. Pp. 172. Rev: *EHR* 79, 359.

[244] Ronald A. Marchant, *The Puritans and the Church Courts in the Diocese of York 1590 – 1642*. L: Longmans: 1960. Pp. xii, 330. Rev: *EHR* 77, 331f.

[245] John H. Primus, *The Vestments Controversy: an historical study of the earliest tensions within the Church of England in the reigns of Edward VI and Elizabeth*. Kampen: Kok: 1960. Pp. xiv, 176.

[246] Donald J. McGinn, *The Admonition Controversy*. New Brunswick, N.J.: Rutgers UP: 1949. Pp. xii, 589.

[247] Donald J. McGinn, *John Penry and the Marprelate Controversy*. New Brunswick N.J.: Rutgers UP: 1966. Pp. xiii, 274. Rev: *EHR* 83, 169f.

[248] W. Schenk, *Reginald Pole, Cardinal of England*. L: Longmans: 1950. Pp. xvi, 176. Rev: *AHR* 56, 338f.

[249] Philip Caraman, ed., *John Gerard: the autobiography of an Elizabethan*. L: Longmans: 1951. Pp. xxiv, 287. – Idem, ed., *William*

minority,[250] while Trimble's book on the same subject makes so many errors in method and understanding that one hardly knows what to do with the result.[251] One of those priest-producing lay families forms the subject of a partisan study,[252] but a discussion of catholic pamphleteering has greater scholarly value.[253]

To conclude with two uncategorizable works: Maclure runs over a century of ecclesiastical propaganda,[254] and Williams, at work on a history of the Welsh Reformation, provides an interim report in a collection of essays.[255]

(E) SOCIAL AND ECONOMIC HISTORY

Here things are very much in flux: the useful short introduction by Ramsey presents more open questions than agreed answers.[256] The most striking phenomenon of the period, the great inflation, is briefly but magisterially explained in Outhwaite's essay;[257] Challis adds detailed information on the debasement which was a major cause of the price rise.[258] The

---

Weston: autobiography of an Elizabethan. L: Longmans: 1955. Pp. xxi, 259. – *See also* n. 169.

[250] John A. Bossy, 'The character of Elizabethan catholicism', *PP* 21 (1962), 39–57.

[251] William R. Trimble, *The Catholic Laity in Elizabethan England, 1558 – 1603.* C (Mass.): Belknap Press: 1964. Pp. xii, 290. Rev: *EHR* 81, 163.

[252] Godfrey Anstruther, *Vaux of Harrowden: a recusant family.* Newport, Mon.: R. H. Johns: 1953. Pp. xv, 552.

[253] Thomas H. Clancy, *Papist Pamphleteers: the Allen-Parsons party in the political thought of the Counter-Reformation in England, 1572 – 1615.* Chicago: Loyola UP: 1964. Pp. xi, 256. Rev: *EHR* 81, 162.

[254] Millar Maclure, *The Paul's Cross Sermons 1534 – 1642.* U of Toronto P: 1958. Pp. ix, 261.

[255] Glanmor Williams, *Welsh Reformation Essays.* Cardiff: U of Wales P: 1967. Pp. 219. Rev: *EHR* 84, 611f.

[256] Peter H. Ramsey, *Tudor Economic Problems.* L: Gollancz: 1963. Pp. 192. Rev: *EcHR*² 16, 366f.

[257] R. B. Outhwaite, *Inflation in Tudor and Early Stuart England.* L: Macmillan: 1969. Pp. 60. Rev: *EcHR*² 22, 559.

[258] C. E. Challis, 'The debasement of the coinage, 1542 – 1551', *EcHR*² 20 (1967), 441–66.

most striking phenomenon in the period's historiography, on the other hand, was the 'storm over the gentry', the attempt to analyse the economic and social fortunes of the landed classes in the belief that thereby the 'real' causes of the Civil War would become apparent. Tawney maintained the 'rise' of the gentry at the expense of crown and aristocracy, and Stone added the 'decline' of the latter; Trevor-Roper had little difficulty in exposing the doubtful methods of this school, but less success in maintaining his own notions of a rising 'court' gentry and a declining 'country' gentry; the debate, often violent, was sympathetically regarded by Zagorin and ironically demolished by Hexter.[259] Meanwhile, several specific attempts have been made to test happy theory by awkward fact, a process which has proved sobering.[260] Then it was again Stone's turn, with his enormous book on the aristocracy (really the parliamentary peerage) which has much of great value in it but cannot, despite all the statistics, substantiate its main thesis, namely that the nobility on the eve of the Civil War was socially and economically stricken.[261] What emerges from the turmoil is

[259] Richard H. Tawney, 'The rise of the gentry 1558 – 1640', *EcHR*[1] 11 (1941), 1–38. – Lawrence Stone, 'The anatomy of the Elizabethan aristocracy', *ibid.* 18 (1948), 1–53. – Hugh R. Trevor-Roper, 'The Elizabethan aristocracy: an anatomy anatomized', *EcHR*[2] 3 (1950 – 1), 279–98. – Idem, *The Gentry 1540 – 1640.* CUP: 1953: Pp. 55. Rev: *EHR* 69, 147f. – Perez Zagorin, 'The social interpretation of the English revolution', *Journal of Econ. Hist.* 19 (1959), 376–401. – J. H. Hexter, 'Storm over the Gentry', *Reappraisals in History* (n. 124), 117–62 (where see also for a full bibliography).

[260] Mary Finch, *The Wealth of Five Northamptonshire Families, 1540 – 1640.* L: OUP: 1956. Pp. xx, 246. Rev: *EcHR*[2] 11, 163f. – Alan Simpson, *The Wealth of the Gentry 1540 – 1640: East Anglian studies.* Chicago UP: 1961. Pp. viii, 226. Rev: *EHR* 78, 774f.; *AHR* 68, 106ff. – J. T. Cliffe, *The Yorkshire Gentry from the Reformation to the Civil War.* L: Athlone: 1969. Pp. xii, 446. – Howell A. Lloyd, *The Gentry of South-West Wales, 1540 – 1640.* Cardiff: U of Wales P: 1968. Pp. 256. Rev: *Hist* 54, 273.

[261] Lawrence Stone, *The Crisis of the Aristocracy.* O: Clarendon: 1965. Pp. xxiv, 841. Rev: *EHR* 81, 562ff.; *PP* 32, 113ff.; *EcHR*[2] 22, 308ff.; *Hist* 51, 165ff.

mainly negative: no essential distinction can be made between gentry and aristocracy, and the Civil War was clearly not the outcome of mainly economic or social strains.

Less exciting but a little more satisfactory has been the progress of agricultural studies. The first volume to appear of a co-operative history of English agriculture covers this period and provides both specific discussion and useful summary right across the board.[262] However, one of the pillars of knowledge in these matters, Tawney's thesis of a capitalist destruction of the traditional rural society, is firmly demolished in Kerridge's demonstration of what the law and its effects really were.[263] Kerridge has also removed the statistical bases of all discussions of enclosure and rent, without so far replacing them by anything new.[264] Habakkuk exterminates several prejudice-ridden errors which had gathered around the sale of secularized lands;[265] his general doubts are confirmed by a particular study of Devon.[266] Fisher emphasizes London's role in creating a specialist agriculture to serve it.[267] Rural housing[268] and fen farming[269] have been studied; Thirsk has usefully summarized what is mostly believed about enclosures;[270]

---

[262] Joan Thirsk, ed., *The Agrarian History of England and Wales: IV, 1500 – 1640*. CUP: 1967. Pp. xl, 919. Rev: *EcHR*² 20, 614ff.; *HJ* 11, 583ff.

[263] Eric Kerridge, *Agrarian Problems in the Sixteenth Century and After*. L: Allen & Unwin: 1969. Pp. xii, 216.

[264] Eric Kerridge, 'The returns of the inquisition of depopulation', *EHR* 70 (1955), 212–28; 'The movement of rent 1540 – 1640', *EcHR*² 6 (1953 – 4), 16–34.

[265] Hrothgar J. Habakkuk, 'The market for monastic property 1549 – 1603', *EcHR*² 10 (1957 – 8), 362–80.

[266] Joyce A. Youings, 'The terms of the disposal of Devon monastic lands', *EHR* 69 (1954), 18–38.

[267] F. J. Fisher, 'The development of London as a centre of conspicuous consumption in the 16th and 17th centuries', *TRHS* (1948), 21–36.

[268] W. S. Hoskins, 'The rebuilding of rural England', *PP* 4 (1954), 44–59.

[269] Joan Thirsk, *Fenland Farming in the Sixteenth Century*. Univ. College of Leicester, Dept. of Local History: Occasional Papers no. 3: 1953. Pp. 45.

[270] Joan Thirsk, *Tudor Enclosures*. L: Routledge: 1959. Pp. 22.

all this valiant work has found ultimate reception in her volume in the general agrarian history.

The historians of trade have met fewer legends and in consequence been less controversial. Ruddock describes the decline of Southampton and its traffic with Italy.[271] We still await a history of the Merchant Adventurers, but at least we have had an important contribution from the other end, from Antwerp.[272] Willan's energy has made the century's other trading companies one of its better known topics.[273] An unorthodox attempt to say something fresh about the companies employs a computer in order to discover who invested in enterprise; the book is unfortunately marred by some crude classifications, nor does it justify its claim that only technical aids of this kind can answer the question posed.[274] At a time when cloth constituted some eighty per cent of exports, the trade in raw wool was of little significance, but we nevertheless have had two books on the subject.[275] The obscure theme of international credit receives some illumination in de Roover's edition of a

[271] Alwyn A. Ruddock, 'London capitalists and the decline of Southampton in the early Tudor period', *EcHR²* 2 (1949 – 50), 135–51. – Eadem, *Italian Merchants and Shipping in Southampton 1270 – 1600.* Southampton: University College: 1951. Pp. xi, 294. Rev: *EHR* 68, 432ff.

[272] Oskar de Smedt, *De Engelske Natie te Antwerpen in de 16e Eeuw,* 2 vols. Antwerp: de Sikkel: 1950, 1954. Pp. viii, 488; vi, 743. Rev: *EHR* 72, 500ff.

[273] T. S. Willan, *The Muscovy Merchants of 1555.* Manchester UP: 1953. Pp. viii, 141. Rev: *EHR* 69, 333. – Idem. *The Early History of the Russia Company 1553–1603.* Manchester UP: 1956. Pp. ix, 295. Rev: *EHR* 72, 316ff.; *EcHR²* 9, 364. – Idem, *Studies in Elizabethan Foreign Trade.* Manchester UP: 1959. Pp. x, 349. Rev: *EHR* 76, 144f.; *EcHR²* 12, 293f. – Idem, 'Some aspects of English trade with the Levant', *EHR* 70 (1955), 399–410.

[274] Theodore K. Rabb, *Enterprise and Empire.* C (Mass.): Harvard UP: 1967. Pp. xii, 420. Rev: *EHR* 85, 171; *EcHR²* 22, 130f.; *Hist* 53, 425f.

[275] Peter J. Bowden, *The Wool Trade in Tudor and Stuart England.* L: Macmillan: 1962. Pp. viii, 246. Rev: *EHR* 79, 593f. – T. C. Mendenhall, *The Shrewsbury Drapers and the Welsh Wool Trade in the XV and XVI Centuries.* L: OUP: 1953. Pp. x, 248. Rev: *EHR* 69, 483f.

tract which he ascribes, possibly incorrectly, to Thomas Gresham.[276] Burwash and Scammell have made a start on the rich
source material available for a study of ship-building and
shipping.[277]

The old certainty that the Tudor state pursued a consciously
mercantilist policy has been severely shaken. Stone sees purely
military ends in what on the face of it looks like an economic
policy; by criticizing the sources, Elton casts doubt on the
whole notion of a policy directed from the centre.[278] Clarkson,
on the other hand, uses the leather industry in order to argue
after all for self-conscious central control in the interests of
economic advance.[279] Another social problem of the century
has been subjected to 'social science' treatment; indeed, it is
arguable that only the concerns of modern sociology have been
at work in inventing the problem at all. Using a 'model', in
order to study social mobility, Stone argues that at this time
the class structure (was there a class structure?) was less rigid
than before or after; but his use of sources is peculiar and the
result neither certain nor striking. Everitt's more modest contribution persuades better but has little new to say.[280]

At this time, economic history also comprehends the story
of exploration and of imperial beginnings. (See also Rowse,
n. 148.) The earliest voyages under English auspices have been
re-studied, with great additions to knowledge and much

---

[276] Raymond de Roover, *Gresham on Foreign Exchange: an essay in early
English mercantilism*. C (Mass.): Harvard UP: 1949. Pp. xx, 348.
Dewar (n. 198) may be right in thinking that the tract was written
by Sir Thomas Smith.

[277] Dorothy Burwash, *English Merchant Shipping, 1460 – 1540*. Toronto
UP: 1947. Pp. xii, 259. Rev: *EcHR*[2] 2, 335ff. – Geoffrey V.
Scammell, 'Shipowning in England, c. 1450 – 1550', *TRHS* (1962),
105–122.

[278] Lawrence Stone, 'State control in sixteenth century England',
EcHR[1] 12 (1947), 103–20. – G. R. Elton, 'State planning in
early Tudor England', *EcHR*[2] 13 (1960 – 1), 433–9.

[279] L. A. Clarkson, 'English economic policy in the 16th and 17th
centuries: the case of the leather industry', *BIHR* 38 (1965),
149–62.

[280] Lawrence Stone and Alan M. Everitt, 'Social mobility in England,
1500 – 1700', *PP* 33 (1966), 16–73.

significant change in interpretation.[281] That the English privateers were active much earlier than used to be supposed is
shown by Connell-Smith;[282] that their activities were much
more profitable than earlier scholarship supposed is shown by
Andrews.[283] Three of the sea-dogs have received new and excellent treatment.[284] Parker supplies an unpretentious and useful survey of the familiar propaganda literature behind the
voyages.[285] The technicalities of navigational science are described by Waters with impressive learning and lucidity.[286]

(f) CULTURE AND CIVILIZATION

Printing was still much practised by foreigners, and Armstrong's account of the Frenchman Robert Estienne is most
useful.[287] Rosenberg shows what may be done with dedicatory
prefaces to books as a source for the study of patronage.[288]
Auerbach uses the sketches of royal personages found in the
initial letters of plea rolls to disentangle chronological prob-

[281] James A. Williamson, *The Cabot Voyages and Bristol Discovery under Henry VII*, with the cartography of the voyages by R. A. Skelton. C: Hakluyt Society: 1962. Pp. xvi, 332. Rev: *EHR* 79, 836f.

[282] Gordon Connell-Smith, *Forerunners of Drake: a study of English trade with Spain in the early Tudor period*. L: Longmans: 1954. Pp. xxii, 264. Rev: *EHR* 69, 657f.

[283] Kenneth R. Andrews, *English Privateering: English privateers during the Spanish war, 1585 – 1603*. CUP: 1964. Pp. xv, 297. Rev: *EHR* 81, 590f.

[284] James A. Williamson, *Hawkins of Plymouth*. L: Black: 1949. Pp. xi, 348. – David B. Quinn, *Raleigh and the British Empire*. L: English Universities Press: 1947, Pp. xiii, 284. – Kenneth E. Andrews, *Drake's Voyages*. L: Weidenfeld: 1967. Pp. ix, 190. Rev: *EcHR*² 20, 391f.

[285] John Parker, *Books to Build an Empire: a bibliographical history of English overseas interests to 1620*. Amsterdam: Israel: 1965. Pp. viii, 290. Rev: *EHR* 83, 167f.

[286] D. W. Waters, *The Art of Navigation in England in Elizabethan and Early Stuart Times*. L: Hollis & Carter: 1958. Pp. xxxix, 696. Rev: *EHR* 75, 303ff.

[287] Elizabeth Armstrong, *Robert Estienne, Royal Printer*. CUP: 1954. Pp. xxi, 310.

[288] Eleanor Rosenberg, *Leicester, Patron of Letters*. New York: Columbia UP: 1955. Pp. xx, 395. Rev: *EHR* 72, 318ff.

lems in the history of art.[289] Strong's studies of the portraits of
Henry VIII and Elizabeth have added much needed precision
to this familiar theme.[290] A mixture of the history of art, the
history of ideas, and some awareness of affairs enables Anglo
to bring out the significance of public display in the Tudor
period;[291] he does, however, rather lose himself in the loving
description of lavish occasions. The same might be said of
Russell's particular study of the most lavish occasion of all, but
the book makes no pretence of trying for more.[292] The
thoroughness and tedium of sixteenth-century preaching are
rather too faithfully reproduced in a study of the subject.[293]
Lehmberg paints a handsome portrait of a well-connected but
second-class humanist;[294] a more conventional humanist,
Roger Ascham, receives a sufficient but suitably conventional
biography.[295] For the least conventional of Tudor writers and
thinkers (and actors), Walter Raleigh, we now possess an
exhaustive and seemingly perceptive analysis of his work.[296]
Raleigh was only one of many who wrote about the new world,
as Blanke (and everybody else) knows: his study of English
writers' treatment of the subject collects a lot of examples but,
rather inevitably, cannot do much with them.[297] Haller uses

---

[289] Erna Auerbach, *Tudor Artists*. L: Athlone: 1954. Pp. xvi, 222;
52 plates. Rev: *EHR* 70, 123ff.

[290] Roy Strong, *Holbein and Henry VIII*. L: Routledge: 1967. Pp. 75. –
Idem, *Portraits of Queen Elizabeth*. O: Clarendon: 1963. Pp. xv, 173.

[291] Sydney Anglo, *Spectacle, Pageantry, and Early Tudor Policy*. O:
Clarendon: 1969. Pp. viii, 375.

[292] Jocelyne G. Russell, *The Field of Cloth of Gold*. L: Routledge: 1969.
Pp. xiii, 248.

[293] J. W. Blench, *Preaching in England in the late 15th and 16th Centuries:
a study of English sermons, 1450 – c. 1600*. O: Blackwell: 1964. Pp.
xv, 378.

[294] Stanford E. Lehmberg, *Sir Thomas Elyot, Tudor Humanist*. Austin:
U of Texas P: 1960. Pp. xv, 218. Rev: *EHR* 77, 556f.

[295] Lawrence V. Ryan, *Roger Ascham*. Stanford UP: 1963. Pp. xii,
352. Rev: *EHR* 81, 158f.

[296] [Pierre Lefranc, *Sir Walter Ralegh Ecrivain: l'œuvre et les ideés*.
Quebec: Presses de l'Université Laval: 1968. Pp. 733. Rev: *EHR*
85, 122ff.; *AHR* 75, 116ff.]

[297] Gustav H. Blanke, *Amerika im englischen Schrifttum des 16. und 17.
Jahrhunderts*. Bochum-Langendreer: Pöppinghaus: 1962. Pp. 336.

John Foxe's book to produce an entrancing and utterly convincing picture of the popular attitudes of the time, formed by low-grade religion and chauvinistic prejudice.[298] The social history of music receives attention from Stephens for the earlier and from Woodfill for the later part of the century.[299] The mass-production industry which serves Shakespeare and other Elizabethan poets cannot be admitted here, but one may mention a book on the activities of English actors in Sweden which is oriented more towards the social than the literary problems.[300] A dissertation which collects English opinions concerning the newly discovered Russia contains some information on trade which Willan's work has rendered out of date.[301] The doyen among historians of mathematics has composed a biographical collection for the sixteenth and seventeenth centuries.[302]

[298] William Haller, *Foxe's Book of Martyrs and the Elect Nation*. L: Cape: 1963. Pp. 259. Rev: *EHR* 80, 589f.

[299] John Stevens, *Music and Poetry in the Early Tudor Court*. L: Methuen: 1961. Pp. xi, 481. Rev: *EHR* 78, 167. – Walter L. Woodfill, *Musicians in English Society from Elizabeth to Charles I*. Princeton UP: 1953. Pp. xv, 372. Rev: *EHR* 69, 665.

[300] Erik Wikland, *Elizabethan Players and Sweden, 1591 – 1592*. Stockholm: Almqvist: 1962. Pp. 192. Rev: *EHR* 79, 413f.

[301] Karl Heinz Ruffmann, *Das Russlandbild im England Shakespeares*. Göttingen: Musterschmidt: 1952. Pp. 185.

[302] E. G. R. Taylor, *The Mathematical Practitioners of Tudor and Stuart England*. CUP: 1954. Pp. xi, 443.

VI

The Seventeenth Century (1603 – 1714)

Also nn. 24–5, 32–4, 38–40, 55–8, 70, 1024–5, 1043–6, 1056–7, 1067, 1072, 1084, 1095, 1108–34, 1169–70, 1185–9, 1211–24, 1237–44.

(A) GENERAL

This period, which is still by many regarded – with some reason – as the crucial and transforming age in the history of English society, has been much studied, but no one has so far attempted to rethink the meaning of this much disturbed century afresh. It remains, too readily, the 'century of revolution', even though it is becoming more and more apparent, all the noise of battle notwithstanding, that few things really changed, and that continuity is at least as notable as revolution. While our understanding of the surrounding territory in the sixteenth and eighteenth centuries has been greatly altered in the past twenty-five years, an orthodoxy created by the men of the seventeenth century themselves, and since buttressed by the doctrinaire preoccupations of liberalism and Marxism, still underlies most books on this period. The tradition may not be altogether misleading, though it is certainly not as obviously correct as seems still to be accepted, but it is a pity that a large number of historians who have done so much valuable work inside the framework fixed by tradition should not have seen that their own labours often disrupt it.

Of more general accounts, only Kenyon's introductions to his collection of documents (n. 24) indicate plainly the probable lines of major re-ordering. Ashley's little book has no independent value, Aylmer's (intended primarily for the schools) has too little space to do more than bring together a highly serviceable version of the usual story, and Hill's thrillingly esoteric treatment demands a good deal of fore-knowledge from the reader.[303] Gough pursues the seventeenth-century commonplace concerning fundamental laws and shows that it became most commonplace when it had ceased to play its part as umpire between prerogative and parliament.[304] A discussion of ministerial responsibility, useful in itself, carries a strangely oldfashioned air of formal constitutional history treated in its own right and without a proper sense of what goes on in politics.[305] Mathew's description of social circumstances is civilized.[306] Bohatec left behind him a strange aberration – reflections on some mid-century writers as representatives of humane thinking; this intellectually very undistinguished book reflects rather the author's unhappy personal experiences and his touching anglomania.[307] Wormuth, too briefly, documents the continued existence of the Interregnum's experiments under the guise of a primitive 'gothic' dream.[308] And Ogg completed his general history of the later Stuarts in a massive volume full of excellence.[309] Plumb outlines a programme of research on a new and vital topic: voters and the franchise.[310]

---

[303] Maurice Ashley, *England in the Seventeenth Century*. Harmondsworth: Penguin Books: 1952. Pp. 256. – Gerald E. Aylmer, *The Struggle for the Constitution 1603 – 1689*. L: Blandford: 1963. Pp. viii, 247. – Christopher Hill, *The Century of Revolution*. Edinburgh: Nelson: 1961. Pp. xii, 340. Rev: *HJ* 5, 80ff.

[304] J. W. Gough, *Fundamental Law in English Constitutional History*. O: Clarendon: 1955. Pp. x, 229. Rev: *EHR* 71, 90ff.; *AHR* 61, 109f.

[305] Clayton Roberts, *The Growth of Responsible Government in Stuart England*. CUP: 1966. Pp. xii, 467. Rev: *EHR* 83, 795ff.; *Hist* 52, 201f.

[306] David Mathew, *The Social Structure of Caroline England*. O: Clarendon: 1948. Pp. 140. – Idem, *The Age of Charles I*. L: Eyre & Spottiswoode: 1951. Pp. xvii, 340. Rev. *EHR* 67, 409ff.

[307] Joseph Bohatec, *England und die Geschichte der Menschen- und Bürgerrechte*. Graz/Köln: Böhlau: 1956. Pp. 136. Rev: *EHR* 72, 750.

[308] Francis D. Wormuth, *The Origins of Modern Constitutionalism*. New York: Harper: 1949. Pp. x, 243.

[309] David Ogg, *England in the Reigns of James II and William III*. O: Clarendon: 1955. Pp. xiii, 567. Rev: *EHR* 71, 297ff.; *CHJ* 12, 195ff.

[310] John H. Plumb, 'The Growth of the Electorate in England from 1600 to 1715', *PP* 45 (1969), 90–116.

(B) 1603 – 1604

The political history of this pre-war period remains astonishingly dominated by S. R. Gardiner and indeed by the so-called
history purveyed in the Grand Remonstrance; the occasional
dissentient tends to be concerned with defending the indefen-
sible, the policy of Charles I. The only attempt at an analytical
survey demolishes a fair number of erroneous suppositions
(Marxist, post-Marxist and anti-Marxist) but comes up with
essentially the same old story of party formation without ever
being able to demonstrate any real identity for the two opposing
camps which form the title of the book.[311] Willson's James I is
the buffoon of tradition;[312] despite the book's solidity and skill,
the less severe judgment, offered by Carter in a work which
contains much of relevance to English affairs, is probably
nearer the truth.[313] That dim creature, bishop Goodman, has
found a biographer who, astonishingly, takes him seriously.[314]
Hulme's careful life of Eliot gathers in all that need be known,
though it is a good deal too drily sober to do justice to its
neurotic and effervescent subject.[315] Hill's collection of
weighty articles contains, in particular, pieces on 'the Norman
yoke' (the legend of the Anglo-Saxons' free constitution which
has had a very long life) and on John Preston, puritan and
politician.[316] A little life of Preston, short on technical scholarly
detail, compensates by showing real historical understanding;
it demonstrates how unrevolutionary and near to political

[311] Perez Zagorin, *The Court and the Country: the beginning of the English
Revolution.* L: Routledge: 1969. Pp. xiv, 366.

[312] David H. Willson, *James VI and I.* L: Cape: 1956. Pp. 480. Rev:
EHR 72, 117ff.

[313] Charles H. Carter, *The Secret Diplomacy of the Habsburgs, 1598 –
1625.* New York: Columbia UP: 1964. Pp. xiv, 321. Rev: *EHR* 82,
164f.

[314] G. T. Soden, *Godfrey Goodman, Bishop of Gloucester, 1583 – 1656.* L:
SPCK: 1953. Pp. xiii, 511. Rev: *EHR* 69, 333f.

[315] Harold Hulme, *The Life of Sir John Eliot, 1592 – 1632.* New York:
New York UP: 1957. Pp. 423. Rev: *AHR* 62, 660f. *See also* J. N.
Ball, 'Sir John Eliot and the Oxford Parliament 1625', *BIHR* 28
(1955), 113–27.

[316] Christopher Hill, *Puritanism and Revolution.* L: Secker & Warburg:
1958. Pp. x, 402. Rev: *EHR* 75, 164f.

success this kind of puritanism was.[317] Charles I's secretary of state has received his tribute from one of his descendants.[318] Wedgwood did the improbable and unusual when she replaced her earlier biography of Strafford by a new one written sixteen years later; in place of the hero on horseback painted by enthusiastic youth, we now have the energetic, self-seeking able, but maladroit man of reality.[319] Cranfield, merchant and politician, has inspired two books: Tawney's contains a brilliant sweep across the commercial scene of the day but little of precise detail, while Prestwich, though perhaps too involved in the detail of her subject's private dealings, also provides the best account of Jacobean politics that at present we have.[320] The story should be completed from Ashton's brilliant investigations into the early Stuarts' disastrous financial policies.[321] Two competent biographies deal with two very different, but equally characteristic, phenomena on the Jacobean stage – the upstart founder of a landed family, and the established aristocrat seeking further satisfaction in puritanism and humanism.[322]

The manifest problems of an age of increasing political tension have been subjected to further investigation which, though tradi-

---

[317] I. Morgan, *Prince Charles's Puritan Chaplain*. L: Allen & Unwin: 1957. Pp. 219. Rev: *EHR* 73, 719f.

[318] Douglas Nicholas, *Mr Secretary Nicholas, 1593 – 1669*. L: Bodley Head: 1955. Pp. 336. Rev: *EHR* 71, 333.

[319] C. Veronica Wedgwood, *Thomas Wentworth, first earl of Strafford, 1593 – 1641: a revaluation*. L: Cape: 1961. Pp. 415. Rev: *EHR* 79, 375ff.

[320] Richard H. Tawney, *Business and Politics under James I: Lionel Cranfield as merchant and minister*. CUP: 1958. Pp. xii, 235. Rev: *EHR* 77, 155ff.; *EcHR*² 11, 515ff. – Menna Prestwich, *Cranfield: profits and politics under the early Stuarts*. O: Clarendon: 1966. Pp. xi, 623. Rev: *EHR* 83, 348f.; *HJ* 11, 189f.

[321] Robert Ashton, *The Crown and the Money Market*. O: Clarendon: 1960. Pp. xvi, 223. Rev: *EHR* 78, 169f.; *EcHR*² 14, 145ff. – Idem, 'Revenue farming under the early Stuarts', *EcHR*² 8 (1955 – 6), 310–22; 'Deficit finance in the reign of James I', *ibid.* 10 (1957 – 1958), 15–29; 'Charles I and the City', *Tawney Ft* (n. 126), 138–63.

[322] A. F. Upton, *Sir Arthur Ingram, c. 1565 – 1642: a study of the origins of an English landed family*. L: OUP: 1961. Pp. x, 274. Rev: *EHR* 77, 764f. – Robert E. L. Strider, *Robert Grenville, Lord Brooke*. C (Mass.): Harvard UP: 1958. Pp. xiv, 252.

tional in form, at times strongly suggests that the traditional interpretation will not do. Thus Judson's study of the ideas that allegedly underlay conflict arrives at the conclusion that it would be quite wrong to think in terms of a constitutional or legal dispute since everybody agreed on all points of essence.[323] What Hinton can discover of Eliot's political ideas supports this view.[324] Mosse, however, dissenting from McIlwain's long-established ruling, does find a conscious struggle for sovereignty in the debates of the half-century before the civil war.[325] The pointless parliament of 1614 receives the most pointful study yet given to an early-Stuart parliament.[326] The revisionary enterprise is potentially supported by a careful discussion of monarchic claims in this period which are shown to have developed from Tudor traditions rather than from a doctrine imported by James I (*contra* McIlwain).[327] Particular political issues have been looked at. Thus Rabb analyses the position of the Stuart's first parliamentary opponent; his views on Edwin Sandys's economic tenets have evoked the justified wrath of Ashton.[328] Elton demonstrates (successfully, despite some doubts) that the *Apology* of 1604 was never accepted by the

---

[323] Margaret A. Judson, *The Crisis of the Constitution*. New Brunswick N.J.: Rutgers UP: 1949. Pp. xi, 444. Rev: *AHR* 55, 887f.

[324] R. W. K. Hinton, 'Government and liberty under James I', *CHJ* 11 (1957), 48–64.

[325] George L. Mosse, *The Struggle for Sovereignty in England from the Reign of Queen Elizabeth to the Petition of Right*. East Lansing: Michigan State College Press: 1950. Pp. vii, 191. Rev: *AHR* 56, 868f.

[326] T. L. Moir, *The Addled Parliament of 1614*. O: Clarendon: 1958. Pp. x, 212. Rev: *EHR* 74, 529f. – On the other hand: William Mitchell, *The Rise of the Revolutionary Party in the English House of Commons*. New York: Columbia UP: 1957. Pp. xvi, 209. The methodological weaknesses and misplaced notions of this book make use of it depend on careful scrutiny of every detail.

[327] Gerhard A. Ritter, 'Divine Right und Prärogative der englischen Könige 1603 – 1640', *Historische Zeitschrift* 196 (1963), 584–625.

[328] Theodore K. Rabb, 'Sir Edwyn Sandys and the Parliament of 1604', *AHR* 69 (1694), 646–70. – Robert Ashton, 'The parliamentary agitation for free trade in the opening years of the reign of James I', *PP* 38 (1967), 40–55. Rabb's rejoinder is in *PP* 40 (1968), 165–73.

commons and must not be used to prove their collective attitude at this time; but he is mistaken in part about the document's later history.[329] Hall establishes that in the well-known
test case on impositions in 1606 neither side could usefully rely
on precedent.[330] The political manœuvres of two faction
centres have been looked at; there is a lot more to do in this
respect.[331] Boynton has given some substance to two of the
complaints raised in 1628 against Buckingham's regime.[332]
Two strictly technical problems of parliamentary history are
discussed by de Villiers and Latham.[333]

The constitutional issue is no longer as clear as it seemed to
Gardiner, but recognition of the fact remains to seek; that of
the Church has been even more drastically reopened, but here
scholars seem more willing to listen. Few would now speak of a
quarrel between puritanism and anglicanism; and those who
would – seeing that until the age of Laud at least puritanism
was a form, even the dominant form, of anglicanism – would
be wrong. The whole concept of puritanism has been much
debated (see also Section 6, D). Hill has remained persuaded
that the political and social consequences of strict Calvinism
produced a class struggle within and without the clergy, and
also that the civil war should be explained by means of this
socio-economic conflict.[334] Though no one has a more ranging

[329] G. R. Elton, 'A high road to civil war?', *Mattingly Ft* (n. 127),
325–47.
[330] G. D. G. Hall, 'Impositions and the courts, 1554 – 1606', *LQR*
69 (1953), 200–18.
[331] Robert W. Kenny, 'Parliamentary influence of Charles Howard,
earl of Nottingham, 1536 – 1624', *JMH* 39 (1967), 215–32. –
Lawrence Stone, 'The electoral influence of the second earl of
Salisbury, 1614 – 1668', *EHR* 71 (1956), 384–400.
[332] Lindsay Boynton, 'Billeting: the example of the Isle of Wight',
EHR 74 (1959), 23–40; 'Martial Law and the petition of right',
ibid. (1964), 255–84.
[333] Elizabeth de Villiers, 'Parliamentary boroughs restored by the
House of Commons, 1621 – 1641', *EHR* 67 (1952), 175–202. –
R. C. Latham, 'Payment of parliamentary wages: the last phase',
ibid. 66 (1953), 27–50.
[334] Christopher Hill, *Economic Problems of the Church from Archbishop
Whitgift to the Long Parliament.* O: Clarendon: 1956. Pp. xiv, 367.

knowledge of one kind of evidence for this period, doubts are increasingly manifesting themselves whether the whole question can be answered by means of his methods which rely on contemporary comment rather than ascertainable fact and articulate things around a highly refined derivation from the Marxist interpretation. Zagorin, for one (n. 311), successfully tackles Hill on precisely his own ground, while the historians of the Church and religion cannot any longer find his kind of puritanism in the record (nn. 371 – 6, 1237).

The difficulties of those who found it impossible simply to conform to the established Church are illustrated briefly by Curtis (puritanism disappointed by James I) and Havran (papists disappointed by Charles I).[335]

A start has at last been made on replacing generalizations about the constitution by facts about the administration. Aylmer's excellent study, which for the first time gives reality to Charles I's government by really looking at his officials (by means of biography, statistics, and unfortunately also sociological abstractions), ought quickly to find imitators for other periods.[336] And Barnes's full-scale investigation of a single shire, at a time when the relations between centre and country became politically crucial, is a model of another kind which one hopes to see widely copied before long.[337]

(c) 1640 – 1660

Roots' fine straight account of the war and Interregnum has plenty of elan but not enough breath when particular problems

Rev: *EHR* 73, 294ff.; *EcHR*² 11, 518f. – Idem, *Society and Puritanism in Pre-Revolutionary England*. L: Secker & Warburg: 1964. Pp. 520. Rev: *EHR* 81, 358ff.; *AHR* 70, 118f.; *EcHR*² 17, 579ff. – *See also* n. 316.

[335] Mark H. Curtis, 'The Hampton Court conference and its aftermath', *Hist* 46 (1961), 1–16. – Martin J. Havran, *The Catholics in Caroline England*. Stanford UP: 1962. Pp. xi, 208. Rev: *EHR* 79, 605f.

[336] Gerald E. Aylmer, *The King's Servants: the civil service of Charles I, 1625 – 1642*. L: Routledge: 1961. Pp. xii, 521. Rev: *EHR* 77, 536ff.; *PP* 20, 76ff.; *HJ* 4, 230ff. – Idem, 'Attempts at administrative reform, 1625 – 1640', *EHR* 72 (1957), 229–59.

[337] Thomas G. Barnes, *Somerset 1624 – 1640*. L: OUP: 1961. Pp. xviii, 369. Rev: *EHR* 78, 330ff.; *EcHR*² 15, 156ff.

need solving.[338] The road to war and the war itself down to Charles I's execution are lavishly recounted in Wedgwood's trilogy which contributes little that is new and tends to pass by the tricky questions of understanding and interpretation.[339] One of these questions engages Hill who has tried to demonstrate essential connections between revolutionary puritanism and the new ideas in science and scholarship, an attempt which has failed to convince and has met with much criticism.[340] Markedly less original but equally doubtful is Eusden's view of a simple alliance between lawyers and parliament against the king;[341] this is a theme crying out for independence of mind, for while the tradition glibly links common law and revolution, the facts demonstrate that the larger part of the profession supported the king, at least till 1640. Freund purports to describe the manner in which parliamentary opposition developed into revolutionary party, but since he admits to relying simply on Gardiner's narration his book has no independent value and is a long way behind the state of research.[342] More important are two studies that look at the time of transition between peace and war. Wormald, tracking Edward Hyde, demonstrates the slow and painful emergence of the king's party from among the fragments of the earlier united opposition;[343] Pearl,

---

[338] Ivan Roots, *The Great Rebellion*. L: Batsford: 1966. Pp. x, 326. Rev: *EHR* 83, 840.

[339] C. Veronica Wedgwood, *The King's Peace 1637 – 1641*. L: Collins: 1955. Pp. 510. – Idem, *The King's War 1641 – 1647*. Ibid.: 1958. Pp. 703. Rev: *EHR* 75, 163f. – Idem, *The Trial of Charles I*. Ibid.: 1964. Pp. 253. Rev: *EHR* 81, 594f.

[340] Christopher Hill, *Intellectual Origins of the English Revolution*. O: Clarendon: 1965. Pp. xiii, 333. Rev: *PP* 31, 111ff.; *HJ* 8, 413ff.; *History and Theory* 5, 61ff.

[341] John D. Eusden, *Puritans, Lawyers and Politics in early 17th Century England*. New Haven: Yale UP: 1958. Pp. xii, 238. Rev; *EHR* 74, 732f.

[342] Michael Freund, *Die grosse Revolution in England: Anatomie eines Umsturzes*. Hamburg: Claassen: 1951. Pp. 529. Rev: *AHR* 58, 105f.

[343] Brian H. G. Wormald, *Clarendon: politics, history and religion, 1640 – 1660*. CUP: 1951. Pp. xiii, 331. Rev: *EHR* 67, 271ff.; *AHR* 57, 127f.

studying the revolution in the capital, shows the stages by which the conservative and royalist pre-war regime was over-thrown by a revolutionary party.[344] It remains to discover just how or why a confrontation occurred which even in November 1640 was out of the question; the one attempt at answering this question, made by Zagorin (n. 311), seems to me to assume too much coherence in Pym's party and policy, and not to recog-nize sufficiently that the bulk of the people involved were in a very real sense surprised by war.

We have two analyses of the Long Parliament. Brunton and Pennington have 'namierized' the members elected in 1640; in the process they have found only one significant difference between those who later joined parliament or king, namely that the latter were on average younger.[345] Keeler presents biographies of all who sat in that parliament during the first two years, describes elections, and offers no conclusions.[346] The parliament's inner history, and especially the crucial problem of Pym's tactics, form the substance of six careful articles from one hand.[347] Pearl takes a closer look at those parliamentarians who hoped to end the war.[348] Trevor-Roper gains useful insights into political ideas and methods from

[344] Valerie Pearl, *London and the Outbreak of the Puritan Revolution*. L: OUP: 1961. Pp. xi, 364. Rev: *EHR* 77, 773f.; *HJ* 5, 93ff.

[345] D. Brunton and Donald H. Pennington, *Members of the Long Par-liament*. L: Allen & Unwin: 1954. Pp. xxi, 256. Rev: *EHR* 71, 652.

[346] Mary Freer Keeler, *The Long Parliament, 1640 – 1641: a biographical study of its members*. Philadelphia: American Philos. Society: 1954. Pp. ix, 410. Rev: *EHR* 70, 286ff.

[347] Lotte Glow, 'Pym and Parliament: the methods of moderation', *JMH* 36 (1964), 373–97; 'The Committee of safety', *EHR* 80 (1965), 289–313; 'The committee men in the Long Parliament, August 1642 – December 1643', *HJ* 8 (1965), 1–15; 'Political affiliations in the House of Commons after Pym's death', *BIHR* 38 (1965), 48–70; 'Manipulation of committees in the Long Par-liament', *JBS* 5 (1966), 31–52; [under married name, Mulligan] 'Peace negotiations, politics, and the Committee of Both King-doms, 1644 – 1646', *HJ* 12 (1969), 3–22.

[348] Valerie Pearl, 'Oliver St John and the "middle group" in the Long Parliament, August 1642 – May 1644', *EHR* 81 (1966), 490–519.

sermons preached in parliament, an unexpected source.[349] The skills of influence used to maintain the war party are analysed by Underdown.[350] A topic on which much more needs still to be written has at least been well opened in various studies of the manner in which the parliament administered its share of the realm. Pennington deals with the committee of finance;[351] with Roots' assistance he describes one of the local instruments, a task performed by Everitt for another region.[352] Everitt has also produced two exemplary general analyses of particular regions in the years of disturbance,[353] while Howell performs a similar service for a town caught in all the cross-currents of the time (including the Scots).[354]

Two new studies of Oliver Cromwell have not replaced the old masterpiece by Firth. Paul emphasizes the protector's religion, while Ashley has recanted his earlier view which saw in Cromwell the prototype of twentieth-century dictators.[355] He has also written some useful brief biographies of Oliver's comrades in arms.[356] Trevor-Roper broke new ground in a

---

[349] Hugh R. Trevor-Roper, 'The fast sermons in the Long Parliament', *Feiling Ft* (n. 130), 85–138.

[350] D. E. Underdown, 'Party management and the recruiter elections 1645 – 1648', *EHR* 83 (1968), 235–64.

[351] Donald H. Pennington, 'The accounts of the kingdom', *Tawney Ft* (n. 126), 182–203.

[352] Donald H. Pennington and Ivan Roots, *The Committee at Stafford*. Manchester UP: 1957. Pp. lxxxiii, 389. – Alan M. Everitt, *The County Committee of Kent in the Civil War*. Leicester: Dept of English Local History, Occasional Papers 9: 1957. Pp. 53. Rev: *EHR* 73, 157ff.

[353] Alan M. Everitt, *The Community of Kent in the Great Rebellion, 1640 – 1660*. Leicester UP: 1966. Pp. 356. Rev: *EHR* 83, 172f.; *EcHR*² 20, 167ff. – Idem, *Suffolk and the Great Rebellion, 1640 – 1660*. Suffolk Record Soc.: 1960. Pp. 141. Rev: *EHR* 77, 775f.

[354] Roger Howell, *Newcastle-upon-Tyne and the Puritan Revolution*. O: Clarendon: 1967. Pp. xiv, 397. Rev: *EHR* 83, 840f.; *EcHR*² 20, 557f.

[355] Robert S. Paul, *The Lord Protector: religion and politics in the life of Oliver Cromwell*. L: Lutterworth Press: 1955. Pp. 438. – Maurice Ashley, *The Greatness of Oliver Cromwell*. L: Hodder & Stoughton: 1957. Pp. 382.

[356] Maurice Ashley, *Cromwell's Generals*. L: Cape: 1954. Pp. 256.

striking study of Cromwell's incompetence at parliamentary management.[357] Particular issues are dealt with in Farnell's demonstration that Barebone's Parliament was manufactured in London, not Wales,[358] and in Heath's attempt to show the devilish cunning behind the constitution of the Protectorate.[359] Grosheide reviews the Dutch reaction to the regicide – mainly hostile.[360] Thomson's article usefully summarizes a longer debate on the conduct of foreign policy.[361] In two books on the royalists, Hardacre attempts a general account while Underdown concentrates on the failed conspiracies.[362] A single good royalist appears in Edgar's study of a useful military man.[363] Thirsk investigates the sale of confiscated estates and concludes that neither this nor the new distribution after the Restoration seriously disturbed the position of the old families.[364] Davies describes the king's return in a heavy-footed volume, intended to complete the general history of Gardiner and Firth.[365] Rather more original is a piece on the influence of the men who

---

[357] Hugh R. Trevor-Roper, 'Oliver Cromwell and his Parliaments', *Namier Ft* (n. 135), 1–48.

[358] James A. Farnell, 'The Usurpation of Honest London House-holders: Barebone's parliament', *EHR* 82 (1967), 24–46.

[359] George D. Heath, 'The making of the Instrument of Government', *JBS* 6 (1967), 15–34.

[360] D. Grosheide, *Cromwell naar het Oordeal van zijn Nederlandse Tijdgenosten*. Amsterdam: Noord-Hollandsche Uitgevers Maatschappij: 1951. Pp. 270.

[361] R. C. Thomas, 'Officers, merchants and foreign policy in the protectorate of Oliver Cromwell', *Historical Studies (Australia and New Zealand)*, 12 (1966), 149–65.

[362] P. H. Hardacre, *The Royalists during the Puritan Revolution*. The Hague: Nijhoff: 1956. Pp. xiv, 185. Rev: *EHR* 72, 543f. – D. E. Underdown, *Royalist Conspiracy in England, 1649 – 1660*. New Haven: Yale UP: 1960. Pp. xvii, 274. Rev: *EHR* 77, 161f.

[363] F. T. R. Edgar, *Sir Ralph Hopton, the King's Man in the West: a study in character and command*. O: Clarendon: 1968. Pp. xx, 248. Rev: *EHR* 84, 847.

[364] Joan Thirsk, 'The sale of royalist lands during the Interregnum', *EcHR*[2] 5 (1952 – 3), 188–207; 'The Restoration land settlement', *JMH* 26 (1954), 315–28.

[365] Godfrey Davies, *The Restoration of Charles II, 1658 – 1660*. L: OUP: 1955. Pp. viii, 383. Rev: *EHR* 73, 688f.; *CHJ* 12, 193ff.

regarded Oliver as a traitor to the 'good old cause'.[366] The part played by the navy in the victory of revolution has been described at length;[367] more surprisingly (and not altogether cogently), the influence of England's disturbances in unsettling the French has been discussed in a book based essentially on a collection of pamphlets and ambassadorial reports.[368] Two typical but very different figures of the day have found their biographers: Gregg, a good democrat, gives uncritical admiration to the democratic John Lilburne, while Lamont thoughtfully and subtly discusses the bitter and heedless William Prynne.[369]

(D) THE PURITANS

Who and what were the English puritans (for those of America are another story still)? What types were there in this 'movement'? Has the concept any sort of analytical value for the historian? Until quite recently, questions of this kind were hardly even asked; it was taken for granted that the puritanism of the age of Cromwell descended directly from that of Elizabeth's reign, and that the so-called revolution was a puritan one formed a simple axiom. All this is today the subject of debate, and in large measure we still await the answers. Admittedly, Hill adheres to the view that the troubles were closely connected with a socio-religious movement to be called puritanism (n. 334), and Haller completed the account of the spiritual and intellectual history of the movement, which he began thirty years ago, without adjusting his categories.[370] On

---

[366] Austin H. Woolrych, 'The good old cause and the fall of the Protectorate', *CHJ* 13 (1957), 133–61.

[367] J. R. Powell, *The Navy in the English Civil War*. L: Archon Books: 1962. Pp. xviii, 240. Rev: *EHR* 80, 171.

[368] Philip A. Knachel, *England and the Fronde: the impact of the English civil war and revolution on France*. Ithaca: Cornell UP: 1967. Pp. xiii, 312. Rev: *Hist* 53, 431.

[369] Pauline Gregg, *Free-Born John: a biography of John Lilburne*. L: Harrap: 1961. Pp. 424. – W. M. Lamont, *Marginal Prynne, 1600 – 1669*. L: Routledge: 1963. Pp. x, 250. Rev: *EHR* 80, 397f.

[370] William Haller, *Liberty and Reformation in the Puritan Revolution*. New York: Columbia UP: 1955. Pp. xv, 410. Rev: *EHR* 71, 286ff.

the other hand, the Georges, in a book whose occasional crudities and lack of comprehension must not be allowed to overshadow its insights, have concluded (from a new and sometimes naïve study of the same body of writings) that no fundamental difference existed between so-called puritan and anglican intellectual attitudes.[371] As doubts began to grow, Walzer restored some spirit to the older view by extracting a kind of revolutionary essence from puritan writings and constructing a morphology of the modern revolutionary, first discernible in these men.[372] Remarkable as his book is, it fails to make some necessary distinctions, but the attempt to do so has led to unresolved debates. Underdown and Yule argue the differences between presbyterians and independents;[373] Foster, with quite unnecessary rudeness and without being able to clinch the point, holds that the question never existed;[374] Kaplan shows that it certainly did, at least at precise moments in time;[375] Pearl finds men of genuine 'independent' convictions who could not stomach the puritan commonwealth.[376] Abernathy is sure that he can treat the presbyterians at least as a definable group, once they had lost the battle for control.[377] The levellers, thanks to their ideas which were 'ahead of their time' and

---

[371] Charles H. and Katherine George, *The Protestant Mind of the English Reformation*. Princeton UP: 1961. Pp. x, 452. Rev: *HJ* 5, 203ff.

[372] Michael Walzer, *The Revolution of the Saints*. C (Mass.): Harvard UP: 1965. Pp. xiv, 334. Rev: *History and Theory* 7, 102ff.; *Hist* 52, 205f.

[373] George Yule, *The Independents in the English Civil War*. CUP: 1958. Pp. viii, 156. Rev: *AHR* 64, 362f. – D. E. Underdown, 'The Independents reconsidered', *JBS* 3 (1964), 57–84. – George Yule, 'Independents and revolutionaries', *JBS* 7 (1968), 11–32.

[374] Stephen Foster, 'The presbyterian independents exorcized: a ghost story for historians', *PP* 44 (1969), 52–75.

[375] Lawrence Kaplan, 'Presbyterians and Independents in 1643', *EHR* 84 (1969), 244–56.

[376] Valerie Pearl, 'The "Royal Independents" in the English civil war', *TRHS* (1968), 69–96.

[377] George R. Abernathy, *The English Presbyterians and the Stuart Restoration, 1648 – 1663*. Philadelphia: American Philos. Soc.: 1965. Pp. 101. Rev: *EHR* 82 170f.

deposited in a mass of writings quite disproportionate to their real influence, have always attracted historians; two good and careful studies have appeared.[378] However, another study casts doubts upon their democratic excellence and shows how authoritarian were the army chaplains who dominated the movement.[379]

Several odd currents in this age of utter upheaval have been restudied. In his life of Hugh Peter, Stearns discusses plain fanaticism;[380] McLachlan seeks the germs of toleration in the ideas of the early unitarians;[381] Barbour deals with the one sect which even the true puritans could not tolerate.[382] Rogers attends to the chiliasts who, for a time, had such powerful influence among the military.[383] Two scholars devote themselves to a somewhat unstable puritan who survived the great age,[384] and Cragg sketches out the continued existence of puritanism in the days when, once again, it became the target rather than the instrument of persecution.[385]

(E) 1660 – 1714

Once the revolution was over, politics again played a more significant part than faith and religious tract; but since English

[378] Perez Zagorin, *A History of Political Thought in the English Revolution*. L: Routledge: 1954. Pp. vii, 208. Rev: *EHR* 70, 490f. – Joseph Frank, *The Levellers: a history of the writings of three 17th century democrats*. C (Mass.): Harvard UP: 1955. Pp. viii, 345.

[379] Leo F. Solt, *Saints in Arms: puritanism and democracy in Cromwell's army*. Stanford UP: 1959. Pp. 150. Rev: *EHR* 76, 155; *HJ* 4, 232f.

[380] Raymond P. Stearns, *The Strenuous Puritan: Hugh Peter, 1598 – 1660*. Urbana: U of Illinois P: 1954. Pp. xii, 463. Rev: *EHR* 69, 666f.

[381] H. J. McLachlan, *Socinianism in Seventeenth Century England*. L: OUP: 1951. Pp. viii, 352.

[382] Hugh Barbour, *The Quakers in Puritan England*. New Haven: Yale UP: 1964. Pp. viii, 272.

[383] P. R. Rogers, *The Fifth Monarchy Men*. L: OUP: 1966. Pp. viii, 168. Rev: *EHR* 83, 397.

[384] [Richard Schlatter, *Richard Baxter and Puritan Politics*. New Brunswick N.J.: Rutgers UP: 1957. Pp. 178. Rev: *EHR* 74, 157f.] – Geoffrey F. Nuttall, *Richard Baxter*. Edinburgh: Nelson: 1965. Pp. ix, 142.

[385] Gerald C. Cragg, *Puritanism in the Period of the Great Persecution, 1660 – 1688*. CUP 1957. Pp. x, 326. Rev: *EHR* 74, 350f.

historians (especially of this period) are only gradually coming to realize that the rude truth is much more interesting than pious legend, there is still a vast deal of work to do here. However, in this period, too, new and disturbing knowledge is accumulating. These terms do not apply to an attempt to write the history of the house of lords in the age of Charles II, a book that can only be called a failure.[386] But Witcombe, intent on proving no points, uses the real sources to show how seriously ambition and distrust from the first disturbed the co-operation of king and parliament;[387] Lee gives us a useful account of the politics of 1667 – 73;[388] and Browning's life of Danby offers the best introduction to the equally troubled politics of the seventies.[389] Even though one may agree that Shaftesbury was a great man, one may still wonder if Haley's biography is not too large, but that he succeeds in recreating and explaining one of the real puzzles of the century must be emphasized.[390] Shaftesbury's great days form the core of the first serious attempt to uncover the inner party history of the reign's central crisis.[391] Nothing new has been specifically done for Charles II, but his brother has received his first scholarly biography (which is a little too kind to this egregious man).[392] The remarkable Sunderland, office-holding survivor of three revolutions, is the subject of the best political biography to

---

[386] Maxwell P. Schoenfeld, *The Restored House of Lords*. The Hague: Mouton: 1967. Pp. 244. Rev: *Hist* 53, 113f.

[387] D. T. Witcombe, *Charles II and the Cavalier House of Commons, 1660 – 1674*. Manchester UP: 1966. Pp. xiv, 218. Rev: *EHR* 83, 177f.

[388] Maurice Lee, *The Cabal*. Urbana: U of Illinois P: 1965. Pp. 275. Rev: *EHR* 82, 391.

[389] Andrew Browning, *Thomas Osborne, Earl of Danby and Duke of Leeds, 1632 – 1712*, vol. 1: the life. Glasgow: Jackson: 1951. Pp. xi, 586. Rev: *EHR* 67, 268ff.

[390] K. H. D. Haley, *The First Earl of Shaftesbury*. O: Clarendon: 1968. Pp. xii, 767. Rev: *HJ* 12, 372ff.

[391] J. R. Jones, *The First Whigs: the politics of the exclusion crisis 1678 – 1683*. L: OUP: 1961. Pp. viii, 224. Rev: *EHR* 78, 788f.

[392] F. C. Turner, *James II*. L: Eyre & Spottiswoode: 1948. Pp. 544. Rev: *AHR* 54, 580ff.

appear on this age.[393] His last master, William III, remains a controversial figure. Haley, studying his secret negotiations with the opponents of Charles II, regards him as skilful and justified;[394] Pinkham's attempt to denigrate his role in 1688 is less convincing.[395] The most balanced, and best written, treatment appears in Baxter's biography.[396] Other figures of the age have had biographies written about them: especially an outstanding whig politician[397] and the one and only Quaker politician, treated in that capacity twice over.[398]

The Glorious Revolution has not been specifically re-analysed, but there have been some tentative contributions. Creswell's study of the year is good on the European setting but does not unravel the politics.[399] Beddard offers two contributions, which show toryism in action both before and after the event.[400] Sachse considers the part played by what politeness may call popular support.[401] And a useful summary-cum-

[393] John P. Kenyon, *Robert Spencer, Earl of Sunderland*. L: Longmans: 1958. Pp. xii, 396. Rev: *EHR* 75, 165; *HJ* 2, 87ff.

[394] K. D. H. Haley, *William of Orange and the English Opposition, 1672 – 1674*. O: Clarendon: 1953. Pp. 231. Rev: *EHR* 69, 337f.

[395] Lucille Pinkham, *William III and the Respectable Revolution*. C (Mass.): Harvard UP: 1954. Pp. ix, 272. Rev: *EHR* 70, 330f.

[396] Stephen B. Baxter, *William III*. L: Longmans: 1966. Pp. xii, 460. Rev: *EHR* 84, 585ff.

[397] G. F. Trevallyn Jones, *Saw-Pit Wharton: the political career from 1640 to 1691 of Philip, fourth lord Wharton*. Sydney UP: 1967. Pp. x, 300. Rev: *EHR* 84, 613.

[398] Joseph E. Illick, *William Penn the Politician: his relations with the English Government*. Ithaca: Cornell UP: 1965. Pp. xi, 267. Rev: *EHR* 83, 178. – Mary M. Dunn, *William Penn: politics and conscience*. Princeton UP: 1967. Pp. xi, 206. Rev: *EHR* 84, 182.

[329] John Creswell, *The Descent on England*. L: Barrie & Rockliff: 1969. Pp. 259.

[400] Robert Beddard, 'The commission for ecclesiastical promotions, 1681 – 1684', *HJ* 10 (1967), 11–40; 'The Guildhall declaration of 11 December 1688 and the counter-revolution of the loyalists', *HJ* 11 (1968), 403–20.

[401] William L. Sachse, 'The mob and the Revolution of 1688', *JBS* 4 (1964), 23–40.

stimulant is applied to the whole post-Revolution era in a collection of analytical essays edited by Holmes.[402]

However, it is in this era that we strike the first serious controversy to have arisen in seventeenth-century political history, the debate over the nature of party and politics. In his analysis of factions and groupings under Anne, Walcott applied a crudely schematic version of Namier's interpretation which was carefully criticized by Horwitz.[403] Criticism of Walcott also appeared, at perhaps too great length, in the important study which Plumb devoted to his demonstration that between Exclusion and Excise English politics moved from party-dominated strife to a deliberately contrived peace without parties.[404] Rubini attempts to show, with a fair measure of success, that at least in William's reign the old distinction between court and country offers a better scheme than the new distinction between whig and tory; on the other hand, for the reign of Anne Holmes demonstrates the active and central position of true party.[405] I am not altogether persuaded that the case has been finally made: clearly, there were times when court-country attitudes are more readily discerned than whig-tory ones. But the most important thing to emerge from the debate is the fact that, though quite genuine and coherent parties existed down to 1714, they did not determine the making of administrations. The next step, therefore, is to study the managerial persons. A start has been made on Harley, perhaps the most significant politician of his age: Hamilton has written

---

[402] Geoffrey S. Holmes, ed., *Britain after the Glorious Revolution.* L: Macmillan: 1969. Pp. ix, 245.

[403] Robert Walcott, *English Politics in the Early Eighteenth Century.* O: Clarendon: 1956. Pp. viii, 291. Rev: *EHR* 72, 126ff. – Henry Horwitz, 'Parties, connections and parliamentary politics, 1689–1714', *JBS* 6 (1966), 45–69.

[404] John H. Plumb, *The Growth of Political Stability in England, 1675 – 1725.* L: Macmillan: 1967. Pp. xi, 206. Rev: *EHR* 83, 570ff.; *HJ* 11, 175ff.

[405] Denis Rubini, *Court and Country, 1688 – 1702.* L: Hart-Davis: 1968. Pp. 304. Rev: *EHR* 85, 175f.; *Hist* 54, 104f. – Geoffrey S. Holmes, *British Politics in the Age of Anne.* L: Macmillan: 1967. Pp. xiv, 546. Rev: *EHR* 84, 358ff.; *JMH* 41, 92ff.

a simple biography;[406] more to the point, McInnes has described his importance at the start of Anne's reign as equal to Marlborough's,[407] and has, somewhat surprisingly, charged him with possessing political ideas,[408] while Holmes and Speck have reviewed the occasion of his first fall.[409] The only other politician of the age to receive a useful biography is the high anglican Nottingham.[410]

The administrative history of the age has produced little, but what there is is vital. Baxter's study of the treasury omits the politics.[411] Finance is continued in Dickson's impressive analysis of public credit in the age in which government finally abandoned the fiscal methods of the past and (under the pressure of war) developed those of a modern state.[412] Carter and Plumb have been able to add significantly to the early history of the cabinet.[413] Fraser accounts for the activities of the secretaries of state in gathering and spreading information.[414] Havighurst does justice to the judges whom he convicts of a narrow but uncorrupt conservatism.[415] The important

---

[406] Elizabeth Hamilton, *The Backstairs Dragon: a life of Robert Harley, earl of Oxford*. L: Hamilton: 1969. Pp. 308. Rev: *Hist* 55, 123f.

[407] Angus McInnes, 'The appointment of Harley in 1704', *HJ* 11 (1968), 255–71.

[408] Angus McInnes, 'The political ideas of Robert Harley', *Hist* 50 (1965), 309–22.

[409] Geoffrey S. Holmes and W. S. Speck, 'The fall of Harley in 1708 reconsidered', *EHR* 80 (1965), 673–98.

[410] Henry Horwitz, *Revolution Politicks: the career of Daniel Finch, second earl of Nottingham, 1647 – 1730*. CUP: 1968. Pp. xii, 306. Rev: *EHR* 85, 173f.; *Hist* 54, 281f.

[411] Stephen B. Baxter, *The Development of the Treasury, 1660 – 1702*. C (Mass.): Harvard UP: 1957. Pp. ix, 301. Rev: *EHR* 73, 159f.

[412] P. M. G. Dickson, *The Financial Revolution in England: a study in the development of public credit, 1699 – 1756*. L: Macmillan: 1967. Pp. xix, 580. Rev: *EHR* 83, 617; *HJ* 11, 378ff.; *EcHR*² 20, 396ff.,

[413] Jennifer Carter, 'Cabinet records for the reign of William III', *EHR* 78 (1963), 95–114. – John H. Plumb, 'The organization of the cabinet in the reign of Queen Anne', *TRHS* (1957), 137–57.

[414] Peter Fraser, *The Intelligence of the Secretaries of State and the Monopoly of Licensed News, 1660 – 1688*. CUP: 1956. Pp. xii, 177. Rev: *EHR* 72, 544f.

[415] Alfred Havighurst, 'The judiciary and politics in the reign of Charles II', *LQR* 66 (1950), 62–78, 229–52.

theme of the civil service remains to be studied; meanwhile, Sainty has shown how much political significance may be extracted from a study of the terms of office-holding.[416] The complicated history of the board of trade has occasioned yet another attempt to unravel it and its connection with affairs: the problems are not yet all solved.[417] As for constitutional ideas, Weston's book on the 'classical constitution' covers too much ground (1642 – 1832) to be able to get beneath the surface.[418] Holmes succeeds in giving new life to a very tired topic of parliamentary opposition.[419] The realities of late-Stuart government need much more work done on them; in particular, if only C. D. Chandaman's enormous dissertation on Restoration finance could achieve its long awaited publication, there would be grounds for rejoicing.

A surprising number of works reminds one that the restored Church continued to exercise a massive political and social influence – but also that this is the area occupied by Norman Sykes and his pupils. Sykes himself established neatly how the conservative settlement of 1661 resulted in the needless maintenance of religious differences.[420] The conservative victory itself is carefully described by Bosher,[421] and Whiteman adds a study of the resumption of traditional organizations.[422] Simon has investigated the bishops' part in general history.[423] The

[416] J. Sainty, 'A reform in the tenure of offices during the reign of Charles II', *BIHR* 41 (1968), 150–71.

[417] Ian K. Steele, *Politics of Colonial Policy: the Board of Trade in colonial administration, 1696 – 1720*. O: Clarendon: 1968. Pp. xvi, 217. Rev: *EcHR*² 22, 134.

[418] Corinne Comstock Weston, *English Constitutional Theory and the House of Lords*. L: Routledge: 1965. Pp. vii, 304. Rev: *HJ* 9, 241f.

[419] Geoffrey S. Holmes, 'The attack on "the influence of the Crown", 1702 – 1716', *BIHR* 39 (1966), 47–68.

[420] Norman Sykes, *From Sheldon to Secker: aspects of English Church History 1600 – 1768*. CUP: 1959. Pp. xi, 273.

[421] R. S. Bosher, *The Making of the Restoration Settlement: the influence of the Laudians, 1649 – 1662*. L: Black: 1951. Pp. xv, 309. Rev: *J. of Eccl. Hist.* 3, 116f.

[422] Anne Whiteman, 'The re-establishment of the Church of England, 1660 – 1663', *TRHS* (1955), 111–31.

[423] Walter G. Simon, *The Restoration Episcopate*. New York: Bookman Associates: 1965. Pp. 238.

fortunes of the Church after the next revolution have also
attracted attention. Thus Every argues that both in name and
fact the high church party belongs to the post-1688 situation.[424]
Straka, on the other hand, defends the view that high-church
doctrines of divine right, inherited from the Stuarts, continued
to be generally preached in the face of all the difficulties even
after the expulsion of James II and with reference to his successor.[425] No fewer than six bishops have found their biographers,
a phenomenon which one may regard as somewhat unnecessary; still, the bunch contains Sykes's chief work.[426] On quite
another track, Vann has produced a most valuable, and
entertaining, social history of the first century of Quakerism,
a book which in its combination of record work, social science
approach, demographic precision, and intellectual penetration
should become a model of its kind.[427]

There is too little to tell of foreign affairs and war. Routledge
examines England's (tiny) role in the peace of 1659.[428] Lachs
attempts something new and much to be desired: a study of the

[424] George Every, *The High Church Party, 1688 – 1718*. L: SPCK: 1956.
Pp. xv, 195. Rev: *EHR* 72, 752.
[425] Gerald M. Straka, *Anglican Reaction to the Revolution of 1698*. Madison: State Hist. Soc. of Wisconsin: 1962. Pp. x, 180. Rev: *HJ* 6,
310ff. – Idem, 'The final phase of divine right theory in England,
1698 – 1702', *EHR* 77 (1962), 638–58.
[426] A. Tindal Hart, *The Life and Times of John Sharp, Archbishop of
York*. L: SPCK: 1949. Pp. xi, 352. – Idem, *William Lloyd, 1627 –
1717*. L: SPCK: 1952. Pp. xii, 282. Rev: *EHR* 69, 151f. – Edward
F. Carpenter, *The Protestant Bishop, being the life of Henry Crompton,
bishop of London, 1632 – 1713*. L: Longmans: 1956. Pp. xiii, 398.
Rev: *CHJ* 13, 86ff. – Idem, *Thomas Tenison, Archbishop of Canter-
bury: his life and times*. L: SPCK: 1948. Pp. x, 466. – Norman
Sykes, *William Wake, Archbishop of Canterbury, 1657 – 1737*, 2 vols.
CUP: 1957. Pp. xiii, 366; 289. Rev: *EHR* 73, 494ff. – G. V.
Bennett, *White Kennett, 1660 – 1728, Bishop of Peterborough*. L:
SPCK: 1957. Pp. xii, 290. Rev: *EHR* 73, 529f.; *CHJ* 13, 192ff.
[427] Richard T. Vann, *The Social Development of English Quakerism,
1650 – 1750*. C (Mass.): Harvard UP: 1969. Pp. xvi, 259. – Idem,
'Quakerism and the social structure in the Interregnum', *PP* 43
(1969), 71–91.
[428] F. J. Routledge, *England and the Treaty of the Pyrenees*. Liverpool
UP: 1953. Pp. x, 136. Rev: *EHR* 69, 667f.

diplomats themselves.[429] With respect to the navy, we have Ollard's solid account of one man's activities, ranging through the era of the Dutch wars,[430] and Ehrman's extensive analysis of fleet and policy in the century's last war.[431] Coombs explains the skill of the parties in working up public opinion in support of this or that foreign policy; he also recounts an episode from the time of England's alliance with the Netherlands.[432] Riley looks at the union with Scotland from the point of view of the English parties.[433] Scouller analyses the large armies produced by England in the war of Spanish succession,[434] and Francis describes the spread of English influence in Portugal at that same time.[435]

Finally two books which rather escape the categories: Ashley's biography of one of Cromwell's rebellious followers who finished up as Charles II's postmaster general,[436] and Thornton's demonstration of the conscious colonial policy developed in this generation with respect to the West Indies.[437]

---

[429] [Phyllis S. Lachs, *The Diplomatic Corps under Charles II and James II*. New Brunswick N.J.: Rutgers UP: 1965. Rev: *EHR* 82, 614f.]

[430] Richard Ollard, *Man of War: Sir Robert Holmes and the Restoration Navy*. L: Hodder & Stoughton: 1969. Pp. 240.

[431] John P. W. Ehrman, *The Navy in the War of William III, 1689 – 1697*. CUP: 1953. Pp. xiii, 710. Rev: *EHR* 70, 128ff.

[432] Douglas C. Coombs, *The Conduct of the Dutch: British opinion on the Dutch alliance during the war of the Spanish succession*. The Hague: Nijhoff: 1958. Pp. viii, 405. Rev: *EHR* 74, 733f. – Idem, 'The Augmentation of 1709: a study in the workings of the Anglo-Dutch alliance', *EHR* 72 (1957), 642–61.

[433] P. W. J. Riley, 'The Union of 1707 as an episode in English politics', *EHR* 84 (1969), 498–527.

[434] R. E. Scouller, *The Armies of Queen Anne*. O: Clarendon: 1966. Pp. xv, 420. Rev: *EHR* 83, 400f.

[435] A. D. Francis, *The Methuens and Portugal, 1691 – 1708*. CUP: 1966. Pp. xv, 397. Rev: *EcHR*² 20, 171f.

[436] Maurice Ashley, *John Wildman, plotter and postmaster*. L: Cape: 1947. Pp. 319.

[437] A. P. Thornton, *West Indian Policy under the Restoration*. O: Clarendon: 1956. Pp. viii, 280. Rev: *EHR* 72, 545f.

(F) ECONOMIC HISTORY

The first half of the century is also, of course, dominated by the debate over the gentry (n. 259).

Wilson's handsome and readable introduction to the age must now be anybody's start on this topic; he explains the origins of the great transformations.[438] Work on agriculture has really concentrated on the eighteenth century and shall be listed under that head. Here we may note that Habakkuk has traced back his earlier study of landownership (1940) into the Interregnum and has also written a piece of more general reflection.[439] Beresford discusses the contemporary debates on the virtues of enclosing.[440] Hammersley draws attention to woodland as a source of crown revenue.[441] And in his study of the rate of interest and the price of land, Habakkuk discovers the surprising fact that while the former fell, the latter remained stable.[442]

On the other hand, there has been a great deal of work done on trade; indeed, historians have virtually come to accept the notion that this century witnessed a 'commercial revolution' in preparation for the industrial revolution of the next. What has appeared is not necessarily very coherent, but all of it supports some such conclusions in demonstrating both the decline of older trades and the growth of new outlets, manufactures and methods. Chaudhuri tackles the early days of the greatest com-

---

[438] Charles H. Wilson, *England's Apprenticeship, 1603 – 1763*. L: Longmans: 1965. Pp. xii, 413. Rev: *EHR* 84, 394f.; *Hist* 52, 83f.

[439] Hrothgar J. Habakkuk, 'Public finance and the sale of confiscated property during the Interregnum', *EcHR*² 15 (1962 – 3), 70–88; 'Landowners and the civil war', *ibid.* 18 (1965 – 6), 130–51; 'Economic functions of English landowners in the seventeenth and eighteenth centuries', *Explorations in Entrepreneurial History 6* (1953), 92–102. - *See also* n. 364.

[440] Maurice Beresford, 'Habitation versus improvement: the debate on enclosure by agreement', *Tawney Ft* (n. 126), 40–69.

[441] George Hammersley, 'The crown woods and their exploitation in the 16th and 17th centuries', *BIHR* 30 (1957), 136–61.

[442] Hrothgar J. Habakkuk, 'The long-term rate of interest and the price of land in the seventeenth century', *EcHR*² 5 (1952 – 3), 26–45.

pany of all.[443] Supple, investigating the major crisis in the established cloth trade, clearly brings out the need for something new.[444] From a different point of view, Hinton explains how the state's withdrawal from control produced a revival after 1660;[445] however 'colonial' the 'system', the intellectual atmosphere of Adam Smith appears to have stretched back a long way. Davis then describes these new departures and developments, especially the phenomenal growth of the re-export trade.[446] In his plain history of a new type of trading company, Davies underlines the transformation from the earlier period's methods and attitudes.[447] Wilson, on the other hand, sees a conscious policy of power in the commercial wars waged against Holland; at any rate, it was conscious in the mind of Sir George Downing.[448] Two specialized studies deal with England's Scandinavian trade in which cloth was exchanged for timber and iron.[449] Shipping and ship-building, ultimately the foundation of the victory over the Dutch, receive thorough attention from Davis.[450]

The foundations of economic growth, capital and labour, still require much hard work from historians. A striking, and

---

[443] K. N. Chaudhuri, *The English East India Company: the study of an early joint-stock company, 1600 – 1640*. L: Cass: 1965. Pp. ix, 245.

[444] Barry E. Supple, *Commercial Crisis and Change in England, 1600 – 1642*. CUP: 1959. Pp. xii, 296. Rev: *EHR* 77, 534ff.; *EcHR*² 13, 124f.

[445] R. W. K. Hinton, *The Eastland Company and the Common Weal in the Seventeenth Century*. CUP: 1959. Pp. xi, 244. Rev: *EHR* 75, 353f.

[446] Ralph Davis, 'English foreign trade, 1660 – 1700', *EcHR*² 7 (1954 – 5), 150–66.

[447] K. G. Davies, *The Royal Africa Company*. L: Longmans: 1957. Pp. ix, 390.

[448] Charles H. Wilson, *Profit and Power: a study of England and the Dutch wars*. L: Longmans: 1957. Pp. vi, 169. Rev: *EHR* 73, 301f.

[449] Sven Tveite, *Engelsk-Norsk Trelasthandel 1640 – 1710*. Bergen/Oslo: Universitetsforlaget: 1961. Pp. 675. – Sven-Erik Åström, *From Cloth to Iron: the Anglo-Baltic trade in the late 17th century*, 2 vols. Helsingfors: Soc. Scientiarum Fennica: 1963, 1965. Pp. 260, 86. Rev: *EHR* 80, 841f.; 82, 394.

[450] Ralph Davis, *The Rise of the English Shipping Industries in the 17th and 18th Centuries*. L: Macmillan: 1962. Pp. ix, 427. Rev: *EHR* 79, 555ff.; *EcHR*² 16, 157ff.

dubious, representative of the former was Sir John Banks, financier and politician, whose dictatorial hand controlled both the East India and Africa Companies.[451] His biographer has also made a first attempt to assess the problem of the supply of labour.[452] In addition to Dickson (n. 412), Horsefield has investigated a number of monetary problems in this age in which private and public credit finally established themselves as safe and permanent features of economic life.[453] To this theme belongs also the great recoinage at the end of the seventeenth century which Isaac Newton supervised and managed.[454] The problem of labour depends, of course in the first instance on what may be known about the population, and here we have the first comprehensive statistics, Gregory King's figures which modern research has cautiously endorsed.[455]

As always, local studies throw light on economic issues. In tackling a whole county, Chalklin provides information about population, agriculture, industry and trade, as well as about the working of an autonomous and hierarchical society.[456] Lord Leconfield, on the other hand, contents himself with two manorial estates which enable him to show what really went on in the countryside.[457] Stephens restricts himself to one town, admittedly Exeter, always a magnet for historians.[458] Dodd's collected papers about seventeenth-century Wales con-

---

[451] Donald C. Coleman, *Sir John Banks, Baronet and Business Man*. O: Clarendon: 1963. Pp. xv, 215. Rev: *EcHR*[2] 17, 414f.

[452] Donald C. Coleman, 'Labour in the English economy in the 17th century,' *EcHR*[2] 8 (1955 – 6), 280–95.

[453] J. Keith Horsefield, *British Monetary Experiments, 1650 – 1710*. L: Bell: 1960. Pp. xix, 344. Rev: *EcHR*[2] 13, 119ff.

[454] Li Ming-Hsun, *The Great Recoinage of 1696 to 1699*. L: Weidenfeld: 1963. Pp. viii, 260.

[455] D. V. Glass, 'Gregory King's estimate of the population of England and Wales, 1695', *Population Studies* 6 (1949 – 50), 338–74.

[456] C. W. Chalklin, *Seventeenth-Century Kent: a social and economic history*. L: Longmans: 1965. Pp. xv, 294. Rev: *EHR* 82, 171f.

[457] Lord Leconfield, *Petworth Manor in the Seventeenth Century*. L: OUP: 1954. Pp. vii, 171. Rev: *EHR* 71, 153f. – Idem, *Sutton and Duncton Manors*. L: OUP: 1956. Pp. vii, 98. Rev: *EHR* 72, 542.

[458] W. B. Stephens, *Seventeenth-Century Exeter*. Exeter: The University: 1958. Pp. xxvi, 203. Rev: *EHR* 75, 352f.

tain not only studies of economic history but also, for instance, of government during the civil war.[459]

(G) CULTURE AND CIVILIZATION

Two by-products of the interest in puritan ideas: Schenk emphasizes the demand for equal rights,[460] while Prall somewhat insufficiently investigates the interesting topic of law reform, the desire for which sprang from the same root.[461] Cotterell offers another small contribution to the same theme; there is much still to be done here.[462] More commonplace, or at least more accustomed, is Cragg's study of the changes which affected religious thinking.[463] Hole writes pleasantly about the women of the time.[464] Two books tackle the highly novel theme of tourist traffic from the two ends possible: Stoye documents the cultural influence exercised by travellers returned from abroad,[465] and Robson-Scott relates the reactions of German visitors to England in a work which, though it extends beyond both ends of this period, yet best fits in here.[466] In this age, London first became the country's main cultural centre, a role which depended a great deal on the new coffee-houses: for these, we now have an exhaustive catalogue.[467]

[459] A. H. Dodd, *Studies in Stuart Wales*. Cardiff: U of Wales P: 1952. Pp. x, 251.

[460] W. Schenk, *The Concern for Social Justice in the Puritan Revolution*. L: Longmans: 1948. Pp. xi, 180.

[461] Stuart E. Prall, *The Agitation for Law Reform in the Puritan Revolution, 1640 – 1660*. The Hague: Nijhoff: 1966. Pp. ix, 159. Rev: *EHR* 83, 173.

[462] Mary Cotterell, 'Interregnum law reform: the Hale Commission of 1652', *EHR* 83 (1968), 689–704.

[463] Gerald R. Cragg, *From Puritanism to the Age of Reason: a study of changes in religious thought within the Church of England, 1660 – 1700*. CUP: 1950. Pp. vii, 247.

[464] Christina Hole, *The English Housewife in the Seventeenth Century*. L: Chatto & Windus: 1953. Pp. 248.

[465] John W. Stoye, *English Travellers Abroad, 1604 – 1667: their influence in English society and politics*. L: Cape: 1952. Pp. 479.

[466] W. D. Robson-Scott, *German Travellers in England, 1400 – 1800*. O: Blackwell: 1953. Pp. xi, 238.

[467] Bryant Lillywhite, *London Coffee Houses*. L: Allen & Unwin: 1963. Pp. 858. Rev: *EHR* 81, 223f.

London was also burned to the ground; Lane discusses the rebuilding.[468] And although Evans's history of one of London's learned societies comes down to 1951 it shall be listed here, for the great age of the Antiquaries was the seventeenth century.[469]

---

[468] Jane Lane, *Rebuilding St Paul's after the Great Fire of London*. L: OUP: 1956. Pp. xii, 269. Rev: *EHR* 72, 707ff.

[469] Joan Evans, *History of the Society of Antiquaries*. O: for the Society: 1956. Pp. xv, 487. Rev: *CHJ* 13, 190ff.

VII

The Eighteenth Century (1714 – 1815)

Also nn. 24, 41–6, 59–62, 71, 1025, 1028, 1062, 1068–71, 1073–6, 1135–52, 1190–7, 1125–30, 1242.

(A) GENERAL

While the historiography of the seventeenth century has not yet really succeeded in absorbing and employing the new insights produced by basic research, that of the eighteenth at times gives the impression of a mildly desperate search for controversies. The main issues, around which debate tends to gather, are two revolutions: that which Namier produced in the history of party politics, and that which took place in the economic life of the time. Unfortunately, both issues are too readily treated as though they were moral ones. Namier's interpretation, disagreeable to many in its lack of sentimentality, provokes the charge that 'he removed the mind from history', while the questions of industrialization are slanted towards an argument about the possible social damage done; and in the outcome, a good deal that one reads seems to be dominated more by moral indignation than by scholarly concern and rigour. However, in both respects there are signs that a phase of controversy is drawing to a close, and that more real issues are moving to the centre of the stage.

The fact that much of the noise is a trifle artificial may be inferred from the few general accounts which have appeared in the last few years but could, in the main, have been written as readily by the previous generation of historians. Plumb's brief introduction stresses social history and material progress.[470] Marshall, with a good deal more space at her disposal, includes more politics in a lucid and straightforward survey.[471]

---

[470] John H. Plumb, *England in the Eighteenth Century*. Harmondsworth: Penguin Books: 1950. Pp. 224.

[471] Dorothy Marshall, *Eighteenth Century England*. L: Longmans: 1962. Pp. xvi, 537. – *See also* n. 625.

She too, however, has her foray into social description, though she confines herself interestingly to the capital in its capital heyday.[472] One would hardly look to Michael, whose monumental history of the first half of the century has now reached completion, for novel concepts or interpretations; his virtues, especially his thorough dissection of international affairs, continue to impress.[473] Perhaps one might have expected rather more from Watson whose contribution to the *Oxford History of England* presents a clear enough account of the years 1760 – 1815 but succeeds neither in bringing them to life nor in renovating an old story.[474] Much more lively, though not very deep, is White's brisk run through the age.[475]

(B) POLITICAL HISTORY

A number of monographs concentrate on the crises of the period. Carswell succeeds in making the bubble of 1721 (crisis of credit) comprehensible, a notable achievement.[476] The new dynasty's uncertain hold on the throne led to the expected conspiracies, and Jones does good service by refusing to confine himself to the two familiar risings.[477] Beattie studies the political influence of the court; Reitan the political consequences of the necessity that the costs of monarchy be covered.[478] The irrational unrest of this age of reason appears formidably in

---

[472] Dorothy Marshall, *Dr Johnson's London*. New York: Wiley: 1968. Pp. xiv, 293. Rev: *Hist* 54, 286.

[473] Wolfgang Michael, *Englische Geschichte im 18. Jahrhundert*, Bd. V: Englands Aufstieg zur Weltmacht. Basel: Verlag für Recht und Gesellschaft: 1955. Pp. xvi, 726. Index to vols. 1–5.

[474] J. Steven Watson, *The Reign of George III, 1760 – 1815*. O: Clarendon: 1960. Pp. xviii, 637. Rev: *EHR* 77, 115ff.; *HJ* 4, 218ff.

[475] Reginald J. White, *The Age of George III*. L: Heinemann: 1968. Pp. ix, 251.

[476] John P. Carswell, *The South Sea Bubble*. L: Cresset: 1960. Pp. xi, 314. Rev: *EcHR*² 16, 361f.

[477] G. H. Jones, *The Mainstream of Jacobitism*. C (Mass.): Harvard UP: 1954. Pp. x, 275. Rev: *EHR* 70, 672.

[478] John M. Beattie, 'The court of George I in English politics', *EHR* 81 (1966), 26–37. – E. A. Reitan, 'The civil list in eighteenth-century British politics: parliamentary supremacy versus the independence of the crown', *HJ* 9 (1966), 318–37.

Rudé's social and political analysis of two events in London: the agitation stirred up by Wilkes, and the occasion when gin and intolerance nearly succeeded in reducing the city once more to ashes.[479] Ritcheson considers the effect which the problems of America had upon politics after 1760.[480] By studying a single year (the year of crisis, 1780, when the loss of America became in effect certain), Butterfield endeavours to disentangle the interaction between government, parliament and public opinion, but it has to be confessed that on occasion he submerges in a morass of detail.[481] A theme of precise circumscription – the political consequences of George III's mental disturbance – offers Derry the opportunity for a precisely circumscribed book.[482] Sutherland chooses a larger ground in her study of the political activities of a solidly founded 'interest', a study which tells much of the political attitudes of the time.[483]

As is always the case in English historical writing, much political history comes out in the form of political biographies. Plumb's massive biography of Walpole still lacks its third volume in which (one may suppose) some of the gaps in the story of political action will no doubt be filled.[484] Walpole's heir, Henry Pelham, has (it would appear) become the victim of an inadequate and misleading book.[485] A very special biography deals with George III's mental health: the authors

[479] George Rudé, *Wilkes and Liberty: a social study of 1763 to 1774*. O: Clarendon: 1962. Pp. xvi, 240. Rev: *EHR* 79, 184f. – Idem, 'The Gordon Riots: a study of the rioters and their victims', *TRHS* (1956), 93–114.

[480] Charles R. Ritcheson, *British Politics and the American Revolution*. Norman: U of Oklahoma P: 1954. Pp. xv, 320. Rev: *AHR* 60, 354f.

[481] Herbert Butterfield, *George III, Lord North, and the People, 1779 – 1780*. L: Bell: 1949. Pp. xi, 407. Rev: *EHR* 65, 526ff.

[482] John W. Derry, *The Regency Crisis and the Whigs, 1788 – 1789*. CUP: 1963. Pp. viii, 244. Rev: *EHR* 80, 852f.

[483] Lucy S. Sutherland, *The East India Company in Eighteenth Century Politics*. O: Clarendon: 1952. Pp. xii, 430. Rev: *EHR* 70, 460ff.

[484] John H. Plumb, *Sir Robert Walpole*, 2 vols. (to date). L: Cresset: 1956, 1960. Pp. xv, 407; xii, 363. Rev: *EHR* 72, 328ff.; 78, 557ff; *CHJ* 13, 80ff.

[485] [John Wilkes, *A Whig in Power*. Evanston: Northwestern UP: 1964. Rev: *EHR* 80, 847f.]

have diagnosed his trouble as porphyria, a deficiency condition, rule out all forms of psychiatric disturbance, and investigate, with becoming reticence, the recurrence of this hereditary disease up and down the royal line.[486] Despite doubts expressed in several quarters (see *EHR* 84, 805f., a note written before the appearance of the big book), the case is winning widespread adherence. Persons not quite in the front rank also receive attention. Brooke completed Namier's last piece of writing, a rehabilitation of that misfortunate politician, Charles Townsend.[487] Guttridge succeeds only in proving that there is little worth saying about the early days of Lord Rockingham,[488] while the unpleasing George Germaine has, surprisingly, found two not very convincing defenders.[489] One of them did even worse by the much maligned North, a man who badly needs a good new life.[490] Francis Dashwood, whose mixture of parliamentary and dilettante activities make him (if one may so put it) a typical oddity, is coolly handled by Kemp.[491] Rather more interesting are two high-born radicals, the duke of Richmond (whose correspondence has been published with a long biographical introduction)[492] and Shelburne whom Norris treats very seriously as a reformer, though he evades the problems posed by a personality which more than any other

[486] Ida Macalpine and Richard Hunter, *George III and the Mad Business.* L: Allen Lane The Penguin Press: 1969. Pp. xv, 407.

[487] Lewis B. Namier and John Brooke, *Charles Townsend.* L: Macmillan: 1964. Pp. ix, 198. Rev: *EHR* 81, 402f. – *See also* Peter G. D. Thomas, 'Charles Townsend and American taxation', *EHR* 83 (1968), 33–51.

[488] G. H. Guttridge, *The Early Career of Lord Rockingham, 1730 – 1765.* Berkeley: U of California P: 1952. Pp. vii, 54.

[489] Alan Valentine, *Lord George Germaine.* L: OUP: 1962. Pp. x, 534. Rev: *EHR* 79, 423f.; *AHR* 68, 1037f. – Gerald S. Brown, *The American Secretary: the colonial policy of Lord George Germain, 1775 – 1778.* Ann Arbor: U of Michigan P: 1963. Pp. ix, 246. Rev: *EHR* 69, 1044f.

[490] Alan Valentine, *Lord North,* 2 vols. Norman: U of Oklahoma P: 1967. Pp. xi, 568; vii, 517. Rev: *HJ* 12, 180f.; *Hist* 53, 442.

[491] Betty Kemp, *Sir Francis Dashwood: an eighteenth-century independent.* L: Macmillan: 1967. Pp. ix, 210. Rev: *EHR* 83, 618.

[492] Alison G. Olsen, *The Radical Duke: career and correspondence of Charles Lennox, 3rd duke of Richmond.* L: OUP: 1961. Pp. 262.

in that age managed to create universal distrust.[493] Shelburne was one of the intellectual heirs of Chatham and as such appears in company with others in an interesting attempt to elucidate politics by means of a group biography.[494] New lives have appeared of the great north and south poles of late-Georgian politics, but neither quite ends the matter. Reid is essentially concerned to explain Fox the orator and leaves the full political account to be written by someone else;[495] while Ehrman, whose enormous life of Pitt has reached vol. 1 and the year 1789, gives the full political and administrative account in which the man is a little bit in danger of disappearing.[496] Though the career of Addington, Pitt's lesser successor and later notorious as that bitter reactionary Sidmouth, extends well beyond 1815, the first – and successful – attempt to bring him to life may be included here.[497] Gray pleasingly demonstrates that more should be remembered about Spencer Percival than that he is the only prime minister (so far) to have died at an assassin's hands.[498]

The very tricky problem of public opinion (did it exist? what does it mean? what did it do?) is at last receiving some attention. Perry's study of the 1753 Jews Naturalization Act attempts to show how political interests managed to exploit worked up opinion in the country at large; but since every facet of this multi-faceted book has been criticized by some expert, it must be confessed that he undertook a task beyond his learning.[499]

[493] John Norris, *Shelburne and Reform*. L: Macmillan: 1963. Pp. xiv, 325. Rev: *EHR* 80, 615f.

[494] Peter Brown, *The Chathamites*. L: Macmillan: 1967. Pp. xv, 516. Rev: *Hist* 54, 109f.

[495] Loren Reid, *Charles James Fox: a man for the people*. L: Longmans: 1969. Pp. xiv, 475.

[496] John P. W. Ehrman, *The Younger Pitt: the years of acclaim*. L: Constable: 1969. Pp. xv, 710.

[497] Philip Ziegler, *Addington*. L: Collins: 1965. Pp. 478. Rev: *EHR* 82, 625.

[498] Denis Gray, *Spencer Percival: the evangelical prime minister, 1762 – 1812*. Manchester UP: 1963. Pp. xii, 506. Rev: *EHR* 80, 564ff.

[499] Thomas W. Perry, *Public Opinion, Propaganda and Politics in 18th Century England: a study of the Jew Bill of 1753*. C (Mass.): Harvard UP: 1962. Pp. xii, 215.

Aspinall's study of the press, which extends beyond this period, is thorough; it contributes usefully to an understanding of how opinion was formed both in support of government and in opposition to it.[500] Marshall describes Manchester's emergence as a centre of radical free thought.[501] An unusual but very important source is exploited by George who places the caricatures of the great age – Gillray and Rowlandson – in the centre of the story.[502]

(C) PARLIAMENT AND PARTIES

Although a large number of historians profess to be concerned with the eighteenth-century parliament, hardly any of them seem to be interested in the institution, its working, or its legislative production. An exception is Lambert who, in addition to drawing attention to the mass of papers produced (n. 17), also shows what may be learned from a proper understanding of seeming technicalities.[503] For the rest, nearly all work concentrates on political organization in the commons, though Turberville completed his rather oldfashioned description of the Lords, and Large contributes a first attempt to trace the decline of government control in the upper house.[504] Kendrick looks at Walpole, the manager of party and parliament, a theme not sufficiently treated by Plumb (n. 484).[505]

---

[500] A. Aspinall, *Politics and the Press, c. 1780 – 1850*. L: Hume & Van Thal: 1949. Pp. xv, 511. Rev: *EHR* 65, 269ff.

[501] Leon S. Marshall, *The Development of Public Opinion in Manchester, 1780 – 1820*. Syracuse UP: 1946. Pp. xi, 247. Rev: *AHR*, 53, 326ff.

[502] M. Dorothy George, *English Political Caricature: a study in opinion and propaganda*, 2 vols. O: Clarendon: 1959. Pp. xii, 236; xii, 275; 96 + 96 plates. Rev: *EHR* 77, 112ff.

[503] Sheila Lambert, 'Guides to parliamentary printing', *BIHR* 38 (1965), 111–7; 'Printing for the House of Commons in the eighteenth century', *Library* (March 1968), 25–46.

[504] A. S. Turberville, *The House of Lords in the Age of Reform, 1784 – 1832*. L: Faber: 1958. Pp. 519. Rev: *EHR* 74, 302ff.; *HJ* 2, 195ff. – David Large, 'The decline of "the party of the crown" and the rise of parties in the House of Lords, 1783 – 1837', *EHR* 78 (1963), 669–95.

[505] T. F. J. Kendrick, 'Sir Robert Walpole, the old whigs, and the bishops, 1733 – 1736: a study in eighteenth century parliamentary politics', *HJ* 11 (1968), 421–45.

Foord probably discovered the existence of a self-conscious opposition party a little earlier than the facts allow, but he offers
a sound exposition of the transition to a new kind of system in
the commons.[506] Kluxen tackles much the same problem from
the standpoint of an historian of ideas, so that what actually
happened remains pretty obscure and the point of the analysis
fails to come across.[507] The making of parliaments has been
studied by Robson in his detailed analysis of a single election,
and by Bonsall in his analysis of a single patron, while Smith
runs too briefly over the history of the men who had to do the
patrons' work.[508]

What about Party? Ever since Namier published his first
book, in 1929, the arguments about whigs and tories have been
going on. Were they real parties, or perhaps invented by
Edmund Burke? What is the place of connexion and of faction
in the making of parliamentary parties, not to mention governments? After the initial resistance to Namier, he became
panjandrumized after the war, and for a time it seemed as
though a rather simplified version of his views would hold the
field for ever. The phase lasted hardly beyond his death, and
at present a kind of semi-respectful compromise is developing
which allows Namier and his school to occupy the area of 'his'
age in parliamentary history (c. 1720 – 1780) but would see
more 'real' parties in existence before and after those dates.
Some of the argument strongly suggests that the questions are
perhaps being put in the wrong way, or at least are put in
different ways by the contestants; and it would be rash for an

---

[506] Archibald S. Foord, 'The waning of the "influence of the crown"',
EHR 62 (1947), 484–507. – Idem, *His Majesty's Opposition, 1714 –
1830*. O: Clarendon: 1964. Pp. xi, 494. Rev: *EHR* 80, 806ff.

[507] Kurt Kluxen, *Das Problem der politischen Opposition: Entwicklung
und Wesen der englischen Zweiparteienpolitik im 18. Jahrhundert*. Frei-
burg/Munich: Alber: 1956. Pp. x, 269.

[508] Robert J. Robson, *The Oxfordshire Election of 1754*. L: OUP: 1949.
Pp. 192. – Brian Bonsall, *Sir James Lowther and Cumberland and
Westmorland Elections, 1754 – 1775*. Manchester UP: 1960. Pp. x,
161. Rev: *EHR* 77, 172f.; *HJ* 4, 104ff. – E. A. Smith, 'The
election agent in English politics, 1734 – 1832', *EHR* 84 (1969),
12–35.

outsider to step between the firing lines. Nevertheless, one may be so foolhardy as to suggest two things. Namier was right in emphasizing the primacy of faction and connexion, as well as the fact that party of a more enduring kind had nothing to do with the formation of administrations until after the decline of George III,[509] but he underestimated the degree to which loyalty, opinion and ideology could hold *part* of the house together through political vicissitudes. On the other hand, those who discover the existence and continuity of parties need to stress more heavily that the groups to be described by this name were very far from comprehending the whole house and ought to look more carefully at what really concerned Namier, the achievement of effective political action and especially the making of governments.

These humble suggestions are offered after a diet of reading the several direct and indirect contributions to the debate. Namier's severity provoked the resistance of those who could not see in politics only the workings of the machine but demanded also to understand the ideas behind action, but of them all only Butterfield had the courage to enter the lists during Namier's lifetime in his attempt to prove that this new 'school' was neither so new nor so sufficient as it thought.[510] The attempt did not altogether succeed, and the fruitful work has been done by those who have at least accepted Namier's precept to study the realities rather than the concepts of tradition. Owen applied the method to the crisis which ensued upon Walpole's fall.[511] Newman added points of interest concerning the politicians who towards the end of George II's reign gathered round his heir.[512] In a remarkable and very important book, Pares succeeded in comprehensively describing Namier's 'own age', that of the young George III, a feat which the

---

[509] Lewis B. Namier, *Monarchy and the Party System*. O: Clarendon: 1952. Pp. 30.

[510] Herbert Butterfield, *George III and the Historians*. L: Collins: 1957. Pp. 304. Rev: *EHR* 74, 300f.

[511] John Owen, *The Rise of the Pelhams*. L: Methuen: 1957. Pp. x, 357. Rev: *EHR* 73, 306ff.

[512] Aubrey N. Newman, 'Leicester House politics, 1748 – 1751', *EHR* 76 (1961), 577–89.

patriarch himself never brought off.[513] The intensive reports
on individual cabinets, which Naimer initiated, have so far
yielded three books which, despite their excessive devotion to
detail, manage to bring much real enlightenment.[514] Coming
originally from the same stable, Cannon, however, wants to
see a change towards real party coming after the disaster of the
American war; his book is nicely enlivened by a firm distaste
for Shelburne and Pitt which no actual supporter of the unhappy coalition could have bettered.[515] Fox, one may say,
turned the Rockingham connexion into the whig party, a
consummation possible only (at the time) to a party out of
office and in continuous decline, as O'Gorman shows.[516]

Though the games played by the parliamentary factions
have attracted most attention, they have not monopolized it,
and very different strands in the nation's political life have not
been forgotten. Robbins collects the evidence for the fact that
the democratic tenets of the seventeenth century found their
adherents in the eighteenth,[517] and Carswell's study of three
'true whigs' active in the century after 1688 offers support.[518]
Black investigates the beginnings of the parliamentary reform
movement by looking at the not altogether spontaneous county
associations,[519] Christie links this phase with the career of John

---

[513] Richard Pares, *George III and the Politicians*. O: Clarendon: 1953.
Pp. 214. Rev: *EHR* 68, 447ff.

[514] John Brooke, *The Chatham Administration, 1766 – 1768*. L: Macmillan: 1956. Pp. xiv, 400. Rev: *EHR* 72, 333ff. – Bernard
Donoughue, *British Politics and the American Revolution; the path to
war, 1773 – 1775*. Ibid.: 1964. Pp. x, 324. Rev: *EHR* 81, 603f.;
HJ 9, 246ff. – Ian R. Christie, *The End of North's Ministry, 1780 –
1782*. Ibid.: 1958. Pp. xiii, 429.

[515] John Cannon, *The Fox-North Coalition: crisis of the constitution,
1782 – 1784*. CUP: 1969. Pp. xiii, 275.

[516] Francis O'Gorman, *The Whig Party and the French Revolution*. L:
Macmillan: 1967. Pp. xv, 270. Rev: *HJ* 12, 712ff.

[517] Caroline Robbins, *The Eighteenth-Century Commonwealthman*. C
(Mass.): Harvard UP: 1959. Pp. viii, 462.

[518] John P. Carswell, *The Old Cause*. L: Cresset: 1954. Pp. xxiii,
402.

[519] Eugene C. Black, *The Association, 1769 – 1793*. C (Mass.): Harvard
UP: 1963. Pp. 344.

Wilkes,[520] and Miller takes a new look at the most dedicated propagandist of them all for the cause of reform.[521]

(D) FOREIGN AFFAIRS AND WAR

A number of works that remind us that this was a century of war and aggressive diplomacy stand far from the controversies. Just before his lamented death, Horn fortunately embodied his special knowledge in a comprehensive treatise.[522] Earlier, he had also demonstrated that for this century one may at last speak of a proper diplomatic service.[523] To this theme, Meyer contributes a piece on the special case of Switzerland.[524] Studies of diplomatic relations deal, in chronological order, with Russia, Sweden and Turkey at the start of the century;[525] with the Netherlands, at about the same time;[526] with Prussia (Schlenke documents the influence of public opinion on foreign policy, while Spencer defends George III's government against the charge that it broke faith in 1762);[527] with the economic

---

[520] Ian R. Christie, *Wilkes, Wyvill, and Reform*. L: Macmillan: 1962. Pp. xii, 247. Rev: *EHR* 79, 861f.

[521] Naomi C. Miller, 'John Cartwright and radical parliamentary reform, 1808 – 1819', *EHR* 83 (1968), 705 – 28.

[522] D. B. Horn, *Great Britain and Europe in the Eighteenth Century*. O: Clarendon: 1967. Pp. xi, 411. Rev: *EHR* 83, 848f.; *HJ* 11, 591f.

[523] D. B. Horn, *The British Diplomatic Service, 1689 – 1789*. O: Clarendon: 1961. Pp. xv, 324. Rev: *EHR* 77, 541ff.

[524] Markus Meyer, *Die diplomatische Vertretung Englands in der Schweiz in 18. Jahrhundert, 1689 – 1789*. Basel: Helbing & Lichterhahn: 1952. Pp. 156.

[525] L. A. Nikiforov, *Russko anglijskie otnoschenija pri Petre I*. Moscow: 1950. Pp. 277. German translation, Weimar, 1954, pp. 377. – Ilse Jacob, *Die Beziehungen Englands zu Russland und zur Türkei in den Jahren 1718 – 1727*. Basel: Helbing & Lichterhahn: 1945. Pp. 159. – John J. Murray, *George I, the Baltic and the Whig Split of 1717*. L: Routledge: 1969. Pp. xv, 366. Rev: *Hist* 55, 125f.

[526] Ragnhild Hatton, *Diplomatic Relations between Great Britain and the Dutch Republic, 1714 – 1721*. L: East & West: 1950. Pp. 283.

[527] Manfred Schlenke, *England und das friderizianische Preussen, 1740 – 1763*. Freiburg/Munich: Alber: 1963. Pp. 435. Rev: *EHR* 80, 36off. – Frank Spencer, 'The Anglo-Prussian breach of 1762, a historical revision', *Hist* 41 (1956), 100–12.

negotiations of the powers on the eve of the French revolutionary wars;[528] with the diplomatic career of one outstanding ambassador in the 1780's;[529] and with the long crisis in the relations with the newly formed United States which did not end until 1820.[530] The twenty years' war with France and Napoleon also produced its diplomatic problems. Helleiner studies the loans by means of which Pitt endeavoured to keep Austria in the war;[531] Sherwig, on the other hand, taking a longer view, concludes that the story of 'Pitt's gold' is largely legend and that heavy subsidizing took place only in the last two years of war.[532] The occupation of Sicily, one successful breach in the wall that Napoleon built round Europe, is the subject properly of diplomatic and not of military history.[533]

Perhaps surprisingly, the army has received more and better attention than the navy. Western's treatment of the militia, the foundation of any British army, is thorough.[534] Robson explains the consequences of promotion by purchase;[535] Savory shows that an army run in that fashion could nevertheless be

---

[528] John P. W. Ehrman, *The British Government and Commercial negotiations with Europe, 1783 – 1793*. CUP: 1962. Pp. viii, 231. Rev: *EHR* 79, 864f.

[529] Alfred B. Cobban, *Ambassadors and Secret Agents: the diplomacy of the first earl of Malmesbury at the Hague*. L: Cape: 1954. Pp. 255. Rev: *EHR* 70, 289ff.

[530] Bradford Perkins, *The First Rapprochement: England and the United States, 1795 – 1805*. Philadelphia: U of Pennsylvania P: 1955. Pp. xii, 257. – Idem, *The Prologue to War: England and the United States, 1805 – 1812*. Berkeley: U of California P: 1961. Pp. xiv, 456. – Idem, *Castlereagh and Adams: England and the United States, 1812 – 1823*. Ibid.: 1964. Pp. x, 364.

[531] Karl F. Helleiner, *The Imperial Loans: a study in financial and diplomatic history*. O: Clarendon: 1965. Pp. ix, 190.

[532] John M. Sherwig, *Guineas and Gunpowder: British foreign aid in the wars with France, 1793 – 1815*. C (Mass.): Harvard UP: 1969. Pp. xi, 393.

[533] John Rosselli, *Lord William Bentinck and the British Occupation of Sicily, 1811 – 1814*. CUP: 1956. Pp. 220. Rev: *EHR* 72, 554f.

[534] J. R. Western, *The English Militia in the Eighteenth Century*. L: Routledge: 1965. Pp. xv, 479. Rev: *EHR* 82, 797f.

[535] Erick Robson, 'Purchase and promotion in the British army in the 18th century', *Hist* 36 (1951), 57–72.

first-class.[536] One improbable but very competent general, a French refugee, receives suitably good treatment.[537] R. Glover breaks new ground in his study of the army reforms which made possible the forces that Wellington commanded in the Peninsula – and which redound to the credit of the much maligned duke of York.[538] The peninsular commanders and their organization have been variously restudied.[539] Roos in his book on Scandinavian prisoners of war treats of a by-product of that sad time.[540] The navy offers much less. Lewis provides an interesting but not very searching description of officers and men, discipline and supply, life on board ship and so forth;[541] Mackay deals with one great admiral and Oman with the greatest of them all;[542] and Haas tackles an entirely different and much more promising line by investigating the conflict between tradition, efficiency and corruption in the dock-yards.[543]

Several particular episodes of the wars have found their chroniclers. Mackesy's history of the American war of indepen-

---

[536] Reginald Savory, *His Britannic Majesty's Army in Germany during the Seven Years' War*. O: Clarendon: 1966. Pp. xxii, 571. Rev: *EHR* 82, 622f.

[537] Reginald H. Whitworth, *Field Marshal Lord Ligonier: a story of the British army, 1702 – 1770*. O: Clarendon: 1958. Pp. xiv, 422.

[538] Richard Glover, *Peninsular Preparation: the reform of the British army, 1795 – 1809*. CUP: 1963. Pp. viii, 315. Rev: *EHR* 82, 132ff.

[539] Carola Oman, *Sir John Moore*. L: Hodder & Stoughton: 1953. Pp. xvi, 700. Rev: *EHR* 69, 453ff. – S. P. G. Ward, *Wellington*. L: Batsford: 1963. Pp. 152. – Idem, *Wellington's Headquarters: a study of administrative problems in the Peninsula, 1809 – 1814*. L: OUP: 1957. Pp. viii, 219. Rev: *EHR* 74, 170f. – Michael Glover, *Wellington as Military Commander*. L: Batsford: 1968. Pp. 288.

[540] [Carl Roos, *Prisonen: Danske og Norske Krigsgefangen i England, 1807 – 1814*. Copenhagen: 1953. Rev: *EHR* 68, 655.]

[541] Michael A. Lewis, *A Social History of the Navy, 1793 – 1815*. L: Allen & Unwin: 1960. Pp. 467. Rev: *EHR*, 76, 736f.

[542] [Ruddock F. MacKay, *Admiral Hawke*. O: Clarendon: 1965. Rev: *EHR* 82, 172f.] – Carola Oman, *Nelson*. L: Hodder & Stoughton: 1947. Pp. xvi, 734.

[543] James M. Haas, 'The introduction of task work into the royal dockyards', *JBS* 8 (1969), 44–68.

dence is particularly impressive.[544] Smith remembers the men
who remained true to their king and supported the mother
country against the rebellious colonists.[545] Patterson remembers an even more readily forgotten story from the same war.[546]
Three regions of the naval warfare which ran alongside the
continental struggle against Napoleon have been described:
Mackesy attends to the Mediterranean, Ryan to the Baltic,
and Parkinson to the very obscure events in the Indian
Ocean.[547]

(E) EMPIRE

We can here treat only of those works concerned with British
expansion overseas that look at the matter from England out-
wards. Two large-scale operations cover the whole story
between them. Gipson has happily concluded his twelve-
volume history of the empire down to the loss of the American
colonies of which five volumes had appeared before 1945.[548]
While this idiosyncratic work carries a mildly oldfashioned air,
Harlow's two volumes, which describe the consequences of that
loss and the start on recovery, constitute a fine example of

---

[544] Piers Mackesy, *The War for America, 1775 – 1783*. L: Longmans:
1964. Pp. xx, 565.

[545] Paul H. Smith, *Loyalists and Redcoats: a study in British revolutionary
politics*. Chapel Hill: U of North Carolina P: 1964. Pp. xii, 199.

[546] A. Temple Patterson, *The Other Armada: the Franco-Spanish attempt
to invade Britain in 1779*. Manchester UP: 1960. Pp. ix, 247. Rev:
EHR 77, 566.

[547] Piers Mackesy, *The War in the Mediterranean, 1803 – 1810*. L:
Longmans: 1957. Pp. xviii, 430. Rev: *EHR* 74, 168ff. – A. P. Ryan,
'The defence of British trade with the Baltic, 1808 – 1813', *EHR*
74 (1959), 444–66. – C. Northcote Parkinson, *War in the Eastern
Seas, 1793 – 1815*. L: Allen & Unwin: 1954. Pp. 477. Rev: *EHR*
70, 156f.

[548] Lawrence H. Gipson, *The British Empire before the American Revolution*, vols. 6–12 (1754 – 1776). New York: Knopf: 1946 – 67. Pp.
xxxvii, 426, xxxviii; xlviii, 467, xxxvi; xxv, 313, xlix; xliv, 345,
xlv; lxxv, 579, xxv; lvii, 372, xxx. Rev: *EHR* 79, 122ff.; 83, 130ff.;
HJ 9, 396ff. Also supplementary vol. 13, in 3 parts: *see EHR* 84,
616.

modern historical writing.[549] Two voyages of discovery, geo-
graphically well separated but concerned with the same des-
tination, are accounted for by Williamson and Williams.[550] In
Graham's general survey of the battle for the Atlantic,
the eighteenth century rightly occupies pride of place.[551]
Feiling writes a solid biography of Warren Hastings, while
Marshall goes into fascinating detail on the governor-general's
political trial.[552] The latter also investigates the manner in
which the home country was affected by the unexpected acqui-
sition of an Indian empire,[553] while Lutnick, utilizing the
newspapers and pamphlets of the time, seeks to discover domestic reaction to the equally unexpected loss of an empire in
America.[554] Madden, who looks at the administrative problems raised by all this expansion, has taken a most valuable
first step in a new direction.[555]

(F) ADMINISTRATION AND GOVERNMENT

A disappointingly small collection of titles draws attention to
the fact that methods of enquiry newly popular among most
historians of England since 1485 have so far largely escaped the

---

[549] Vincent T. Harlow, *The Founding of the Second British Empire,
1763 – 1793*, 2 vols. L: Longmans: 1952, 1964. Pp. viii, 664; x, 820.
Rev: *EHR* 68, 282ff.; *HJ* 10, 113ff.

[550] James A. Williamson, *Cook and the Opening of the Pacific*. L: English
Universities Press: 1946. Pp. xii, 251. – Glyndwr Williams, *The
British Search for the Northwest Passage in the Eighteenth Century*. L:
Longmans: 1962. Pp. xvi, 306.

[551] Gerald S. Graham, *Empire of the North Atlantic: the maritime struggle
for North America*. Toronto UP: 1950. Pp. xiii, 338. Rev: *EHR* 66,
597f.

[552] Keith Feiling, *Warren Hastings*. L: Macmillan: 1954. Pp. xi, 420.
Rev: *EHR* 71, 462ff. – Peter J. Marshall, *The Impeachment of
Warren Hastings*. L: OUP: 1965. Pp. xix, 217. Rev: *EHR* 82, 404f.

[553] Peter J. Marshall, *Problems of Empire: Britain and India, 1742 – 1813*.
L: Allen & Unwin: 1968. Pp. xii, 239.

[554] Solomon Lutnick, *The American Revolution and the British Press,
1775 – 1783*. Columbia, Mo: U of Missouri P: 1967. Pp. xi, 249.
Rev: *EHR* 84, 404.

[555] A. F. McC. Madden, 'The imperial machinery of the younger
Pitt', *Feiling Ft* (n. 130), 173–93.

attention of specialists in the eighteenth century. The massive sources available, and the fundamental importance of the theme, will, one hopes, soon alter this situation.

The only book on that central office, the treasury, confines itself to a rather simple collecting of points about the office's duties in colonial administration.[556] More learned, but not much better digested, is Aspinall's large essay on the cabinet: he gathers the materials but leaves it to someone else to make historical sense of them.[557] Very little is known so far of the active officialdom of this period, though Ward has bravely dipped a toe into that uncharted sea.[558] He has also produced a straight dissertation on the century's main tax.[559] Binney has made the only attempt to seek general significance in the interaction of finance and policy, an attempt which stands out at least in part because of its isolation.[560] A few institutions have been investigated. Thus Ellis writes about the post office and Mitchison about the unreformed board of agriculture,[561] but the most substantial efforts belong to the beginning of the period – Beattie's important and comprehensive analysis of the place and function of the king's court and household,[562] and Baugh's intensive study of naval administration in an era of peace and retrenchment.[563]

---

[556] Dora Mae Clark, *The Rise of the British Treasury: colonial administration in the eighteenth century*. New Haven: Yale UP: 1960. Pp. x, 249. Rev: *EHR* 78, 179f.

[557] A. Aspinall, *The Cabinet Council, 1783 – 1835*. L: OUP: 1953. Pp. 108. Rev: *EHR* 70, 680f.

[558] W. R. Ward, 'Some eighteenth-century civil servants: the English revenue commissioners, 1754 – 1798', *EHR* 70 (1955), 25–54.

[559] W. R. Ward, *The English Land Tax in the Eighteenth Century*. L: OUP: 1953. Pp. 188. Rev: *EHR* 69, 109f.

[560] J. E. D. Binney, *British Public Finance and Administration, 1774 – 1892*. O: Clarendon: 1958. Pp. xii, 320. Rev: *EcHR*[2] 13, 124f.

[561] Kenneth L. Ellis, *The Post Office in the Eighteenth Century*. L: OUP: 1958. Pp. xvi, 176. Rev: *EHR* 73, 726f. – Rosalind Mitchison, 'The old Board of Agriculture, 1793 – 1822', *EHR* 74 (1960), 41–69.

[562] John M. Beattie, *The English Court in the Reign of George I*. CUP: 1967. Pp. xii, 306. Rev: *EcHR*[2] 21, 395f.

[563] Daniel A. Baugh, *British Naval Administration in the Age of Walpole*. Princeton UP: 1965. Pp. xvi, 557. Rev: *EHR* 82, 618f.

(G) THE CHURCH

In this period, the idea was dead that a national Church should comprehend all the king's subjects, but full civil rights remained reserved to anglicans, though the disabilities often operated more in theory than in practice. These facts are reflected in the concerns of modern research. Carpenter's urbanely pompous and discursively chatty survey admittedly stands outside both modern interests and modern research.[564] Best, on the other hand, starting from a study of the organization which administered Queen Anne's modest Bounty, achieves a genuine social history of the Church.[565] The first volume has appeared of a co-operative history of methodism.[566] The methodists left the Church; the later evangelicals tried (successfully) to regenerate it from within and were also politically very active, especially in the struggle against the slave trade.[567] Their methods owed a good deal to those of the earlier nonconformists who throughout the century recognized the need to organize themselves politically if they were to achieve anything in a world which treated them as second-class citizens. Manning has described the organization of elected committees exercising influence upon parliament from outside; Hunt has dissected the energetic methods particularly employed by the quakers.[568] Three interesting studies deal with the religious thought of this often deistic century. Stromberg explores the orthodox reaction

---

[564] S. C. Carpenter, *Eighteenth Century Church and People*. L: Murray: 1959. Pp. x, 290. Rev: *EHR* 75, 527.

[565] Geoffrey F. A. Best, *Temporal Pillars: Queen Anne's Bounty, the Ecclesiastical Commissioners, and the Church of England*. CUP: 1964. Pp. xiv, 582.

[566] Rupert Davies and E. Gordon Rupp, eds., *A History of the Methodist Church of Great Britain*, vol. 1. L: Epworth: 1965. Pp. xl, 332.

[567] G. C. B. Davies, *The Early Cornish Evangelicals, 1735 – 1760*. L: SPCK: 1951. Pp. ix, 229. – Ernest M. Howse, *Saints and Politics: the Clapham Sect and the growth of freedom*. Toronto UP: 1952. Pp. xv, 215. Rev: *AHR* 58, 605f.

[568] B. L. Manning, *The Protestant Dissenting Deputies*. CUP: 1952. Pp. ix, 498. Rev: *EHR* 69, 111ff. – Norman C. Hunt, *Two Early Political Associations: the quakers and the dissenting deputies in the age of Sir Robert Walpole*. O: Clarendon: 1961. Pp. xvi, 231. Rev: *EHR* 77, 779f.

against deism and against Wesley's anti-calvinism.[569] Barlow
refutes the opinion that toleration had effectively been achieved
by the start of the period.[570] Cragg, who usefully expounds the
debate between reason and authority, tends rather to leave out
the enlightenment, thereby liberating religion from secular
philosophy to a very misleading extent.[571]

(H) ECONOMIC HISTORY

In contrast to the topics discussed in the last sections, this is an
area of immense and profitable activity. The fact of the Industrial Revolution sees to that. The best general account has
already been mentioned (n. 106); and although other works to
be listed stretch well beyond the limits of the present section, it
will be best to gather everything together here, in one place.

Ashton has left us two fine general surveys of the century;
with these may be linked an article of Habakkuk's which, so to
speak, sums up the Ashton stage of knowledge.[572] However,
this stage has already been left behind in a good many respects,
not only in particulars but especially in its fundamental interpretative scheme. The reason for this is to be found in the
continuing and continuous debate about the Industrial Revolution. Some twenty years ago Ashton produced a brilliant
summary which proved extraordinarily influential and indeed
still has much serious value.[573] This book, like his others, was

---

[569] Roland H. Stromberg, *Religious Liberalism in Eighteenth-Century England*. L: OUP: 1954. Pp. xi, 192.

[570] Richard B. Barlow, *Citizenship and Conscience: a study in the theory and practice of religious toleration in England during the 18th century*. Philadelphia: U of Pennsylvania P: 1962. Pp. 348.

[571] Gerald R. Cragg, *Reason and Authority in the Eighteenth Century*. CUP: 1964. Pp. ix, 349. Rev: *EHR* 81, 170f.

[572] Thomas S. Ashton, *An Economic History of England: the Eighteenth Century*. L: Methuen: 1955. Pp. vii, 257. Rev: *EHR* 70, 674f. – Idem, *Economic Fluctuations in England, 1700 – 1800*. O: Clarendon: 1959. Pp. viii, 199. Rev: *EHR* 76, 158f. – Hrothgar J. Habakkuk. 'The eighteenth century: an essay in bibliography and criticism'. *EcHR*² 8 (1955 – 6), 434–8.

[573] Thomas S. Ashton, *The Industrial Revolution, 1760 – 1820*. L: OUP: 1948. Pp. 167. Rev: *EcHR*² 1, 159ff.

dominated by his conviction that the key to the problem was to be found in the accumulation of transferable capital, the fluctuations of the rate of interest, and the activities of the newly founded banks. The revolution was to be explained by the availability of money. All this is now subject to serious doubt. Pollard has specifically emphasized a fact that also emerges from many particular studies, namely the small amount of capital needed at the start of industrial expansion.[574] Joslin and Presnell demonstrate that neither London nor the provinces possessed the sort of banking system demanded by Ashton's view,[575] and to top it all, Presnell has comprehensively criticized Ashton's interpretation of the changes in interest rates.[576] The facts of capital accumulation and investment do not appear to support Ashton's main scheme.

On the other hand, it is clearly not yet time for a new synthesis, though attempts have been made. Deane's contribution, originally a set of lectures directed at students of economics, is too schematic, starts a bit too firmly with the revolution, and seems unaware of some of the real difficulties.[577] One may prefer Hartwell's sketch, just because he refuses to draw major conclusions.[578] Much more successful is Landes's remarkable treatment of industrialization which deliberately concentrates on one main aspect, the changes in technique; this splendid sweep through one continent and two centuries contains perhaps the best study of the English Indus-

---

[574] Sidney Pollard, 'Investment, consumption, and the Industrial Revolution', *EcHR*² 11 (1958 – 9), 215–26; 'Fixed capital in the Industrial Revolution', *Journal of Econ. History* 24 (1964), 299–314.

[575] David M. Joslin, 'London private bankers, 1720 – 1785', *EcHR*² 7 (1954-5), 167–86; 'London bankers in war time, 1739 – 84', *Ashton Ft* (n. 136), 156–77. – L. S. Pressnell, *Country Banking in the Industrial Revolution*. O: Clarendon: 1956. Pp. xvi, 553. Rev: *EcHR*² 9, 366f.

[576] L. S. Pressnell, 'The rate of interest in the eighteenth century', *Ashton Ft* (n. 136), 178–214.

[577] Phyllis Deane, *The First Industrial Revolution*. CUP: 1965. Pp. viii, 295. Rev: *EHR* 82, 799ff.; *EcHR*² 20, 402ff.

[578] R. Max Hartwell, *The Industrial Revolution in England*. L: Routledge: 1965. Pp. 26. – Idem, 'The causes of the Industrial Revolution: an essay in methodology', *EcHR*² 18 (1965 – 6), 164–82.

trial Revolution at present available.[579] However, clearly we need a lot more work on every sort of problem, and we are getting it. Studies of particular areas, as John's on South Wales and Rowe's on Cornwall, have their uses,[580] but the major work is being done with respect to single themes and single industries. A French attempt to describe English society in the age of industrialization rests on the secondary literature, lacks annotation, and contributes nothing fresh.[581]

A great debate, which unfortunately at once slid sideways into the bog of moral indignation, has arisen over the effects of industrialization on the living standard of the labouring classes. An earlier generation judged this mainly from the extraordinarily ill-analysed evidence of parliamentary committees and was sure that everything was going rapidly downhill. The view was attacked by Clapham and Ashton, with the ideological support of Hayek.[582] Taylor, too, in a thoughtful article, took the line that industrialization generally brought amelioration.[583] All this finally led to a sharp exchange between Hartwell (representing the new views which are dubbed politically conservative) and Hobsbawm (a progressively oriented defender of the old notions), which has extracted, especially from the latter, rather more heat than light.[584] It may perhaps be

---

[579] David S. Landes, *The Unbound Prometheus: technological change and industrial development in Western Europe from 1750 to the present*. CUP: 1969. Pp. ix, 566.

[580] A. H. John, *The Industrial Development of South Wales, 1750 – 1850*. Cardiff: U of Wales P: 1950. Pp. xii, 201. – John Rowe, *Cornwall in the Age of the Industrial Revolution*. Liverpool UP: 1953. Pp. xii, 367. Rev: *EHR* 69, 165; *EcHR²* 9, 148ff.

[581] André Parreaux, *La societé anglaise de 1760 à 1810*. Paris: Presses Universitaires de France: 1966. Pp. xii, 118. Rev: *EHR* 83, 619.

[582] F. A. Hayek, ed., *Capitalism and the Historians*. L: Routledge: 1954. Pp. vii, 192. See particularly the essays by Ashton and Hutt.

[583] Arthur J. Taylor, 'Progress and poverty in Britain, 1780 – 1850: a reappraisal', *Hist* 45 (1960), 16–31.

[584] Eric J. Hobsbawm, 'The British standard of living, 1790 – 1850', *EcHR²* 10 (1957 – 8), 46–68. – R. Max Hartwell, 'The rising standard of living in England, 1800 – 1850', *ibid.* 12 (1959 – 60), 397–416. – Hobsbawm and Hartwell, 'The standard of living during the Industrial Revolution: a discussion', *ibid.* 16 (1963 – 4), 120–46.

concluded that the 'new view' is right on the figures, but one need
not forget that the social life of England's industrialized towns
should not be understood only from the statistical facts. This
conclusion is also supported by the most recent contributions
which look closely at particular cases.[585] This is where one
must place Thompson's impressive, but also rather impressionistic, work on the class situation of the industrialized workers,
a book whose substance and passion render it distinguished
despite the manifest double standard applied to the judging of
evidence wherever ideologically important points are touched.[586]
A study of the domestic situation of the cotton operatives appeared too late for consideration by the disputants.[587]

We leave the field of battle and enter the forge and armoury.
The slow but extensive changes in agriculture, nowadays no
longer regarded as simply an aspect of industrial change, are
smoothly summarized by Chambers and Mingay (but see n. 100
for the view that the real changes came a century earlier).[588]
Grigg does a thorough job for one of the most agrarian regions.[589]
Jones gives solid substance to the view that agrarian change
failed to provide the sort of increase in domestic purchasing
power which was needed to stimulate economic growth in the
manufacturing sector.[590] The prehistory of the changes is

---

[585] J. E. Williams, 'The British standard of living, 1750 – 1850',
and R. S. Neale, 'The standard of living, 1780 – 1844: a regional
and class study', *EcHR*[2] 19 (1966), 581–606.

[586] Edward P. Thompson, *The Making of the English Working Class.*
L: Gollancz: 1963. Pp. 848. Rev: *HJ* 8, 271ff.; *EcHR*[2] 18, 633ff.

[587] Frances Collier, *The Family Economy of the Working Classes in the
Cotton Industry, 1784 – 1833.* Manchester UP: 1964. Pp. x, 94.
Rev: *EHR* 82, 174f.

[588] J. D. Chambers and G. E. Mingay, *The Agricultural Revolution, 1750 – 1880.* L: Batsford: 1966. Pp. ix, 222. Rev: *EHR* 83,
184f.

[589] D. Grigg, *The Agricultural Revolution in South Lincolnshire.* Cambridge UP: 1965. Pp. xiv, 219. Rev: *Hist* 52, 346ff.

[590] E. L. Jones, 'Agriculture and economic growth in England,
1650 – 1750: agricultural change', *Journal of Econ. History* 25
(1965), 1–18. *See also* his introduction to a collection of readings:
Agriculture and Economic Growth in England, 1650 – 1815. L: Methuen:
1967. Pp. xi, 195.

discussed by John and Mingay.[591] The latter also discusses very thoroughly everything that touches all layers of rural society,[592] while Habakkuk sticks to the upper layers.[593] Rural problems include those of river navigation, twice tackled by Willan.[594]

With respect to industry, there seems to be widespread agreement that unsolved problems of population history remain fundamental. The sudden increase is still a puzzle, and there is even still debate (with no end in sight) about whether it owed more to a rising birth rate or a falling death rate. At one time, we were taught the latter, with much stress on improvements in hygiene, the end of plague, and such medical points. Against this, Habakkuk has shown a lowering in the age of marriage, presumably productive of a higher birth rate.[595] Krause, McKeown and Brown have demonstrated that the medical details beloved by earlier historians were largely mythical; they, too, ascribe the increase to the greater fertility produced by earlier marriage.[596] There things stood until recently when Razzell once again advanced the death rate to the forefront of explanation and revived the medical arguments; he cannot suppose that the spread of inoculation against smallpox played no part in the growth of population.[597]

[591] A. H. John 'The course of agricultural change, 1660 1760', *Ashton Ft* (n. 136), 125–55. – G. E. Mingay, 'The agricultural depression, 1730 – 1750', *EcHR²* 8 (1955 – 6), 323–38.

[592] G. E. Mingay, *English Agricultural Society in the Eighteenth Century*. L: Routledge: 1963. Pp. x, 292. Rev: *EHR* 80, 403; *EcHR²* 17, 146ff.

[593] Hrothgar J. Habakkuk, 'Marriage settlements in the 18th century', *TRHS* (1950), 15–30.

[594] T. S. Willan, *The Navigation of the River Weaver in the 18th Century*. Manchester: Chetham Soc., 3rd Series, vol. 3: 1951. Pp. ix, 235. Rev: *EHR* 67, 411ff. – Idem, *The Early History of the Don Navigation*. Manchester UP: 1965. Pp. ix, 165.

[595] Hrothgar J. Habakkuk, 'English population in the 18th century', *EcHR²* 6 (1953 – 4), 117–33.

[596] J. T. Krause, 'Changes in English fertility and mortality, 1781 – 1850', *EcHR²* (1958 – 9), 52–80. – T. McKeown and R. G. Brown, 'Medical evidence relating to English population changes in the 18th century', *Population Studies* 9 (1955 – 6), 199–41.

[597] P. E. Razzell, 'Population change in the 18th century England: a reinterpretation', *EcHR²* 18 (1965 – 6), 312–32.

He has also argued (pursuing his faith in physiology rather than economics) that, so far from being the product of industrial growth, population increases preceded the latter and stand in direct causal relationship to it, a point of view once popular, then discredited, but now again worth considering.[598] Krause, however, has not remained silent and on balance seems to carry the bigger guns.[599] One thing only would appear to be certain: the massive labour force required by industry was produced by numerical increase, not by the expulsion of a peasantry which, driven from its lands, moved into the towns.[600] Just another legend.

Still, by and large the situation at present is that neither capital nor labour can be credited with playing a fundamental and causal role in the sudden expansion of production; that technological progress alone will not explain it has long been recognized and is not at all contradicted by Landes, despite his main concern for changes in technique (n. 579).[601] This mildly desperate situation leaves nothing over except the existence of the entrepreneur, a scientifically pretty inaccurate concept. We thus note a tendency to explain by describing the work of individuals,[602] an uncomfortable tendency for economic historians with their preference for the assurance of tables and graphs, but a development which has done much good both in

---

[598] P. E. Razzell, 'Population growth and economic change in eighteenth and early nineteenth century England and Ireland', *Chambers Ft* (n. 134), 260–81.

[599] J. T. Krause, 'Some aspects of population change, 1690 – 1790', *Chambers Ft* (n. 134), 187–202.

[600] J. D. Chambers, 'Enclosure and labour supply in the Industrial Revolution', *EcHR*² 5 (1952 – 3), 319–43; 'Population changes in a provincial town: Nottingham 1700 – 1800', *Ashton Ft* (n. 136), 97–124.

[601] In an interesting article about transport and supplies, E. A. Wrigley attempts to open up a new line of thought; but it seems to me that his answer will not really serve: 'The supply of raw materials in the Industrial Revolution', *EcHR*² 15 (1962 – 3) 1–16.

[602] Sidney Pollard, *The Genesis of Modern Management: a study in the Industrial Revolution in Great Britain.* C (Mass.): Harvard UP: 1965. Pp. 328. Rev: *VS* 10, 93f.

general, by recalling these historians to the existence of people, and in particular by stimulating some very important research. Thus McKendrick has impressively highlighted the role of the entrepreneur by studying Josiah Wedgwood.[603] Pollard, too, stresses the central importance of the organized factory.[604] Fitton and Wadsworth describe a textile enterprise which got off to an early start.[605] Raistrick discusses the best known iron works of all;[606] less familiar but more interesting are the Crowleys who even before the beginning of the century built themselves an empire in Sunderland, applied technical and organizational innovation all along the line, and even made a reality of schemes of paternalistic welfare which elsewhere had to wait another 200 years.[607] Minchinton studies another metal industry which experienced a sudden expansion towards the end of the century.[608] Brewing offers the example of an industry which suffered from several clearly defined problems of production and distribution, problems which were solved by a series of remarkable entrepreneurs.[609] Two biographies of men rather characteristic for their time: John Rennie was a great transport engineer who built canals and viaducts, J. J. Gurney

[603] Neil McKendrick, 'Josiah Wedgwood: an 18th century entrepreneur in salesmanship and marketing techniques', *EcHR*² 12 (1959 – 60), 408–33; 'Josiah Wedgwood and Thomas Bentley: an inventor-entrepreneur partnership in the Industrial Revolution', *TRHS* (1964), 1–33; 'Josiah Wedgwood and factory discipline', *HJ* 4 (1961), 30–55.

[604] Sidney Pollard, 'Factory discipline in the Industrial Revolution', *EcHR*² 16 (1963 – 4), 254–71.

[605] R. S. Fitton and A. P. Wadsworth, *The Strutts and the Arkwrights, 1758 – 1830*. Manchester UP: 1958. Pp. xii, 361. Rev: *EcHR*² 12, 292f.

[606] Arthur Raistrick, *Dynasty of Ironfounders: the Darbys and Colebrookdale*. L: Longmans: 1953. Pp. xvi, 308.

[607] M. W. Flinn, *Men of Iron: the Crowleys in the early iron industry*. Edinburgh UP: 1962. Pp. xii, 270. Rev: *EHR* 80, 174f.; *EcHR*² 6, 562f.

[608] W. E. Minchinton, *The British Tinplate Industry*. O: Clarendon: 1957. Pp. xviii, 286. Rev: *EHR* 74, 507ff.

[609] Peter Mathias, *The Brewing Industry in England, 1700 – 1820*. CUP: 1959. Pp. xxviii, 595. Rev: *EHR* 76, 108ff.

a quaker and financier who also displayed an interest in political reforms.[610] One obvious line of interpretation – obvious but wrong – has been well demolished by Elliott who shows that any attempt to link the entrepreneurism of the eighteenth century with Weber's 'protestant ethic' flies in the face of all the evidence.[611]

Though it has not been forgotten that industrial growth could not have taken place without a similar growth in trade, we do hear less of merchants' problems than for earlier centuries. Davis continues his analysis.[612] Using the papers of the Radcliffe family firm, he also gives an account of near eastern trade,[613] while Gill's somewhat romantic book helps to illumine that with the far east.[614] The activities of the East India Company provide Furber with the grounds for a well generalized thesis.[615] Sheridan's description of the inner organization of the slave trade is too brief;[616] one hopes to hear more. The effects of long years of war, to which the new textile industry owed its sudden explosive expansion, are brought out by Edwards.[617] Starting similarly from problems of trade, Crouzet has in fact produced a remarkable history of the whole British

---

[610] C. T. G. Boucher, *John Rennie, 1761 – 1821: the life and work of a great engineer*. Manchester UP: 1963. Pp. x, 149. – David E. Swift, *Joseph John Gurney: banker, reformer, and quaker*. Middletown (Conn.): Wesleyan UP: 1962. Pp. xix, 304.

[611] Charles M. Elliott, 'The ideology of economic growth: a case study', *Chambers Ft* (n. 134), 76–99.

[612] Ralph Davis, 'English foreign trade 1700 – 1774', *EcHR*² 15 (1962 – 3), 285–303.

[613] Ralph Davis, *Aleppo and Devonshire Square: English traders in the Levant in the eighteenth century*. L: Macmillan: 1967. Pp. xiv, 258. Rev: *EHR* 84, 397f.

[614] Conrad Gill, *Merchants and Mariners in the Eighteenth Century*. L: Arnold: 1961. Pp. 176. Rev: *EHR* 78, 389f.

[615] Holden Furber, *John Company at Work: a study of European expansion in India in the late 18th century*. C (Mass.): Harvard UP: 1948. Pp. xiii, 407. Rev: *EHR* 64, 526ff.

[616] R. B. Sheridan, 'The commercial and financial organisation of the British slave trade, 1750–1807', *EcHR*² 11 (1958–9), 249–63.

[617] Michael M. Edwards, *The Growth of the British Cotton Trade, 1780 – 1815*. Manchester UP: 1967. Pp. viii, 276. Rev: *EHR* 84, 620f.; *EcHR*² 22, 348f.

economy during the Napoleonic wars.[618] It may be remarked that John has shown war to have been equally favourable to industrialization in the earlier part of the century.[619] And a very important article by Eversley reminds us that in this period it becomes for the first time really possible to consider consumption at home and not only export abroad when estimating the state of industry.[620]

Even the story of economics is not always solid. We are asked to shed scepticism and believe that the entrepreneurs learned their business from the natural scientists.[621] We are asked to regard the notions which the century applied to the care of its poor as less primitive than we used to think them.[622] And we are asked to believe that all those treatises on agricultural improvements were particularly influential in France.[623]

Two local studies, in the main concerned with economic history but also very useful for explaining the local politics of the provinces at a time when their importance was steadily increasing: Chambers describes the great highway from the industrial Midlands to the sea, and Patterson describes what happened to a town in which an ancient, nearly decayed, tradition of manufacture suddenly experienced a most active revival.[624]

Lastly, one may note a few examples of social history.

[618] François M. J. Crouzet, *L'économie britannique et le blocus continental 1806 – 1813*, 2 vols. Paris: Presses Universitaires: 1958. Pp. 949. Rev: *EHR* 75, 699ff.

[619] A. H. John, 'War and the English economy, 1700 – 1763', *EcHR*² 7 (1954 – 5), 329–44.

[620] D. E. C. Eversley, 'The home market and economic growth in England, 1750 – 1780', *Chambers Ft* (n. 134), 206–59.

[621] A. E. Musson and E. Robinson, *Science and industry in the Industrial Revolution*. Manchester UP: 1969. Pp. viii, 509. Rev: *Hist* 55, 134.

[622] A. W. Coats, 'Economic thought and poor law policy in the 18th century', *EcHR*² 13 (1960 – 1), 39–51.

[623] André J. Bourde, *The Influence of England on the French Agronomes, 1750 – 1789*. CUP: 1963. Pp. xi, 250.

[624] J. D. Chambers, *The Vale of Trent*. CUP: 1957. Pp. 63. – A. Temple Patterson, *Radical Leicester: a history of Leicester, 1780 – 1850*. Leicester: University College: 1954. Pp. x, 405. Rev: *EHR* 70, 339f.

Marshall's study of various layers of the population is pleasant rather than searching.[625] Though he confines himself to the north, Hughes' two volumes rest upon much the same methods and principles.[626] Hecht has taken on the servant class in two studies of which one deals with immigrant servants and the other more generally with domestic service of a type that was really new in the eighteenth century – essentially different from the household organizations of the past.[627] A different probe produces a similar treatment for scientists: Hamilton tells of the social background and standing of medical men,[628] while Schofield demonstrates the support which science and progress received in the provinces.[629] A pretty book about the Chinese mania of the century suitably concludes the list.[630]

[625] Dorothy Marshall, *English People in the Eighteenth Century*. L: Longmans: 1956. Pp. xvi, 258. Rev: *EHR* 73, 163.

[626] Edward Hughes, *North Country Life in the Eighteenth Century*, 2 vols. (1: The North East, 1700 – 1750; 2: Cumberland and Westmorland, 1700 – 1830). L: OUP: 1955, 1965. Pp. xxi, 435; viii, 426. Rev: *EHR* 70, 455ff.; 82, 175.

[627] J. Jean Hecht, *Continental and Colonial Servants in Eighteenth Century England*. Northampton (Mass.): Smith College Studies in History, vol. 40: 1954. Pp. v, 61. – Idem, *The Domestic Servant Class in Eighteenth Century England*. L: Routledge: 1956. Pp. xii, 240.

[628] Bernice Hamilton, 'The medical profession in the 18th century', *EcHR*² 4 (1951 – 2), 141–69.

[629] Robert E. Schofield, *The Lunar Society of Birmingham: a social history of provincial science and industry in eighteenth century England*. O: Clarendon: 1963. Pp. xi, 491. Rev: *EHR* 81, 36off.

[630] William W. Appleton, *A Cycle of Cathay: the Chinese vogue in England during the 17th and 18th centuries*. New York: Columbia UP: 1951. Pp. xii, 182.

VIII

The Nineteenth Century (1815 – 1914)

Also nn. 22, 24, 47–52, 63–6, 1025–7, 1029–31, 1035–6, 1047–54,
1059–62, 1064, 1077–8, 1097, 1153–65, 1171–7, 1198–1209,
1231–4, 1243–5.

(A) GENERAL

This is the period which has attracted more work and more historians than any other. The reasons are plain enough: the vast mass of materials and the great number of unsolved problems. Foreign relations apart, the history written about this age before the war was well behind that current for earlier centuries, and in most respects only the last twenty-five years have seen a move from the surface into the depths. The primitive condition of so much that is written about the nineteenth century is well illustrated by the fact that a man who would wish to know the details of constitutional or administrative history, for instance, must still too often laboriously disinter them from political biographies, sometimes written by intelligent amateurs not much interested in the fundamental questions that exercise the historians. And though we may record respectable progress, we are still a good way from the end of the tunnel. There are still many questions unasked, and many more are disputed over than are at a stage of knowledgeable agreement. One trouble is that the advance of learning has on too many occasions met with the sort of resistance that grows from political prejudice. Historical research usually demolishes legends, and for the nineteenth century the legends are mainly liberal. The story of the last 150 years is less simple than that legend liked to think: the progressive angels, who trod the path that ultimately led to the labour party, and the reactionary devils whom selfishness alone drove to reject the commonplaces of democracy, tend to look quite a bit different in the searchlight of research.

It is, therefore, little wonder that no really comprehensive or firm general accounts have yet been produced, though we have several useful books on parts of the period. Briggs has attempted to refresh study of the age by choosing unusual terminal dates for his contribution to a general series, but the real value of the book lies in its concentration on social questions seen from the point of view of the provinces.[631] Beales also covers a solid chunk of years in a survey which does excellently, considering the brevity imposed on the author; here politics play the main role.[632] Kitson Clarke both assimilates and introduces some novel notions in two essentially consecutive surveys which avoid the manner of the textbook and are distinguished by the author's marked humanity; but they do not attempt to provide more than a sketch of events.[633] Burn covers only one decade, but there is much originality in the writing of a professor who was also a justice of the peace and who recalled the commonly forgotten fact that even as late as 1850 most Englishmen still lived rural lives.[634] Perkin attempts a general survey concentrated on the problems of social transformation; necessarily in part premature, the book will prove as stimulating for further work as it is useful in indicating work done.[635] More simply, Derry traces one particular strand by means of biographical essays touching on a mixed collection of people.[636] Briggs's essays, respectively, on people and towns similarly attempt to paint a picture by col-

[631] Asa Briggs, *The Age of Improvement*. L: Longmans: 1959. Pp. xii, 547. Rev: *EHR* 75, 173f.

[632] Derek E. D. Beales, *From Castlereagh to Gladstone, 1815 – 1885*. L: Nelson: 1969. Pp. 328.

[633] G. Kitson Clark, *The Making of Victorian England*. L: Methuen: 1962. Pp. xii, 312. Rev: *EHR* 80, 129ff. – Idem, *An Expanding Society: Britain 1830 – 1900*. CUP: 1967. Pp. xv, 188. Rev: *EHR* 84, 127ff.; *EcHR*[2] 20, 407f.

[634] W. L. Burn, *The Age of Equipoise: a study of the mid-Victorian generation*. L: Allen & Unwin: 1964. Pp. 340. Rev: *EHR* 81, 192f.; *HJ* 8, 417ff.

[635] Harold Perkin, *The Origins of Modern English Society, 1780 – 1880*. L: Routledge: 1969. Pp. xiv, 465.

[636] John W. Derry, *The Radical Tradition: Tom Paine to Lloyd George*. L: Macmillan: 1967. Pp. xi, 435. Rev: *EHR* 84, 197f.

lecting instances.[637] Using the techniques of the sociologist, Guttsman professes to track the history and changing social composition of Britain's leaders, but since his definition of an elite is both too large and too far removed from the realities of the nineteenth century, the result has limited value.[638]

(B) POLITICAL HISTORY

It will be best to list, chronologically, a series of works which between them destroy much of the old picture but have not yet really made possible a new one. The Peterloo Massacre has attracted three serious studies: Read and White modify the blood-and-thunder tradition, while Walmsley, who altogether exonerates the traditional villains, probably goes much too far.[639] The activities of the century's first reforming administration are expounded by Fay in a 'life and times' type of study.[640] The powerful influence upon policy and parliamentary elections of one of the problems requiring reform is shown up by Machin's study of catholic emancipation.[641] A peculiar incident in the peculiar career of the most familiar of extra-parliamentary radicals is described by Harrison.[642] One topic that has received much attention is the real effect of the first reform bill: Gash shows how little things changed – in particular, how

---

[637] Asa Briggs, *Victorian People*. L: Odham: 1954. Pp. 317. Rev: *EHR* 71, 502. – Idem, *Victorian Cities*. *Ibid*. 1963. Pp. 416. Rev: *EHR* 80, 634f.; *EcHR*² 16, 563f.

[638] W. L. Guttsman, *The British Political Elite*. L: MacGibbon & Kee: 1963. Pp. 398. Rev: *EHR* 80, 647.

[639] Donald Read, *Peterloo: the 'massacre' and its background*. Manchester UP: 1958. Pp. ix, 234. Rev: *EHR* 74, 172f. – Reginald J. White, *Waterloo to Peterloo*. L: Heinemann: 1957. Pp. ix, 202. Rev: *EHR* 73, 167f. – Robert Walmsley; *Peterloo: the case reopened*. Manchester UP: 1969. Pp. xx, 585. Rev: *Hist* 55, 138ff.

[640] C. R. Fay, *Huskisson and his Age*. L: Longmans: 1951. Pp. xv, 398. Rev: *EcHR*² 6, 86ff.

[641] G. I. T. Machin, *The Catholic Question in English Politics, 1820 – 1830*. O: Clarendon: 1964. Pp. xi, 227. Rev: *EHR* 80, 865f.

[642] Brian Harrison, 'Two roads to social reform: Francis Place and the "drunken committee" of 1834', *HJ* 11 (1969), 272–300.

surprisingly important the relations of Church and state remained in the shaping of politics.[643] The utopian ideals of the age in action are pursued by Harrison both in Britain and in America, in a book of which nearly a quarter is filled by a remarkable bibliography.[644] Some political by-products of the industrial changes appear in Ward's study of the movement for the statutory control of the new factories.[645] Similarly, Parris shows briefly the political consequences of railway building.[646] That those years, especially the forties, were seething with the possibility and reality of revolt has not escaped attention. Hobsbawm and Rudé recount the last peasant rising, a pale reflection of the real thing.[647] The new form of social unrest was better represented by the chartists, with their ever fluctuating numbers of men rendered desperate by the trade-cycle. Briggs has written a collection of studies which track the movement through the localities;[648] Schoyen investigates one of its obscurer leaders;[649] Read and Glasgow attend to the best known of them.[650] Middle-class agitation revolved around the corn laws, alleged to be keeping the price of bread high in the interests of landowners and aristocrats. Kitson Clark well demonstrates the political core in this allegedly disinterested

---

[643] Norman Gash, *Reaction and Reconstruction in English Politics, 1832 – 1852*. O: Clarendon: 1965. Pp. 227. Rev: *EHR* 82, 579f.; *HJ* 10, 313ff.

[644] J. F. C. Harrison, *Robert Owen and the Owenites in Britain and America: the quest for a new moral world*. L: Routledge: 1969. Pp. xi, 392. Rev: *Hist* 55, 141f.

[645] John T. Ward, *The Factory Movement*. L: Macmillan: 1962. Pp. xi, 515. Rev: *EHR* 79, 623f.; *HJ* 7, 179f.

[646] Henry Parris, 'Railway policy in Peel's administration', *BIHR* 33 (1960), 181–94.

[647] Eric J. Hobsbawm and George Rudé, *Captain Swing*. L: Lawrence & Wishart: 1969. Pp. 384. Rev: *HJ* 12, 716f.; *EcHR²* 22, 354f.

[648] Asa Briggs, ed., *Chartist Studies*. L: Macmillan: 1959. Pp. xi, 423. Rev: *EHR* 76, 170f.

[649] A. Schoyen, *The Chartist Challenge: a portrait of G. J. Harney*. L: Heinemann: 1958. Pp. viii, 300. Rev: *HJ* 2, 89ff.

[650] Douglas Read and E. Glasgow, *Feargus O'Connor, Irishman and Chartist*. L: Arnold: 1961. Pp. 160. Rev: *EHR* 77, 801f.

movement,[651] while McCord reveals the high sophistication
and lack of scruple displayed by Cobden's league.[652] Wales's
special revolutionary enterprise – a strange transvestite outbreak in which justified complaint mingled with unmistakable
criminality – has also been properly studied.[653] As the troubled
years passed and the mid-century approached, politics of a
more conventional sort, by contrast, went into a phase of con-
fusion produced by the collapse of Peel's party. Here we have
two very different studies. Conacher patiently unravels events
and interactions in a most instructive way, but can by this
means cover few years only in a long book.[654] Anderson, taking
the problem of England's one major war in this century, tries
to establish a number of general conclusions about the ability
of a constitutional state to wage war or the effects of war upon
a nation deeply divided by social strife (the answers are very
negative) which need some further development and perhaps
refutation but should also prove a jumping-off stage of real
significance.[655]

In the second half of the century, reform at last began to
have some effect on the miseries of the poor, though among
the reformers were a good many of the odd cranks of which
the age produced so many.[656] The highly complex story of the
second reform bill has evoked three centenary celebrations of
varied approach and conclusions: Smith writes a straight

---

[651] G. Kitson Clark, 'The electorate and the repeal of the corn laws',
TRHS (1951), 109–26; 'The repeal of the corn laws and the
politics of the forties', *EcHR*² 4 (1951 – 2), 1–13.

[652] Norman McCord, *The Anti-Corn Law League, 1838 – 1846*. L: Allen
& Unwin: 1958. Pp. 226. Rev: EHR 74, 542f.; *HJ* 2, 89ff.

[653] David Williams, *The Rebecca Riots: a study in agrarian discontent*.
Cardiff: U of Wales P: 1955. Pp. xi, 377. Rev: *EHR* 72, 339ff.

[654] James B. Conacher, *The Aberdeen Coalition, 1852 – 1855*. CUP:
1968. Pp. xiv, 607. Rev: *EHR* 84, 811ff.; *HJ* 12, 720ff.

[655] Olive Anderson, *A Liberal State at War: English politics and economics
during the Crimean war*. L: Macmillan: 1967. Pp. xi, 306. Rev:
EHR 83, 416f.; *VS* 11, 408ff.

[656] Herman Ausubel, *In Hard Times: reformers among the late Victorians*.
New York: Columbia UP: 1960. Pp. x, 403. Rev: *EHR* 77, 802f.;
*EcHR*² 15, 167f.

account demolishing legends,[657] Cowling employs a very detailed method of his own in order to bring out the way in which the whole story turned on the concerns of the inner ring of politicians,[658] and Himmelfarb endeavours not very successfully to restore an air of high principle to the whole business.[659] Another legend dies at the hands of Shannon who demonstrates that Gladstone, so far from creating a moral outcry, merely knew well how to use it in the cause of party politics.[660] Arnstein studies the occasion which removed all religious tests from the house of commons.[661] That there were limits to the extent to which the age would surrender its prejudices is the substance of Lyons' investigation of Parnell's destruction by adultery.[662] The political events of Edward VII's reign have yielded several studies of varying worth. Rowland puts the skids under the famous last liberal administration: he shows that there was no programme of social reform nor any propaganda for it at the elections, argues that little enough was ever achieved, and holds that a turning point was encountered in 1909 when for political reasons ministers who had little interest in radical measures found themselves forced to espouse them.[663] It is too early to say whether this iconoclasm will catch on. Fraser and Blewett cast shorter glances at the internal politics of the unionist party.[664] The various crises and move-

---

[657] F. Barry Smith, *The Making of the Second Reform Bill*. CUP: 1966. Pp. vii, 297. Rev: *HJ* 11, 205ff.

[658] Maurice Cowling, *1867: Disraeli, Gladstone and Revolution*. CUP: 1967. Pp. xi, 451. Rev: *HJ* 11, 594ff.; *JMH* 41, 99ff.

[659] Gertrude Himmelfarb, 'The politics of democracy: the English reform act of 1967', *JBS* 6 (1966), 97–138. For the subsequent debate, see *ibid.* 9 (1969), 96–104.

[660] R. T. Shannon, *Gladstone and the Bulgarian Atrocities, 1876*. Edinburgh: Nelson: 1963. Pp. xxviii, 308. Rev: *EHR* 81, 204f.

[661] Walter L. Arnstein, *The Bradlaugh Case*. O: Clarendon: 1965. Pp. 348.

[662] F. S. L. Lyons, *The Fall of Parnell, 1890 – 1891*. L: Routledge: 1960. Pp. xii, 362. Rev: *HJ* 4, 113f.

[663] Peter Rowland, *The Last Liberal Governments: the promised land, 1905 – 1910*. L: Barrie & Rockliff: 1968. Pp. xviii, 404.

[664] Peter Fraser, 'Unionism and tariff reform: the crisis of 1906', *HJ* 5 (1962), 149–66; 'The Unionist debacle of 1911 and Balfour's

ments of protest are treated by Jenkins (a smart and biased account of the lords' resistance to reform),[665] Steward (who at last gives the Ulster crisis the comprehensive treatment long called for),[666] and Rover (a plain and not adequate treatment of the battle for women's franchise which, as usual, over-estimates the part played by the militants).[667] Morgan shows how strong the political influence of Welsh radicalism with its religious overtones was from disestablishment to the fall of Lloyd George.[668] An unusual viewpoint, not altogether dis-passionate, is provided for the understanding of those hundred years in the anonymous history of *The Times* newspaper (written by Stanley Morison).[669]

Despite all this, political biographies still appear in which political history must be hunted down, and despite everything the sometimes gifted amateur continues to operate. We confine ourselves in the main to the more professional works. Rolo's attempt to cope with the large and varied figure of Canning has partial success only.[670] Two very different radical poli-ticians appear in New's solemn book on the lively, brilliant and irresponsible Brougham (New died before the work was finished) and in Driver's account of that honest and limited man, the tory reformer Oastler.[671] Much more important is Gash's life of Peel, a work in the grand tradition of which only

---

retirement', *JMH* 35 (1963), 354–65. – Neal Blewett, 'Free Fooders, Balfourites, Whole Hoggers: factionalism within the Unionist party, 1906 – 1910', *HJ* 11 (1968), 95–124.

[665] Roy Jenkins, *Mr Balfour's Poodle*. L: Heinemann: 1954. Pp. 224.

[666] A. C. Q. Steward, *The Ulster Crisis*. L: Faber: 1967. Pp. 284.

[667] Constance Rover, *Women's Suffrage and Party Politics*. L: Routledge: 1967. Pp. xvi, 240. Rev: *EHR* 84, 427f.; *HJ* 12, 725f.

[668] Kenneth O. Morgan, *Wales in British Politics, 1868 – 1922*. Cardiff: U of Wales P: 1963. Pp. xii, 353.

[669] *The History of the Times*, vols. 3 and 4: 1884 – 1920. L: Times Publishing Company: 1947, 1952. Pp. xv, 862; xvi, 534.

[670] P. J. V. Rolo, *George Canning: three biographical studies*. L: Macmillan: 1965. Pp. ix, 276. Rev: *EHR* 81, 613f.

[671] Chester W. New, *The Life of Henry Brougham to 1830*. O: Clarendon: 1961. Pp. xi, 458. Rev: *EHR* 78, 739ff. – Cecil H. Driver, *Tory Radical: the life of Richard Oastler*. L: OUP: 1946. Pp. ix, 597.

the first volume has so far appeared.[672] Goderich, one of the most readily forgotten prime ministers of any age, is not rendered more memorable by his biographer.[673] Peel's chief assistant, James Graham, has drawn two works: Erickson's adds mainly error to knowledge, while Ward gives a good straight account.[674] Palmerston's astounding personality continues to defeat the biographers.[675] Eyck, on the other hand, does all that is necessary for the prince consort.[676] The heavenly twins of mid-Victorian radicalism appear together in one book (which finds Cobden to be the more radical of the two);[677] Bright alone forms the subject of Ausubel's honest revelations of the great man's moral dubieties,[678] and of Sturgis's less critical review of his attitude to Britain's overseas expansion (animated by a liberal belief in self-determination, but totally unaware of the existence of nationalism).[679] Gladstone has still not achieved a book of scholarly worth; of Magnus's biography all one can say is that it reads well.[680] On the other hand, his great opponent now stands forth – if that is the right word – in Blake's splendid book which really brings him to

---

[672] Norman Gash, *Mr Secretary Peel: the life of Sir Robert Peel to 1830*. L: Longmans: 1961: Pp. xix, 693. Rev: *EHR* 78, 738ff.

[673] Wilbur D. Jones, *Prosperity Robinson: the life of Viscount Goderich, 1782 – 1859*. L: Macmillan: 1967. Pp. x, 324. Rev: *EHR* 84, 198.

[674] Arvel B. Erickson, *The Public Career of Sir James Graham*. O: Blackwell: 1952. Pp. vii, 433. Rev: *EHR* 67, 588ff. – John T. Ward, *Sir James Graham*. L: Macmillan: 1967. Pp. xx, 356. Rev: *Hist* 53, 142.

[675] Donald Southgate, '*The Most English Prime Minister*': *the policies and politics of Palmerston*. L: Macmillan: 1966. Pp. xxx, 647. Rev: *EHR* 83, 135ff.

[676] Frank Eyck, *The Prince Consort*. L: Chatto & Windus: 1959. Pp. 269. Rev: *EHR* 76, 171f.

[677] Donald Read, *Cobden and Bright: a Victorian political partnership*. L: Arnold: 1967. Pp. ix, 275. Rev: *EHR* 84, 424f.; *HJ* 12, 377ff.

[678] Herman Ausubel, *John Bright, Victorian Reformer*. New York: Wiley: 1966. Pp. xvi, 250. Rev: *JMH* 40, 290f.

[679] James L. Sturgis, *John Bright and the Empire*. L: Athlone: 1969. Pp. x, 206.

[680] Philip Magnus, *Gladstone*. L: Murray: 1954. Pp. xiv, 402. Rev: *EHR* 70, 292ff.

life.[681] Lewis is rather more tolerant of the mixture of calcula-
tion and principle which characterized this statesman.[682]
Disraeli's boss – sometimes active, sometimes distracted by the
horses – receives an undeservedly tedious biography.[683] Amery
has now completed the life of Joseph Chamberlain, still essentially in the hagiographical vein in which Garvin so many years
ago started it.[684] Howard somewhat corrects Garvin's account
of the man's radical programme,[685] while in a curiously elusive
book Fraser attempts to give an independent account of his
public life (with bits about his private life, too).[686] The First
Lord who never went to sea gets a biography which very
properly respects him;[687] its author also commemorates his own
ancestor, Salisbury's chief whip.[688] James takes care of two
politicians whose careers were ruined for different reasons and
in very different ways;[689] the inadequacies which doctrinaire
liberalism instilled in the man who replaced Churchill at the
exchequer are brought out by Spinner.[690] Kennedy writes a
simple book about the complex and mysterious marquess of

---

[681] Robert Blake, *Disraeli*. L: Eyre & Spottiswoode: 1966. Pp. xxv, 819. Rev: *EHR* 83, 360ff.

[682] Clyde J. Lewis, 'Theory and expediency in the policy of Disraeli', *VS* 4 (1960 – 1), 237–58.

[683] Wilbur D. Jones, *Lord Derby and Victorian Conservatism*. O: Black-well: 1956. Pp. xi, 367.

[684] Julian Amery, *The Life of Joseph Chamberlain*, vols. 4 and 5. L: Macmillan: 1951, 1969. Pp. xvi, 533; xiii, 1146. Rev: *EHR* 67, 278ff.

[685] Christopher H. D. Howard, 'Joseph Chamberlain and the "un-authorised programme" ', *EHR* 65 (1950), 477–91.

[686] Peter Fraser, *Joseph Chamberlain: nationalism and empire, 1868 – 1914*. L: Cassell: 1966. Pp. xv, 349. Rev: *EHR* 83, 364ff.

[687] Viscount Chilston, *W. H. Smith*. L: Routledge: 1965. Pp. xii, 380. Rev: *EHR* 82, 440f.; *VS* 10, 99f.

[688] Viscount Chilston, *Chief Whip: the political life and times of Aretas Akers-Douglas, first Viscount Chilston*. L: Routledge: 1961. Pp. xiii, 270. Rev: *EHR* 79, 212f.

[689] Robert V. R. James, *Lord Randolph Churchill*. L: Weidenfeld: 1959. Pp. 384. – Idem, *Rosebery. Ibid.* 1963. Pp. xiv, 534. Rev: *EHR* 80, 197f.

[690] Thomas J. Spinner, 'George Joachim Goschen, the man Lord Randolph Churchill "forgot" ', *JMH* 39 (1967), 405–24.

Salisbury.[691] Morley's political career, one of self-imposed failure, is studied by Hamer, who analyses the part his ideas played in his actions, and by Koss who investigates his contribution to the beginnings of the end of empire in India.[692] Five interesting essays deal with Haldane, that man of influence; they discuss his part in law reform, education, army reform, and administrative change; there is now also a good biography, mainly concerned with the private man in public life.[693] Gollin, who made his name with a book on Garvin in which he generously shared his subject's inflated self-esteem, then turned to Milner and produced a study which, though it rests on hitherto unused materials, hardly seems to deserve the praise showered upon it.[694] Blake's biography of Bonar Law, on the other hand, which restores remembrance to one forgotten, is a model which more might follow.[695] The journalist who descended upon the fastidious Balfour cannot be said to have done so; the book deserves mention only because it gives much detail and uses some inaccessible sources.[696] More influential than most politicians was Beatrice Webb; a new life of her does not make her personality more agreeable.[697] And a liberal poli-

---

[691] A. L. Kennedy, *Salisbury, 1830 – 1903: portrait of a statesman*. L: Murray: 1953. Pp. xiv, 409. Rev: *EHR* 69, 169f.

[692] David A. Hamer, *John Morley, liberal intellectual in politics*. O: Clarendon: 1968. Pp. xvi, 412. Rev: *VS* 13, 105ff.; *Hist* 54, 316. – Stephen E. Koss, *John Morley at the India Office, 1905 – 10*. New Haven: Yale UP: 1969. Pp. ix, 231.

[693] Viscount Waverley, Earl Jowitt, John F. Lockwood, Cyril Falls, Lord Bridges, 'Haldane Centenary Essays', *Public Administration* 35 (1957), 217–66. – Stephen E. Koss, *Lord Haldane: scapegoat for liberalism*. New York: Columbia UP; 1969. Pp. xv, 263. Rev: *Hist* 55, 150f.

[694] A. M. Gollin, *The Observer and J. L. Garvin, 1908 – 1914*. L: OUP: 1960. Pp. xiii, 445. – Idem, *Proconsul in Politics: a study of Lord Milner in opposition and power*. L: Blond: 1964. Pp. xi, 627. Rev: *EHR* 81, 209f.

[695] Robert Blake, *The Unknown Prime Minister: the life and times of Andrew Bonar Law, 1858 – 1923*. L: Eyre & Spottiswoode: 1955. Pp. 556.

[696] Kenneth Young, *Arthur James Balfour*. L: Beil: 1963. Pp. xxvi, 516.

[697] Kitty Muggeridge and Ruth Adam, *Beatrice Webb: a life, 1858 – 1943*. L: Secker & Warburg: 1967. Pp. 272. Rev: *VS* 12, 470ff.

tician who consistently overestimated his own importance left behind such masses of paper that the formal biography could not be avoided.[698]

(C) PARLIAMENT AND PARTIES

Amongst the truly important developments of the century, we must reckon the first appearance of undoubted modern parties, a phenomenon which both reflected and provoked fundamental changes in the relation between the executive and the representative assembly. It would be good to know more about what actually went on in the commons, and the lords remain, as usual, dark. However, Fraser has opened (no more) one of the central themes by looking at cabinet control over the lower house,[699] Beales considers the position of the non-party man in the first age of ascendant parties,[700] and Cromwell, entitling her piece misleadingly so as to suggest that the eighteenth-century commons controlled the executive, runs swiftly over a long period of parliamentary management.[701] Venturing into much the same area, Close firmly places the emergence of two exclusive parties in the age of Melbourne and Peel.[702] Aydelotte, engaged for many years in the task of taking apart the commons of the forties in order to glue them together again in different patterns, has produced both progress reports warning against rash conclusions, and some tentative analytical pieces which build up a picture of controlling parties in the face of which neither social nor economic interests determined the alignment of members on even the most crucial issues of the

---

[698] James Pope-Hennessy, *Lord Crewe, 1858 – 1945*. L: Constable: 1955. Pp. xvii, 205.

[699] Peter Fraser, 'The growth of ministerial control in the nineteenth-century house of commons', *EHR* 75 (1960), 444–63.

[700] Derek E. D. Beales, 'Parliamentary parties and the "independent" member', *Kitson Clark Ft* (n. 137), 1–19.

[701] Valerie Cromwell, 'The losing of the initiative by the house of commons, 1780 – 1914', *TRHS* (1968), 1–24.

[702] David Close, 'The formation of the two-party alignment in the house of commons between 1832 and 1841', *EHR* 84 (1969), 257–77.

day.[703] Blewett considers voting rights and emphasizes the inadequacy of electoral registers.[704] The advantages which such registers offered to the organizers of party attract the somewhat preliminary attention of Thomas.[705] Winter brings out the parliamentary opposition to further reform before 1867.[706] Vincent shows how much political sociology may be extracted from Victorian poll books, a source destroyed by the introduction of the secret ballot.[707] The parliaments of the latter part of the period have been patchily studied. Pelling surveys elections in general, in a tentative effort to link political attitudes with region, class and religion.[708] Lloyd fails to prove that the methods of modern students of elections can usefully be applied to earlier occasions which were unfortunately not aware of the evidence they were supposed to accumulate.[709] And Thomas, with less ambition and greater care, manages to start on another transfer backwards of modern concerns – a description of the Edwardian commons in terms of members' backgrounds.[710]

---

[703] William O. Aydelotte, 'The house of commons in the 1840s', *Hist* 39 (1954), 249–62; 'Voting patterns in the house of commons in the 1840s', *Comparative Studies in Society and History* 5 (1962 – 3), 134–63; 'Parties and issues in early-Victorian England', *JBS* 5 (1966), 95–114; 'The conservative and radical interpretations of early Victorian social legislation', *VS* 11 (1967 – 8), 225–36; 'The country gentlemen and the repeal of the corn laws', *EHR* 82 (1967), 47–60. *See also* his appendix to Kitson Clark's book, n. 633.

[704] Neal Blewett, 'The franchise in the United Kingdom, 1885 – 1918', *PP* 32 (1965), 27–56.

[705] J. Alun Thomas, 'The system of registration and the development of party organisation, 1832 – 1870', *Hist* 35 (1950), 81–98.

[706] James Winter, 'The Cave of Adullam and parliamentary reform', *EHR* 81 (1966), 38–55.

[707] John R. Vincent, *Poll Books: how Victorians voted*. CUP: 1967. Pp. xi, 194.

[708] Henry Pelling, *The Social Geography of British Elections, 1885 – 1910*. L: Macmillan: 1967. Pp. xxxi, 455. Rev: *EHR* 84, 428f.

[709] Trevor Lloyd, *The General Election of 1880*. L: OUP: 1968. Pp. 175. Rev: *EHR* 84, 871f.; *EcHR²* 20, 409.

[710] J. Alun Thomas, *The House of Commons 1906 – 1911: an analysis of its economic and social character*. Cardiff: U of Wales P: 1958. Pp. 53. Rev: *EHR* 74, 546.

The interaction of party organization, electoral manipulation, and parliamentary management has been investigated at several points. The three solid volumes in which Jennings discursively, personally and often vapidly ran his eye over the party-political situation of nearly 200 years are so seriously lacking in scholarly rigour that they cannot really be used.[711] Gash discusses the consequences of the first reform act and demonstrates the surprising continuance of old methods, more particularly of the dominance of patrons in the constituencies.[712] The story is taken on in Conacher's short study of the parties during a time of decomposition.[713] Hanham takes over at the point where at long last 'modern' parties exist beyond possibility of doubt.[714] Gwyn concerns himself with the problems raised by the increasing charges upon political activities, themselves the product of an increasing electorate,[715] and O'Leary tells the remarkable story of electoral corruption, not ended till the early eighties.[716]

We turn to the individual parties. The tories, most continuous of parties, have probably received least attention, though Gash (n. 712) deals mainly with them. McDowell's gallant attempt to discern behind the continuity of party also a continuity of principle fails to plumb the depths.[717] Gash

[711] Ivor Jennings, *Party Politics*, 3 vols. CUP: 1960 – 2. Pp. xxxiv, 388; vii, 404; x, 493. Rev: *EHR* 77, 200f. and 795f.; *HJ* 5, 191ff.
[712] Norman Gash, *Politics in the Age of Peel*, L: Longmans: 1953. Pp. xxi, 496. Rev: *EHR* 69, 457ff.
[713] James B. Conacher, 'Party politics in the age of Palmerston', *1859: entering an age of crisis* (P. Appleman *et al.*, eds.: Bloomington: Indiana UP: 1959), 163–80.
[714] H. J. Hanham, *Elections and Party Management: politics in the time of Disraeli and Gladstone*. L: Longmans: 1959. Pp. xvii, 468. Rev: *EHR* 77, 121ff. – Idem, 'The sale of honours in late Victorian England', *VS* 3 (1959 – 60), 277–89.
[715] William B. Gwyn, *Democracy and the Cost of Politics in Britain*. L: Athlone: 1962. Pp. 256. Rev: *EHR* 79, 195f.
[716] Cornelius O'Leary, *The Elimination of Corrupt Practices in British Elections, 1868 – 1911*. O: Clarendon: 1962. Pp. 253. Rev: *EHR* 78, 814.
[717] R. B. McDowell, *British Conservatism, 1832–1914*. L: Faber: 1959. Pp. 191. Rev: *EHR* 76, 742f.

underlines Peel's negative attitude to party (a phenomenon
sufficiently manifest in his day) and the influence of professional
politicians.[718] The echoes of Peel's sudden fall, which long
reverberated through politics, are tracked by Conacher.[719] The
structure and tenets of Disraeli's tory party have been analysed
twice: Smith finds no evidence for a serious concern with reform, but Feuchtwanger thinks that claims made at elections
had a better foundation.[720] The latter also contributes usefully
to our understanding of the new organization of the party
demanded by the consequences of the second reform act.[721]
Much of the not-too-much that was done was the work of
Randolph Churchill's dynamism and his belief in democratic
'participation'.[722] Cornford offers a solid discussion of the important fact that in the last quarter of the century conservatism
and the conservative party were virtually rebuilt from the
ground up under the pressure of new political circumstances;[723]
more conventionally, he also shows how the long Cecil ascendancy rested on the fluctuations of management in the house
of commons.[724]

Liberalism has attracted more historians by its decline (to
be considered in the next section) than its rise; for some reason,
it has always been easier to look at the liberals out of office

---

[718] Norman Gash, 'Peel and the party system', *TRHS* (1951), 47–69;
'F. R. Bonham, conservative "political secretary", 1832 – 1847',
EHR 63 (1948), 502–22.

[719] James B. Conacher, 'Peel and the Peelites', *EHR* 73 (1958), 431–52.

[720] Paul Smith, *Disraelian Conservatism and Social Reform.* L: Routledge:
1967. Pp. x, 358. Rev: *EHR* 84, 596ff.; *HJ* 11, 594ff.; *JMH* 41,
245ff. – E. J. Feuchtwanger, *Disraeli, Democracy and the Tory Party.*
O: Clarendon: 1968. Pp. xiv, 268. Rev: *HJ* 12, 578f.

[721] E. J. Feuchtwanger, 'J. E. Gorst and the central organization of
the conservative party, 1870 – 1882', *BIHR* 37 (1959), 192–208;
'The conservative party under the impact of the second reform
act', *VS* 2 (1958 – 9), 289–304.

[722] Francis H. Herrick, 'Lord Randolph Churchill and the popular
organization of the conservative party', *Pacific History Review* 15
(1946), 178–91.

[723] James P. Cornford, 'The transformation of conservatism in the
late nineteenth century', *VS* 7 (1963 – 4), 35–66.

[724] James P. Cornford, 'The parliamentary foundations of the Hotel
Cecil', *Kitson Clark Ft* (n. 137), 268–311.

than in. This even applies to their whig predecessors, twice studied in just such a situation.[725] The most significant book to have been written on this party is Vincent's which sought to analyse the manner of its emergence, but it is not easy to say in just what its significance lies.[726] He has clearly destroyed some pious legends about the influence of principle, morality and religion; but it remains hard to tell what in fact happened. At least we hope to hear less in future of the part played by middle classes and nonconformists. McGill and Tholfsen contribute to our understanding of liberal party organization.[727] While McCaffrey still sought the cause of the electoral débâcle of 1874 in Gladstone's conversion to home rule for Ireland, Maehl more subtly finds it in Gladstone's incompetent handling of his party.[728] Hurst uses Birmingham as the centre of a discussion of the changes produced by the home rule split of 1886; at greater length, he also deals with the narrower question of why peace-making failed in 1887.[729] The disastrous failure of the party to come to terms with Gladstone's disappearance, and the battles for the succession, are handsomely narrated by Stansky.[730] Decline had now started. Butler shows

---

[725] Austin Mitchell, *The Whigs in Opposition, 1815 – 1830*. O: Clarendon: 1967. Pp. xi, 266. Rev: *EHR* 84, 407f. – Abraham D. Kriegel, 'The politics of the whigs in opposition, 1834 – 1835', *JBS* 7 (1968), 64–91.

[726] John R. Vincent, *The Foundation of the Liberal Party, 1857 – 1868*. L: Constable: 1966. Pp. xxxv, 281. Rev: *EHR* 82, 802ff.; *HJ* 12, 181ff.; *Hist* 57, 358f.

[727] Barry McGill, 'Francis Schnadhorst and the liberal party organization', *JMH* 34 (1962), 19–39. – Trygve R. Tholfsen, 'The origins of the Birmingham caucus', *HJ* 2 (1959), 161–84.

[728] Lawrence J. McCaffrey, 'Home rule and the general election of 1874', *Irish Hist. Studies* 9 (1953 – 4), 190–212; W. H. Maehl, 'Gladstone, the liberals and the election of 1874', *BIHR* 36 (1963), 53–69.

[729] Michael C. Hurst, 'Joseph Chamberlain, the conservatives and the succession to John Bright, 1886 – 1889', *HJ* 7 (1954), 64–93. – Idem, *Joseph Chamberlain and Liberal Reunion: the round table conference of 1887*. L: Routledge: 1967. Pp. xv, 407. Rev: *HJ* 11, 394.

[730] Peter Stansky, *Ambitions and Strategies: the struggle for the leadership of the liberal party in the 1890s*. O: Clarendon: 1964. Pp. ix, 312. Rev: *EHR* 81, 424f.

how party politicians used the enquiry into the complicity of Joseph Chamberlain in the Jameson Raid in order to discredit one another; here liberalism, for the sake of its internal quarrels, preserved the conservatives' chief asset.[731] McCready, similarly, demonstrates that during the tory ascendancy the liberal party tried to follow suit by dropping home rule and preaching empire.[732] The oldfashioned radicalism, a central component of mid-Victorian liberalism, receives oldfashioned treatment from Maccoby.[733]

The newer radicals were, in the main, the ancestors of the labour party. Harrison wishes to pinpoint the political position of the working classes before the day of working-class parties; the result is not very clear.[734] Pelling and Poirier between them consider the spring days of the party which was to claim the right to speak for the workers.[735] An evanescent extra-parliamentary workers' organization has also been discussed.[736] One wonders if the history of the labour party needs to lack excitement to quite the extent so far apparent. Still, the various contributory streams of the movement have also been investigated. The trade unions, on whose money the party was in the end to grow, have been briefly dealt with by Pelling;[737]

[731] Jeffrey Butler, *The Liberal Party and the Jameson Raid*. O: Clarendon: 1968. Pp. xii, 336. Rev: *EHR* 84, 872f.

[732] H. W. McCready, 'Home rule and the liberal party, 1899 – 1906', *Irish Hist. Studies* 13 (1962 – 3), 316–48.

[733] S. Maccoby, *English Radicalism, 1886 – 1914*. L: Allen & Unwin: 1953. Pp. 540. Rev: *EHR* 69, 462ff. – Idem, *English Radicalism – the End? Ibid.*: 1961. Pp. 640. These are the last volumes of an enterprise started some time ago.

[734] Royden Harrison, *Before the Socialists*. L: Routledge: 1965. Pp. xiii, 369.

[735] Henry Pelling, *The Origins of the Labour Party, 1880 – 1900*. New ed. O: Clarendon: 1965. Pp. ix, 256. – Philip P. Poirier, *The Advent of the Labour Party, 1900 – 1906*. L: Allen & Unwin: 1958. Pp. 288. Rev: *EHR* 74, 373f.

[736] F. W. Bealey and Henry Pelling, *Labour and Politics, 1900 – 1906: a history of the Labour Representative Committee*. L: Macmillan: 1958. Pp. xi, 314. Rev: *EHR* 74, 373f.

[737] Henry Pelling, *A History of British Trade Unionism*. L: Macmillan: 1963. Pp. xi, 287. Rev: *EHR* 80, 637f.

a much larger co-operative work has achieved its first volume only.[738] A history of the T.U.C. has the virtues (if any) and deficiencies of a semi-official account.[739] Hobsbawm has looked at the efforts of the lowest layers to organize themselves,[740] while of the elite unions only the railway-men's has received reasonably scholarly treatment.[741] An odd aspect of trade union history, of which little is known, was the unions' share in promoting emigration – in the end to the detriment of their own funds.[742] The upright ineffectuals of the I.L.P., bearers of the true faith, have found their historian.[743] The influence of the Fabians is uncritically hymned by Cole, herself involved, while the beginnings of a more doubtful attitude, of which more will be heard, appear in the book by McBriar which, in consequence, met with some execration.[744] Some individuals receive their due, or more than their due. It took a Japanese scholar to cope with H. M. Hyndman, a socialist John Bull of essentially tory character;[745] Masterman attends to a more typical figure, the sentimental christian J. M. Ludlow.[746] Foreign prophets, too, make their appearance: Collins and Abramsky look into the relations between England and the

---

[738] H. A. Clegg, A. Fox, A. F. Thompson, *A History of British Trade Unionism since 1889*, vol. 1: 1889 – 1910. O: Clarendon: 1964. Pp. xi, 514. Rev: *EHR* 80, 872f.; *EcHR*[2] 20, 359ff.

[739] Benjamin C. Roberts, *The Trades Union Congress, 1868 – 1921*. L: Allen & Unwin: 1958. Pp. 408.

[740] Eric J. Hobsbawm, 'General labour unions, 1882 – 1914', *EcHR*[2] 1 (1948 – 9), 123–42.

[741] P. S. Gupta, 'Railway trade unionism in Britain, c. 1880 – 1900', *EcHR*[2] 19 (1966), 124–53.

[742] Charlotte Erickson, 'The encouragement of emigration by British trade unions, 1850 – 1900', *Population Studies* 3 (1949 – 50), 248–73.

[743] Robert E. Dowse, *Left in the Centre: the independent labour party, 1873 – 1940*. L: Longmans: 1966. Pp. xi, 231.

[744] Margaret Cole, *The Story of Fabian Socialism*. L: Heinemann: 1961. Pp. xv, 361. Rev: *EHR* 78, 816. – A. M. McBriar, *Fabian Socialism in British Politics, 1884 – 1918*. CUP: 1962. Pp. x, 388. Rev: *EHR* 80, 200f.

[745] Chushichi Tsuzuki, *H.M. Hyndman and British Socialism*. L: OUP: 1961. Pp. viii, 304. Rev: *EHR* 77, 809.

[746] Neville C. Masterman, *John Malcolm Ludlow, the builder of Christian Socialism*. CUP: 1963. Pp. vii, 299.

First International,[747] while Bünger contributes a book on the part played by Engels which, despite its immaculate dogmatic foundations, has much value on account of its careful treatment of important materials.[748] Lastly we may note a promising new departure: a study of what happened instead of what people wrote. Thompson demonstrates that in the political battle for the control of London the Fabians' part has been 'grossly exaggerated', while the organized social democrats did much better than the gradualist legend supposes.[749]

The history of the Irish party, influential beyond its numbers, belongs in the main to the history of Ireland where it shall be treated (nn. 1318 – 37). But Lyons' treatise on the twenty years between Parnell's fall and the revival of the struggle for independence looks at it almost entirely in the context of the Westminster parliament – quite rightly, for that period.[750]

(D) GOVERNMENT

It is no news to anyone that the nineteenth century witnessed a full-scale revolution in the nature and tasks of government. Twice as many people in the same territory, increasingly gathered in towns and in an industrial economy: the facts posed masses of social problems and demanded administrative changes which were for ever calling old concepts of freedom and legal rights in doubt. Though many details still remain obscure, historians have at last moved from comfortable generalizations and the reading of approved prophets to the rigorous study of the sources. Inevitably, this situation has led to some necessary but premature conclusions and some under-

---

[747] Henry Collins and Chimen Abramsky, *Karl Marx and the British Labour Movement*. L: Macmillan: 1965. Pp. xi, 356. Rev: *VS* 10, 91f.

[748] S. Bünger, *Friedrich Engels und die britische sozialistische Bewegung, 1881 – 1895*. Berlin: Rütter u. Loening: 1962. Pp. 242. Rev: *EHR*, 79, 634.

[749] Paul Thompson, *Socialists, Liberals and Labour: the struggle for London, 1885 – 1914*. L: Routledge: 1967. Pp. viii, 376. Rev: *HJ* 11, 599ff.

[750] F. S. L. Lyons, *The Irish Parliamentary Party, 1890 – 1910*. L: Faber: 1951. Pp. 284.

standably but unnecessarily sharp exchanges. Thus Mac-
Donagh has endeavoured to show that the old 'model', according to which the changes were the direct consequence of
Benthamite ideas, is false; in his view, offices and officers simply
and pragmatically followed the call of necessity and in the
process discovered new methods of central control and initiative.[751] This revisionary interpretation, in itself convincing
enough to anyone who has ever had to handle administrative
problems, rests too exclusively on his own researches into
governmental provision for emigration to America.[752] It also
underlies his brief glance at the process by which parliament
vested legislative power in the executive.[753] To Parris, on the
other hand, it seems that the new 'model' just happens to fit
MacDonagh's sole example, and that in general developments
were more commonly imposed from above by politicians
trained in Bentham's school; by way of proof he offers his own
work on the railways.[754] Bentham's direct influence is also
revived, without excessive claims, by Hume.[755] A debate,
which was already lively enough, was needlessly exacerbated
by Hart who saw nothing but political prejudice in the new
view and discovered a tory conspiracy against the liberal
gospel.[756]

That, however, is nonsense.[757] The real work that is going

---

[751] Oliver MacDonagh, 'The nineteenth-century revolution in government', *HJ* 1 (1958), 52–67.

[752] Oliver MacDonagh, *A Pattern of Government Growth, 1800 – 1860: the passenger acts and their enforcement*. L: Macgibbon & Kee: 1961. Pp. 368. Rev: *EHR* 78, 56off.; *HJ* 6, 140ff.

[753] Oliver MacDonagh, 'Delegated legislation and administrative discretion in the 1850s', *VS* 2 (1958 – 9), 29–44.

[754] Henry Parris, 'The nineteenth-century revolution in government: a reappraisal reappraised', *HJ* 3 (1960), 1–18. – Idem, *Government and the Railways in nineteenth-century Britain*. L: Routledge: 1965. Pp. xii, 244.

[755] L. J. Hume, 'Jeremy Bentham and the nineteenth-century revolution in government', *HJ* 10 (1967), 361–75.

[756] Jennifer Hart, 'Nineteenth-century social reform: a tory interpretation of history', *PP* 31 (1965), 39–61.

[757] Valerie Cromwell, 'Interpretations of 19th century administration: an analysis', *VS* 9 (1966), 245–56. Mentions a number of contributions which space prevents me from including here.

forward demonstrates that there is a lot in the MacDonagh thesis. New tasks compelled government to undertake reforming activities which unquestionably owed something to a new intellectual climate but in the main followed in the wake of necessity. How early all this started is shown in Roberts' book on welfare legislation, though the book tries to do too much and brings too little to a firm conclusion.[758] Edwin Chadwick, the leading reformer, has been thoroughly discussed by Finer and Lewis who in part raise and in part lower his contribution from the level credited by tradition.[759] Lambert has saved from oblivion a less well known but more interesting reformer, John Simon, medical man and medical administrator.[760] Other pioneering works about social reform, in part derived from Kitson Clark's Cambridge seminar, are still on the anvil; of the few conclusions to have reached print one may cite as typical Collins' important analysis of the beginnings of national insurance.[761]

On the fundamental problem of the staffing of government service, we now possess a comprehensive but still tentative introduction by Parris.[762] A lot of work is still needed here, and what has appeared has rarely escaped the temptation to seek 'major significance' in place of simply discovering the facts. Thus Torrance makes a creative hero out of the unlikely figure of the first permanent under-secretary of the treasury.[763]

---

[758] David Roberts, *Victorian Origins of the British Welfare State*. New Haven: Yale UP: 1960. Pp. xiii, 368.

[759] S. E. Finer, *The Life and Times of Sir Edwin Chadwick*. L: Methuen: 1952. Pp. xi, 555. Rev: *EHR* 68, 101f. – Richard A. Lewis, *Sir Edwin Chadwick and the Public Health Movement, 1832 – 1854*. L: Longmans: 1952. Pp. viii, 411. Rev: *EcHR*[2] 5, 419.

[760] Royston Lambert, *Sir John Simon, 1816 – 1904, and English Social Administration*. L: MacGibbon & Kee: 1963. Pp. 669. Rev: *EcHR*[2] 19, 211ff.; *EHR* 80, 626f.

[761] Doreen Collins, 'The introduction of old age pensions in Great Britain', *HJ* 8 (1966), 246–59.

[762] Henry Parris, *Constitutional Bureaucracy*. L: Allen & Unwin: 1969. Pp. 324.

[763] J. R. Torrance, 'Sir George Harrison and the growth of bureaucracy in the early nineteenth century', *EHR* 83 (1968), 52–88.

Hughes endeavours to seek out the real meaning of the supposedly basic reforms of the 1850's,[764] while Kitson Clark,
more interestingly, reflects upon the new idea that civil servants
should have no politics (and places its arrival too early).[765]
Wright's massive treatise on the treasury's control over the
administration, which greatly reduces its influence and, so to
speak, trivialises its interference, sounds right enough, but until
informed criticism has done its work on the thesis one must,
perhaps, withhold judgment.[766]

A few institutions have been well described. Willson briefly
summarizes the amazing expansion of ministries and indicates
the commons' changing attitudes towards the executive.[767]
Gosses and Steiner analyse the running of the foreign office
towards the end of the period; here there are signs of premature
thesis making.[768] Thanks to Young, we know most about the
colonial office at the start of the period;[769] later years have to
be content with a modest, and modestly useful, article about
treasury control.[770] Two books study the board of trade: Prouty
describes its development into a full-scale ministry of trade,
while Brown elucidates its relations with the tariff reforms of

---

[764] Edward Hughes, 'Sir Charles Trevelyan and civil service reform,
1853 – 1855', *EHR* 64 (1949), 53–88, 206–34; 'Civil service reforms
of 1853 – 1855', *Public Administration* 32 (1954) 17–51; 33 (1955),
299–306.

[765] G. Kitson Clark, ' "Statesmen in disguise"? Reflections on the
history of the neutrality of the civil service', *HJ* 2 (1959), 19–
39.

[766] Maurice W. Wright, *Treasury Control of the Civil Service, 1854 – 1874.*
O: Clarendon: 1969. Pp. xxxv, 406.

[767] F. M. G. Willson, 'Ministries and boards: some aspects of administrative developments since 1832', *Public Administration* 33 (1955),
43–58.

[768] F. Gosses, *The Management of British Foreign Policy before the First
World War, especially during the period 1880 – 1914.* Leyden: Sijthoff:
1948. Pp. 172. – Zara Steiner, 'The last years of the old foreign
office, 1898 – 1905', *HJ* 6 (1963), 59–90.

[769] D. Murray Young, *The Colonial Office in the Early Nineteenth Century.*
L: Longmans: 1961. Pp. x, 310. Rev: *EHR* 78, 806.

[770] Ann M. Burton, 'Treasury control and colonial policy in the late
19th century', *Public Administration* 44 (1966), 169–92.

the first half of the century.[771] Tucker criticizes the common
view of Caldwell's army reforms as fundamental and successful,
and pursues the matter to a later date.[772] A few new things
have been said about local government. Mather shows that at
a time when England in effect knew nothing of modern police
methods public order was in the main maintained, despite the
prevalence of misery and active discontent.[773] Lambert looks
at the relations between centre and extremities,[774] Hart at the
first moves to introduce a genuine police force in the towns,[775]
and Dunbabin at the organizations which finally ended the
rule of the JPs.[776]

(E) FOREIGN AFFAIRS

Nineteenth-century diplomatic history has for long been one
of the truly established disciplines in the English historical
canon, but even here new stirrings – the asking of new
questions and exploitation of different materials – have been
noticeable. Two brief studies touch on the vexed question of
parliament's interference: Cromwell shows that this was much
smaller than is usually supposed, and Lambert, reviewing the
reprint of an old and influential book, shows that traditional
views rest on fundamental misunderstandings concerning the

---

[771] Roger Prouty, *The Transformation of the Board of Trade, 1830 – 1855.*
L: Heinemann: 1957. Pp. viii, 123. Rev: *EcHR*² 10, 493f. – Lucy
Brown, *The Board of Trade and the Free Trade Movement, 1830 – 1842.*
O: Clarendon: 1958. Pp. 245. Rev: *EHR* 75, 361f.

[772] Albert V. Tucker, 'Army and society in England, 1870 – 1900: a
reassessment of the Cardwell reforms', *JBS* 2 (1962), 110–41; 'The
issue of army reform in the unionist government, 1903 – 1905',
HJ 9 (1966), 90–100.

[773] F. C. Mather, *Public Order in the Age of the Chartists.* Manchester
UP: 1959. Pp. ix, 260. Rev: *EHR* 76, 169f.; *EcHR*² 13, 128f.

[774] Royston Lambert, 'Central and local relations in mid-Victorian
England; the local government act office, 1858 – 1871', *VS* 6
(1962 – 3), 121–50.

[775] Jennifer Hart, 'Reform of the borough police, 1835 – 1856',
EHR 70 (1955), 411–27.

[776] J. P. D. Dunbabin, 'The politics of the establishment of county
councils', *HJ* 6 (1963), 226–52; 'Expectations of the new county
councils and their realization', *ibid.* 8 (1965), 353–79.

crucial documents.[777] Steiner, on the other hand, attempts to discover the part played by permanent officials; the book should lead to prolonged debate.[778] The fact that foreign policy is not all diplomacy is beginning to leave its mark on the writings of scholars: thus Platt attempts a survey of the inter-action of policy and trade, with case studies ranging from Egypt to Chile.[779] A particular case-study also leans more to matters economic than political.[780] However, the traditional methods still dominate this field, in great part because the opening of the archives has demanded much initial sorting out of the basic diplomatic story; Taylor, our leading historian in these matters, has publicly declared his ignorance of and in-difference to economic problems, and most specialists still treat diplomacy as self-sufficient. This is a marked feature even of the one general book on a particular relationship which has been attempted – Bourne's otherwise powerful review of policy towards the United States which brings out the remarkable degree to which that policy was determined by convictions that war would sooner or later become inevitable.[781] It will be best to run through the particular studies in chronological order.

Ward's study of the slave trade is lively but essentially popular; the importance of the problem in international rela-tions is insufficiently illumined.[782] The well known problem

---

[777] Valerie Cromwell, 'The private member of the house of commons and foreign policy in the nineteenth century', *Liber Memorialis Sir Maurice Powicke* (Louvain/Paris: Nauwelaerts: 1965), 191–218. – Sheila Lambert, 'A Century of Diplomatic Blue Books: review article', *HJ* 10 (1967), 125–31.

[778] Zara Steiner, *The Foreign Office and Foreign Policy, 1898 – 1914*. CUP: 1969. Pp. xii, 262.

[779] D. C. M. Platt, *Finance, Trade and Politics in British Foreign Policy, 1815 – 1914*. O: Clarendon: 1968. Pp. xli, 454. Rev: *EcHR*² 22, 142f.

[780] H. S. Ferns, *Britain and Argentina in the Nineteenth Century*. O: Clarendon: 1960. Pp. xiv, 517.

[781] Kenneth Bourne, *Britain and the Balance of Power in North America, 1815 – 1908*. L: Longmans: 1967. Pp. xii, 439. Rev: *EHR* 84, 408f.; *VS* 12, 410ff. – *See also* Frederick Merk, *The Oregon Question: essays in Anglo-American politics*. C (Mass): Belknap Press: 1967. Pp. xvi, 427.

[782] W. E. F. Ward, *The Royal Navy and the Slavers*. L: Allen & Unwin: 1969. Pp. 248. *See also* n. 841.

of English relations with Latin America in the age of Canning has led to a somewhat superfluous book which does not even rely on new materials in its criticisms of better scholars.[783] Rosselli's gigantic tome deals with English policy towards Piedmont-Sardinia, but covers in effect the whole of Sardinian foreign policy;[784] less thoroughly but more interestingly, Beales once more tackles Britain's part in the creation of a united Italy.[785] Gleason's heavy-footed study of English apprehensions concerning Russian expansion finds their origins in the policy of the Holy Alliance.[786] Death unhappily interrupted Webster's last work, a large-scale investigation of Palmerston's foreign policy.[787] One of the gaps is filled by Gillesen who refutes the old charge that Palmerston in 1848 – 50 prevented German unification by means of a European coalition.[788] More detailed studies of Palmerston's policy are provided by Barié (Italy, 1846 – 9) and Holger (the Baltic, 1848 – 50);[789] while Mosse looks briefly at a problem of the fifties.[790] British support for

---

[783] William W. Kaufmann, *British Policy and the Independence of Latin America, 1804 – 1824.* New Haven: Yale UP: 1951. Pp. ix, 238.

[784] Nello Rosselli, *Inghilterra e regno di Sardegna del 1815 al 1847.* Turin: Einaudi: 1954. Pp. xxviii, 940. Rev: *AHR* 60, 356f.

[785] Derek E. D. Beales, *England and Italy, 1859 – 1860.* Edinburgh: Nelson: 1961. Pp. xii, 196. Rev: *EHR* 78, 810f.

[786] John H. Gleason, *The Genesis of Russophobia in Great Britain.* C (Mass.): Harvard UP: 1950. Pp. xi, 314. Rev: *EHR* 67, 587f.

[787] Charles K. Webster, *The Foreign Policy of Palmerston, 1830 – 1841,* 2 vols. L: Bell: 1951. Pp. xii, 914. Rev: *EHR* 67, 421ff.

[788] Günther Gillesen, *Lord Palmerston und die Einigung Deutschlands.* Lübeck: Matthiesen: 1961. Pp. 160.

[789] Ottavio Barié, *L'Inghilterra e il problema italiano nel 1846 – 1848.* Naples: Edizioni Scientifiche Italiane: 1960. Pp. xii, 251. Rev: *EHR* 78, 196f. – Idem, *L'Inghilterra e il problema italiano nel 1848 – 1849.* Milan: Giuffrè: 1965. Pp. viii, 298. – Holger Hjelholt, *British Mediation in the Danish-German Conflict, 1848 – 1850,* 2 vols. Copenhagen: Historisk-Filosofiske Meddelelser udgivet af det kgl. danske videnskabernes selskab, 41–42: 1965 – 6. Pp. 236; 252. Rev: *EHR* 82, 419; 83, 631f.

[790] Werner E. Mosse, 'The triple treaty of 15 April 1856', *EHR* 67 (1952), 203–29.

Swiss independence at the time when this fact of European life was finally confirmed is described by Imlah.[791]

The age of Palmerston was succeeded by the age of Bismarck. Foot describes British reactions to the crisis of 1867.[792] Two valuable studies investigate Britain's position before the war of 1870 and the problems of Europe after Bismarck's rise to dominance.[793] A conventionally organized book takes care of eight years of Anglo-French relations during the first phase of 'revanche'.[794] A much less conventional book tries to present a comprehensive survey of the manner in which an unwanted imperial expansion came to affect foreign policy.[795] The new crisis of 1887 forms the substance of a doctoral dissertation from Bern.[796] This takes one into the era of political realignments and the formation of alliances which produced the antagonists of the first world war. Here the most important contribution is Grenville's demonstration that Salisbury's policy rested on a principled rejection of the 'new course', a rejection which his successors attempted to maintain without adhering to his principles.[797] A less original contribution to the

---

[791] Ann G. Imlah, *Britain and Switzerland, 1845 – 60: a study of Anglo-Swiss relations during some critical years for Swiss neutrality*. L: Longmans: 1966. Pp. xv, 208. Rev: *EHR* 83, 631.

[792] M. R. D. Foot, 'Great Britain and Luxemburg, 1867', *EHR* 67 (1952), 352–79.

[793] R. Millman, *British Foreign Policy and the Coming of the Franco-Prussian War*. O: Clarendon: 1965. Pp. x, 238. Rev: *EHR* 82, 414. – W. N. Medlicott, *Bismarck, Gladstone, and the Concert of Europe*. L: Athlone: 1956. Pp. xiv, 353. Rev: *EHR* 74, 138f.

[794] Charles Bloch, *Les relations entre la France et la Grande-Bretagne, 1871 – 1878*. Paris: Éditions Internationales: 1955. Pp. 287. Rev: *EHR* 73, 181f.

[795] Cedric J. Lowe, *The Reluctant Imperialists: British foreign policy, 1878 – 1902*, 2 vols. L: Routledge: 1967. Pp. x, 261; xvi, 139. Rev: *EHR* 84, 630f.; *VS* 12, 410ff.

[796] Klaus Römer, *England und die europäischen Mächte im Jahre 1887*. Aarau: Sauerländer: 1957. Pp. 153. Rev: *EHR* 73, 182f.

[797] John A. S. Grenville, *Lord Salisbury and Foreign Policy: the close of the nineteenth century*. L: Athlone: 1964. Pp. xi, 451. Rev: *EHR* 81, 205f.; *HJ* 7, 340ff.

same theme comes from Germany.[798] The changing situation after Salisbury's retirement is skilfully analysed by Monger.[799] Though no one any longer accepts the term 'splendid isolation' as correctly describing British policy, it remains true that a new willingness to undertake entangling alliances began with the Japanese treaty of 1902.[800] One effect of these new alliances is traced in a study of far eastern policy down to 1915.[801]

European expansion involved policy in all sorts of new parts of the globe, as British governments found themselves most reluctantly drawn into actions which they believed to be unwise and uncalled for. British interests helped to bring Brazil out of its old sleep,[802] through the defence of established concerns came to be involved in suppressing the Taiping rebellion,[803] and assisted powerfully in the early and later peaceful invasion of Japan by westernization.[804] The Mediterranean formed a traditional area of operations,[805] the Sudan a very new but ominously active one;[806] the attempts to gain a foothold in Morocco owed more to the second than the first.[807] The

[798] Theodor A. Bayer, *England und der neue Kurs*. Tübingen: Mohr: 1955. Pp. vii, 128.

[799] G. W. Monger, *The End of Isolation: British foreign policy, 1900 – 1907*. Edinburgh: Nelson: 1963. Pp. vi, 343. Rev: *EHR* 80, 638f.; *HJ* 7, 340ff.

[800] Zara Steiner, 'Great Britain and the creation of the Anglo-Japanese alliance', *JMH* 31 (1959), 27–36. – Ian H. Nish, *The Anglo-Japanese Alliance: the diplomacy of two island empires*. L: Athlone: 1966. Pp. xi, 420. Rev: *EHR* 82, 869f.

[801] Peter Lowe, *Great Britain and Japan, 1911 – 1915: a study of British far eastern policy*. L: Macmillan: 1969. Pp. 343.

[802] R. Graham, *Britain and the Onset of Modernisation in Brazil, 1850 – 1914*. CUP: 1968. Pp. xvi, 385.

[803] John S. Gregory, *Great Britain and the Taipings*. L: Routledge: 1969. Pp. xvi, 271.

[804] William G. Beasley, *Great Britain and the Opening of Japan, 1834 – 1858*. L: Luzac & Co.: 1951. Pp. xix, 227. – Grace Fox, *Britain and Japan, 1858 – 1883*. O: Clarendon: 1969. Pp. xviii, 627.

[805] Cedric J. Lowe, *Salisbury and the Mediterranean, 1886 – 1896*. L: Routledge: 1965. Pp. x, 123. Rev: *EHR* 81, 871f.; *VS* 9, 168f.

[806] G. N. Sanderson, *England, Europe, and the Upper Nile, 1882 – 1899*. Edinburgh UP: 1965. Pp. xiv, 456. Rev: *EHR* 82, 194f.

[807] Alan J. P. Taylor, 'British policy in Morocco, 1886 – 1902', *EHR* 66 (1951), 342–74.

problem of Persia (fundamentally the problem of a station on the road to India and therefore also a bone of contention with Russia) has produced no fewer than six studies, some of them markedly overlapping, perhaps less a tribute to the importance of the issue than to the availability of documents.[808] Hauser shows more generally how Germany could utilize the enmity between Britain and Russia.[809] Moving over to Turkey, Chapman looks at the negotiations over the Baghdad railway, and Smith looks at the last influential British ambassador at Istanbul.[810] Two mildly twin-like studies deal with the first stages of an Anglo-American rapprochement; of them, that listed second is rather the better and especially exercises more proper scepticism in the face of politicians' public statements.[811] The shortage of Ph.D. subjects available to Swiss graduate students has produced two specialized and somewhat ordinary

---

[808] P. C. Terenzio, *La rivalité anglo-russe en Perse et en Afghanistan jusqu'aux accords de 1907*. Paris: Rousseau: 1947. Pp. 179. – Rose L. Greaves, *Persia and the Defence of India, 1884 – 1892: a study in the foreign policy of the third Marquess of Salisbury*. L: Athlone: 1959. Pp. xii, 301. Rev: *EHR* 75, 748f.; *HJ* 3, 301ff. – Jens B. Plass, *England zwischen Deutschland und Russland: der persische Golf in der britischen Vorkriegspolitik 1899 1907*. Hamburg: Institut für auswärtige Politik: 1966. Pp. viii, 507. Rev: *EHR* 83, 872f. – John Barrett Kelly, *Britain and the Persian Gulf, 1795 – 1880*. O: Clarendon: 1968. Pp. xvi, 911. Rev: *HJ* 12, 374f.; *VS* 12, 410ff. – Firuz Kazemzadeh, *Russia and Britain in Persia, 1864 – 1914: a study in imperialism*. New Haven: Yale UP: 1968. Pp. xii, 711. Rev: *EHR* 85, 198f.; *Hist* 54, 310f. – Briton C. Busch, *Britain and the Persian Gulf, 1894 – 1914*. Berkeley & Los Angeles: U of California P: 1967. Pp. xv, 432. Rev: *VS* 12, 410ff.

[809] Oswald Hauser, *Deutschland und der englisch-russische Gegensatz, 1900 – 1914*. Göttingen: Musterschmidt: 1958. Pp. viii, 288. Rev: *EHR* 75, 371f.

[810] Maybelle K. Chapman, *Great Britain and the Baghdad Railway, 1888 – 1914*. Northampton (Mass.): Smith College Studies in History, 31: 1948. Pp. x, 248. – Colin L. Smith, *The Embassy of Sir William White at Constantinople, 1886 – 1891*. L: OUP: 1957. Pp. xii, 183. Rev: *EHR* 74, 184f.

[811] Charles S. Campbell, *Anglo-American Understanding, 1898 – 1903*. Baltimore: Johns Hopkins UP: 1957. Pp. vii, 385. Rev: *EHR* 73, 738f. – A. E. Campbell, *Great Britain and the United States, 1895 – 1903*. L: Longmans: 1960. Pp. viii, 216. Rev: *EHR* 77, 583ff.

books on relations between England and Switzerland; the second shows that the good relations established by the mid-century accord had virtually vanished by 1914 under the influence of the Boer war.[812]

All this is reasonably traditional. Anything but traditional is Taylor's approach to the problems of foreign policy in a book which both thoroughly stimulates and frequently annoys by its splendidly wild passages. It treats not of those who made policy but of those who thought themselves influential from outside: the author shares their illusions.[813] To the same complex of questions belongs an article which discusses various attitudes to the attempts to replace international disputes by settled arbitration.[814]

(F) THE EMPIRE

From the point of view of England, the problems of imperial expansion (hindered as a rule, or at least not supported, by one government after another) appeared very similar to those of foreign policy. The century falls into two parts: the years without a conscious positive notion of imperialism, and the years with one. Six studies deal with the period before the popular thirst for expansion: Knaplund explains James Stephens' share in the development of the 'white' empire;[815] Galbraith brings out the dislike with which leading circles at home regarded the forward activities of the men on the spot in South Africa;[816]

---

[812] Lotti Genner, *Die diplomatischen Beziehungen zwischen England und der Schweiz.* Basel/Stuttgart: Albig u. Lichterhahn: 1956. Pp. 228. Rev: *EHR* 74, 371f. – Othmar Uhl, *Die diplomatisch-politischen Beziehungen zwischen Grossbritannien und der Schweiz in den Jahrzehnten vor dem ersten Weltkrieg.* Basel/Stuttgart: Helbing u. Lichterhahn: 1961. Pp. 193. Rev: *EHR* 79, 438f.

[813] Alan J. P. Taylor, *The Trouble-Makers: dissent over foreign policy, 1792 – 1939.* L: Hamilton: 1957. Pp. 207. Rev: *EHR* 74, 126ff.

[814] Maureen M. Robson, 'Liberals and "vital interests": the debate on international arbitration, 1815 – 1872', *BIHR* 32 (1959), 38–55.

[815] Paul Knaplund, *James Stephen and the British Colonial System, 1813 – 1847.* Madison: U of Wisconsin P: 1953. Pp. ix, 315.

[816] J. S. Galbraith, *Reluctant Empire: British policy on the South African frontier, 1834 – 1854.* Berkeley: U of California P: 1963. Pp. xi, 293. Rev: *EHR* 80, 622f.

Graham describes the less controversial uses of naval supremacy in the south seas;[817] Bloomfield sees in Wakefield's radical imperialism a premature manifestation of modern ideas of commonwealth relations;[818] Eddy, more fruitfully, shows what governing very distant territories meant in the first part of the century;[819] and Norris demonstrates that even the seeming aggression in Afghanistan resulted only from partly justified fears of Russian advances in central Asia.[820]

In turning to the age of true imperialism (national, not governmental), one must first of all share Fieldhouse's doubts whether there is anything at all in the widely held view (held especially by Lenin) that this European expansion was driven on by the search for profit and by a crisis in the capitalist system.[821] Stokes inclines to give Lenin better credit by arguing that he never held the crude version of this view which is characteristic of Leninism.[822] At any rate, a very different picture emerges from the joint work of two historians who discern purely political motives directly derived from the problem of a European balance of power.[823] Barié's very old-fashioned review of imperialist teaching and preaching, in which he relies in the main on the writings of literary men, does not, of course, affect the truth of the new view;[824] but the

---

[817] Gerald S. Graham, *Great Britain in the Indian Ocean: a study of maritime enterprise, 1810 – 1850*. O: Clarendon: 1967. Pp. xiii, 479. Rev: *EHR* 84, 362ff.

[818] Paul Bloomfield, *Edward Gibbon Wakefield: builder of the British commonwealth*. L: Longmans: 1961. Pp. xi, 378.

[819] J. J. Eddy, *Britain and the Australian Colonies, 1818 – 1831: the technique of government*. O: Clarendon: 1969. Pp. xviii, 326.

[820] John A. Norris, *The First Afghan War, 1838 – 1842*. CUP: 1967. Pp. xvi, 500. Rev: *EHR* 84, 418f.; *HJ* 12, 573ff.

[821] D. K. Fieldhouse, ' "Imperialism": a historical revision', *EcHR²* 14 (1961 – 2) 187–209.

[822] Eric Stokes, 'Late nineteenth century colonial expansion and the attack on the theory of economic imperialism: a case of mistaken identity?', *HJ* 12 (1969), 285–301.

[823] Ronald E. Robinson and John Gallagher, *Africa and the Victorians: the official mind of imperialism*. L: Macmillan: 1961. Pp. xii, 491. Rev: *EHR* 78, 345ff.; *HJ* 7, 154ff.

[824] Ottavio Barié, *Idee e dottrine imperialistiche nell' Inghilterra vittoriana*. Bari: Laterze: 1953. Pp. xii, 326. Rev: *EHR* 69, 682f.

discussion has not really started yet. Porter, at any rate, has usefully reminded us of the existence of men who loudly criticized imperialism at the height of its popularity;[825] it remains to note that the views of these men, who had a case to make, still underlie the Marxist interpretation of the whole phenomenon. Particular treatises add nothing much to the more fundamental discussion. Boahen described the advance into the Sahara.[826] Coombs tackles a similar subject – the replacement of Dutch influence by British on the Gold Coast.[827] Gillard slightly arrests the universal feeling that British governments tried to keep out of colonial involvement, by showing how consistently Salisbury defended those interests against Germany.[828] One of the greatest of the proconsuls, the founder of Nigeria, has received a biography as large as life;[829] an earlier and less praised representative of the type who occupied leading positions in several regions is put forward as a paragon of colonial policy.[830] South Africa has provoked several touchily political studies. Schreuder removes some of the anti-colonial halo from Gladstone's head;[831] Drus and Van der Poel leave no doubt that Chamberlain knew beforehand of Jameson's intention to invade;[832] Galbraith

---

[825] Bernard Porter, *Critics of Empire: British attitudes to colonialism in Africa, 1895 – 1914*. L: Macmillan: 1968. Pp. xvi, 369. Rev: *EHR* 84, 873; *Hist* 54, 317f.

[826] A. Adu Boahen, *Britain, the Sahara, and the Western Sudan, 1788 – 1861*. O: Clarendon: 1964. Pp. xiii, 268. Rev: *EHR* 80, 617f.

[827] Donald Coombs, *The Gold Coast, Britain and the Netherlands, 1850 – 1874*. L: OUP: 1963. Pp. xiii, 160.

[828] D. R. Gillard, 'Salisbury's African policy and the Heligoland offer, 1890', *EHR* 75 (1960), 631–53.

[829] Margery Perham, *Lugard: the Years of Adventure, 1858 – 1898; the Years of Authority, 1898 – 1945*, 2 vols. L: Collins: 1959, 1960. Pp. xv, 750; xx, 748. Rev: *EHR* 73, 116ff.

[830] James K. Chapman, *The Career of Arthur Hamilton, first Lord Stanmore, 1829 – 1912*. Toronto UP: 1964. Pp. x, 387. Rev: *EHR* 81, 621f.

[831] D. M. Schreuder, *Gladstone and Kruger: liberal government and colonial 'home rule', 1880 – 1885*. L: Routledge: 1967. Pp. xviii, 558.

[832] Ethel M. Drus, 'The question of imperial complicity in the Jameson Raid', *EHR* 68 (1953), 582–93. – Jean Van der Poel, *The Jameson Raid*. L: OUP: 1951. Pp. 251.

describes the anti-war propaganda in England;[833] Curtis recorded his own memories of the Boer war;[834] Pyrah shows how the anti-imperialist traditions of the liberal party influenced policy towards the defeated Boers.[835] The activities of men variously favourable towards the empire have also been written about. Judd shows how Balfour came to be – mildly – bitten by the bug;[836] Dilks (in the first volume of a projected two-volume work) shows Curzon heartily enjoying his great days in India;[837] and Hyam shows how the labours of liberal imperialists helped to transform empire into commonwealth.[838] Lastly a work that has nothing to do with anything else: it treats of the attempts by British missionaries to settle in Palestine and to combine the promotion of religion with the advancement of Britain's political interests.[839]

The empire, we know, rested almost solely on sea-power, but there is little to tell of that. Lewis provides a competent description of the navy in the years between the heroic age of Nelson and the revolution produced by steam and iron.[840] Lloyd investigates that navy's chief active duty, the suppression of the slave trade.[841] Peace naturally brought much

---

[833] J. S. Galbraith, 'The pamphlet campaign on the Boer war', *JMH* 24 (1952), 111–26.

[834] Lionel Curtis, *With Milner in South Africa*. O: Blackwell: 1951. Pp. xiv, 254. Rev: *EHR* 69, 508.

[835] G. B. Pyrah, *Imperial Policy and South Africa, 1902 – 1910*. O: Clarendon: 1955. Pp. xvi, 272.

[836] Denis Judd, *Balfour and the British Empire: a study in imperial evolution, 1874 – 1932*. L: Macmillan: 1968: Pp. 392. Rev: *VS* 13, 107f.

[837] David Dilks, *Curzon in India*, vol. 1: Achievement. L: Hart-Davis: 1969. Pp. 296.

[838] Ronald Hyam, *Elgin and Churchill at the Colonial Office, 1905 – 1908: the watershed of the empire-commonwealth*. L: Macmillan: 1968. Pp. xvi, 574.

[839] A. L. Tibawi, *British Interests in Palestine, 1800 – 1901: a study of religious and educational enterprise*. L: OUP: 1961. Pp. ix, 280. Rev: *EHR* 78, 397.

[840] Michael A. Lewis, *The Navy in Transition*. L: Hodder & Stoughton: 1965. Pp. 287.

[841] Christopher Lloyd, *The Navy and the Slave Trade*. L: Longmans: 1949. Pp. xiii, 314. Rev: *EHR* 66, 600ff. *See also* n. 782.

debate about naval policy, especially its cost.[842] The problems
before the first world war receive much attention in a book
listed below.[843] The army is represented by only one book in
which the usually critical writings of British soldiers against
their superiors' methods and tenets are reviewed.[844] Another
book deals similarly with naval strategical thought.[845] Army
and navy: their mention reminds one of the cost of empire.
The nation had, up to a point, to choose between imperial and
social ends. A book which treats of the fluctuations between
the two provides illumination but is a little too much marked
by the technical stigmata of the history of ideas.[846]

(G) ECONOMIC HISTORY

Since one frequently feels tempted to think that the history of
the nineteenth century is effectively all economic history, it
comes as a surprise to find that much less work has been done
in this area than in those of domestic politics or international
relations. On the other hand, there is rather more disputatious
vigour in what has been written. For this, some thanks are
due to Rostow whose essay on the causes of industrialization
has proved very influential – mostly by rousing energetic
resistance and denial.[847] Possibly less brilliant but certainly
more reliable general accounts have also appeared. Chambers
and Sayers between them offer a readily comprehended intro-

---

[842] C. J. Bartlett, *Great Britain and Sea Power, 1815 – 1853*. O: Clarendon: 1963. Pp. xviii, 364. Rev: *EHR* 80, 185f.

[843] See n. 984.

[844] Jay Luvaas, *The Education of an Army: British military thought,
1815 – 1940*. Chicago: U of Chicago P: 1964. Pp. xiii, 454. Rev:
EHR 81, 850f.; *VS* 10, 95f.

[845] Don M. Schurman, *The Education of a Navy: the development of
British naval thought, 1867 – 1914*. L: Cassell: 1965. Pp. 213. Rev:
EHR 82, 195f.

[846] Bernard Semmel, *Imperialism and Social Reform: English social-
imperialist thought, 1895 – 1914*. L: Allen & Unwin: 1960. Pp. 283.
Rev: *EHR* 76, 752f.

[847] Walt W. Rostow, *The British Economy of the Nineteenth Century*. O:
Clarendon: 1948. Pp. 240.

duction.[848] Checkland succeeds in overcoming the limitations of space sufficiently to provide a genuinely learned explanation of the complications of economic development;[849] Ashworth, tackling the next period, does not manage quite so well.[850] His book should be used in conjunction with Court's valuable selection from the sources.[851] Habakkuk has opened up a more general theme in his comparative study of England and America: the former disposed of more capital and of no less inventive genius or entrepreneurial zeal, but a surplus of available labour arrested the drive for explosive innovation.[852] That the major problems of the early stages of industrialization arose in the main from the uncertainties of investment and the market is recognized in two studies which thoroughly analyse the consequent sharp crises for two important decades.[853] A general survey of trading policy is undertaken in a work whose title, appropriate really only for one fifth of the time covered, betrays its American origin.[854] Church maintains the solid tradition of town histories, which has provided

[848] J. D. Chambers, *The Workshop of the World: British economic history from 1820 to 1880*. L: OUP: 1961. Pp. viii, 239. Rev: *EHR* 77, 796f. – R. S. Sayers, *A History of Economic Change in England, 1880 – 1939*. L: OUP: 1967. Pp. viii, 179. Rev: *EHR* 84, 631f.

[849] Sidney G. Checkland, *The Rise of Industrial Society in England, 1815 – 1885*. L: Longmans: 1964. Pp. xiv, 471. Rev: *EHR* 81, 420f.; *EcHR*[2] 18, 650f.

[850] W. Ashworth, *An Economic History of England, 1870 – 1939*. L: Methuen: 1960. Pp. ix, 438. Rev: *EHR* 77, 405f.; *EcHR*[2] 15, 561f.

[851] W. H. B. Court, *British Economic History, 1870 – 1914: commentary and documents*. CUP: 1965. Pp. xxviii, 495.

[852] Hrothgar J. Habakkuk, *American and British Technology in the Nineteenth Century*. CUP: 1962. Pp. ix, 222.

[853] R. C. O. Mathews, *A Study in Trade Cycle History: economic fluctuations in Great Britain, 1833 – 1842*. CUP: 1954. Pp. xiv, 228. – J. R. T. Hughes, *Fluctuations in Trade, Industry and Finance: a study of British economic development, 1850 – 1860*. O: Clarendon: 1960. Pp. xviii, 344.

[854] Robert L. Schuyler, *The Fall of the Old Colonial System: a study in British free trade, 1770 – 1870*. L: OUP: 1945. Pp. vii, 344.

so much material for more imaginative studies, in his portrayal of a century of development in Nottingham.[855]

Although agriculture remained the leading industry almost to the end of the century, the shifting centre of gravity leaves its mark on the work of historians. Thompson, who believes in yet another agricultural revolution,[856] nevertheless is forced to conclude in his general analysis of all matters agrarian that things were going downhill.[857] Spring, confining himself to the large estates and describing rather than analysing, also cannot escape a certain elegiac air.[858] The only technical problem that seems to have been studied is that of the corn laws, a theme in which political and economic matters link almost beyond hope of disentanglement. By studying farming methods, Moore arrives at the conclusion that in a changed situation the repeal of the laws offered landlords the best of opportunities.[859] Fairlie, on the other hand, starting from the world production of wheat, argues that Peel's government became convinced that in the foreseeable circumstances a maintenance of the laws would result in a grave shortage of bread.[860] Possibly those three articles complement one another; to me they seem to be in contradiction. Admittedly, the landlords themselves were far from clear about the situation.[861]

[855] Roy A. Church, *Economic and Social Change in a Midland Town: Victorian Nottingham, 1815 – 1900*. L: Cass: 1966. Pp. xxiv, 409. Rev: *EcHR*[2] 22, 151f.

[856] F. M. L. Thompson, 'The second agricultural revolution, 1815 – 1880', *EcHR*[2] 21 (1968), 62–77.

[857] F. M. L. Thompson, *English Landed Society in the Nineteenth Century*. L: Routledge: 1963. Pp. xii, 374. Rev: *EHR* 80, 428f.; *EcHR*[2] 17, 146ff.

[858] David Spring, *The English Landed Estate in the Nineteenth Century: its administration*. Baltimore: Johns Hopkins UP: 1963. Pp. vii, 216. Rev: *EHR* 80, 633f.; *Agric. Hist. Rev.* 13, 65ff. – Idem, 'The role of the aristocracy in the late nineteenth century', *VS* 4 (1960 – 1), 55–64.

[859] D. C. Moore, 'The corn laws and high farming', *EcHR*[2] 18 (1965 – 6), 544–61.

[860] Susan Fairlie, 'The 19th century corn laws reconsidered', *EcHR*[2] 18 (1965 – 6), 562–75; 'The corn laws and British wheat production', *ibid.* 22 (1969), 88–116.

[861] John T. Ward, 'West Riding landowners and the corn laws', *EHR* 81 (1966), 256–72.

The war against the corn laws ended in the triumph of the Manchester economists.[362] But while these were preaching the faith of *laissez faire* and self-help, reality compelled the state to intervene as protector and organizer in the nation's economic life. Thus Bruce regards the new poor law of 1834, once abominated as a triumph of *laissez faire*, as the beginnings of the welfare state;[363] Huzel, incidentally, maintains that, despite Malthus, the old poor law had not assisted a rise in population.[364] The history of medical welfare offers some support to Bruce's views.[365] Nevertheless, there should be no doubt that despite all this growing social concern, both private and public, the typical figure of the age (at least down to the seventies) remained the energetic and self-reliant entrepreneur, left essentially free in his enterprising.[366] Three of the best-known engineers have received pretty naïve biographies, from one hand.[367] The England of that day produced a good many examples of an odd mixture of selfmade wealth and conscientious philanthropy, often associated with off-key fixed ideas: Briggs presents one such in his book about the chocolate manufacturer Rowntree, Armytage another in his about the politically active manufacturer Mundella.[368]

Several industries have been studied, mostly by means of

---

[362] W. D. Grampp, *The Manchester School of Economics*. Stanford UP: 1960. Pp. ix, 155. Rev: *EHR*, 77, 337f.

[363] Maurice Bruce, *The Coming of the Welfare State*. L: Batsford: 1961. Pp. xi, 308. Rev: *EHR* 78, 818f.; *EcHR*² 15, 564f.

[364] James P. Huzel, 'Malthus, the poor law, and population in early nineteenth-century England', *EcHR*² 22 (1969), 430–51.

[365] Brian Abel-Smith, *The Hospitals, 1800 – 1948: a study in social administration in England and Wales*. L: Heinemann: 1964. Pp. xiii, 574.

[366] Asa Briggs, 'The welfare state in historical perspective', *Archives Européennes de Sociologie*, 2 (1961), 221–58.

[367] L. C. T. Rolt, *George and Robert Stephenson: the railway revolution*. L: Longmans: 1960. Pp. xix, 356. – Idem, *Isambard Kingdom Brunel. Ibid.*: 1957. Pp. xv, 345.

[368] Asa Briggs, *Social Thought and Social Action: a study of the work of Seebohm Rowntree, 1871 – 1954*. L: Longmans: 1961. Pp. x, 371. – W. H. G. Armytage, *A. J. Mundella, 1825 – 1897: the liberal background to the labour movement*. L: Benn: 1951. Pp. 386.

the history of given firms. In Lancashire, cotton manufacture went modern;[869] in Yorkshire, linen and wool moved far more slowly.[870] In these last industries are found the worst sufferers from technological unemployment.[871] The age of great transformations in iron and steel is comprehensively covered.[872] South Wales signifies coal and iron.[873] Musson looks at the early days of the chemical industry, at this time backward by comparison with other countries.[874] The building industry remains much less explored than its importance deserves; however, there is a start to record.[875] The notorious decline in primacy which hit Britain towards the end of the century is too often explained on the grounds that the 'spirit of enterprise' had fled the island. Aldcroft corrects the legend and discerns a situation which, though difficult, was hardly serious.[876] Musson casts doubts on the established concept of a 'great depression' in the nineties; he argues instead that there was a well justified shift from older forms of enterprise to

---

[869] Arthur J. Taylor, 'Concentration and specialisation in the Lancashire cotton industry, 1825 – 1850', *EcHR*² 1 (198–9), 114–122. – Arthur W. Silver, *Manchester Men and Indian Cotton, 1847 – 1872.* Manchester UP: 1966. Pp. xi, 349.

[870] W. G. Rimmer, *Marshall's of Leeds, Flaxspinners, 1788 – 1886.* CUP: 1960. Pp. xiii, 342. Rev: *EHR* 78, 801ff.; *EcHR*² 14, 153f. – E. M. Sigworth, *Black Dyke Mills: a history.* Liverpool UP: 1958. Pp. xvii, 385. Rev: *EHR* 75, 367f.

[871] Duncan Bythell, *The Handloom Weavers.* CUP: 1969. Pp. xiv, 302. Rev: *EcHR*² 22, 567ff.

[872] Alan Birch, *The Economic History of the British Iron and Steel Industry, 1784 – 1879.* L: Cass: 1967. Pp. xv, 398. Rev: *EHR* 84, 862; *EcHR*² 21, 404f.

[873] J. H. Morris and L. J. Williams, *The South Wales Coal Industry, 1841 – 1875.* Cardiff: U of Wales P: 1958. Pp. xiv, 289. – John P. Addis, *The Crawshay Dynasty. Ibid.* 1957. Pp. xiv. 184. Rev: *EHR* 74, 507ff.

[874] A. E. Musson, *Enterprise in Soap and Chemicals: John Crossfield & Sons Ltd., 1815 – 1965.* Manchester UP: 1965. Pp. xi, 384. Rev: *EHR* 82, 861f.; *EcHR*² 21, 178f.

[875] S. B. Saul, 'Building in England, 1890 – 1914', *EcHR*² 15 (1962–3), 119–37.

[876] D. H. Aldcroft, 'The entrepreneurs and the British economy', *EcHR*² 17 (1964–5), 113–34.

new.[877] Harrison tells the undoubted success story of the English bicycle, unexpected victor over foreign competitors with an earlier start.[878] A more obscure and controversial point is raised by Trebilcock in what one hopes may be the beginning of extensive studies: the question of the industrial role of the armaments industry.[879] Problems of high finance and investment are tackled in a general sketch of the central control of the monetary system since 1873;[880] in studies of banking activities in London, the country and overseas;[881] and in a collection of papers on the use of financial resources which corrects some well entrenched errors.[882]

Trade is not forgotten. Imlah takes on various aspects of the earlier part of the period, and Saul does much the same for the later; both have a good deal to say about intercourse with the empire.[883] Redford has completed his work on Manchester's world-wide trade.[884] One of the most important

[877] A. E. Musson, 'The great depression in Britain, 1873 – 1896, a reappraisal', *Journal of Econ. Hist.* 19 (1959), 199–228; 'British industrial growth during the "great depression": some comments', *EcHR*[2] 15 (1962 – 3), 529–33.

[878] A. E. Harrison, 'The competitiveness of the British cycle industry, 1890 – 1914', *EcHR*[2] 22 (1969), 287–303.

[879] Clive Trebilcock, ' "Spin-off" in British economic history: armaments and industry, 1760 – 1914', *EcHR*[2] 22 (1969), 474–90.

[880] Richard S. Sayers, *Central Banking after Bagehot.* O: Clarendon: 1957. Pp. 149.

[881] Richard S. Sayers, *Gilletts: in the London money market, 1867 – 1967.* O: Clarendon: 1968. Pp. x, 204 – Audrey M. Taylor, *Gilletts: banking at Banbury and Oxford. A story in local economic history.* O: Clarendon: 1964. Pp. xiii, 247 – Ralph W. Hiddy, *The House of Baring in American Trade and Finance, 1763 – 1861.* C (Mass.): Harvard UP: 1949. Pp. xxv, 631.

[882] A. K. Cairncross, *Home and Foreign Investment, 1870 – 1913.* CUP: 1953. Pp. xvi, 251. Rev: *EHR* 69, 503f.; *EcHR*[2] 8, 251ff.

[883] Albert H. Imlah, *Economic Elements in the Pax Britannica.* C (Mass.): Harvard UP: 1958. Pp. 224. Rev: *EHR* 75, 701ff. – S. B. Saul, *Studies in Overseas Trade, 1870 – 1914.* Liverpool UP: 1960. Pp. ix, 246. Rev: *EHR* 78, 142ff. – Idem, 'Britain and world trade, 1870 – 1914', *EcHR*[2] 7 (1954 – 5), 49–66.

[884] A. Redford, *Manchester Merchants and Foreign Trade*, vol. 2: 1850 – 1939. Manchester UP: 1956. Pp. xxii, 307. Rev: *EHR* 72, 341f.

of the new markets was China, and the archives of a pioneering firm (Jardine Mathieson) have made possible a thorough description of those beginnings.[885] The story of another business similarly engaged continues the story.[886] Several useful books have been written about the splendidly active shipping concerns of Victorian England.[887] The indefatigable Briggs contributes the model history of a large department store.[888] Another type of multiple shop – food-retailing chains – is studied by Mathias.[889] These are among the signs that the end of the individual enterprise was drawing close; Payne opens a very necessary assault on the problem of mergers and giant companies.[890]

Apart from the books on trade unionism, which have already been mentioned,[891] little has been written about the history of labour, though attention may in general be drawn to a specialist periodical, *The British Journal of Labour History*. Hobsbawm's interesting collection of articles touches in the main on the least known aspects of the working classes.[892] Pollard provides a chronicle of the workers employed in a town equipped with mixed industries; he covers the years

[885] Michael Greenberg, *British Trade and the Opening of China, 1800 – 1842*. CUP: 1951. Pp. xii. 238. Rev: *EcHR²* 5, 140ff.

[886] Sheila Marriner, *The Rathbones of Liverpool, 1845 – 1873*. Liverpool UP: 1961. Pp. xiii, 246. Rev: *EHR* 78, 142ff.

[887] Marischal Murray, *Union Castle Chronicle, 1853 – 1953*. L: Longmans: 1953. Pp. xvii, 392. Rev: *EHR* 69, 172f. – Francis E. Hyde and J. R. Harris, *Blue Funnel: a history of Alfred Holt and Company of Liverpool from 1865 to 1914*. Liverpool UP: 1956. Pp. xvii, 201. Rev: *EHR* 72, 764f. – Francis E. Hyde, *Shipping Enterprise and Management, 1830 – 1939: Harrison's of Liverpool*. Liverpool UP: 1967. Pp. xx, 208. Rev: *EcHR²* 20, 561f.; *Hist* 53, 455ff.

[888] Asa Briggs, *Friends of the People: the centenary history of Lewis's*. L: Batsford: 1956. Pp. 242.

[889] Peter Mathias, *Retailing Revolution*. L: Longmans: 1967. Pp. xix, 425. Rev: *EHR* 83, 869f.; *EcHR²* 20, 410f.

[890] P. L. Payne, 'The emergence of the large-scale company in Great Britain, 1870 – 1914', *EcHR²* 20 (1967), 519–42.

[891] See nn. 737–41.

[892] Eric J. Hobsbawm, *Labouring Men: studies in the history of labour*. L: Weidenfeld: 1964. Pp. viii, 401. Rev: *EcHR²* 20, 178ff.

1850 – 1939.[893] Gartner tackles Jewish immigration from the east, a development which had marked effects upon the clothing industry in London and Manchester.[894] A suitably sentimental study is devoted to the lower orders of rural England.[895]

(H) THE CHURCH

It is only in recent years that historians have fully grasped the central importance of religious and ecclesiastical issues in the age of Victoria. Thus Kitson Clark and Burn, for instance, are instinctively conscious of the fact in ways which differ greatly from the attitudes of earlier writers (nn. 633–4). Best's book also, of course, covers this period (n. 565). A rather too admiring book on the Victorian Church traces the growth of an active 'social gospel' through the problems of the clergy, the establishment and the intellectual tenets.[896] Chadwick's monumental history, intent to do justice to all forms of Christianity, covers a lot of ground but not, perhaps, too much depth.[897] Brown describes the Church's reinvigoration by the energies and the deadly seriousness of the evangelicals;[898] Newsome shows something about the later collapse of this movement.[899] However revived the Church might be, it clearly could not resume its old relationship to a state that had become fully secularized, a fact which resulted in problems not

---

[893] Sidney Pollard, *A History of Labour in Sheffield*. Liverpool UP: 1959. Pp. xix, 372. Rev: *EHR* 76, 374f.; *EcHR*² 13, 127f.

[894] Lloyd P. Gartner, *The Jewish Immigrant in England, 1870 – 1914*. L: Allen & Unwin: 1960. Pp. 320.

[895] E. W. Martin, *The Secret People: English village life after 1750*. L: Phoenix House: 1954. Pp. 319.

[896] Desmond Bowen, *The Idea of the Victorian Church: a study of the Church of England, 1833 – 1889*. Montreal: McGill UP: 1968. Pp. xiii, 421. Rev: *EHR* 85, 136f.; *HJ* 12, 718ff.

[897] Owen Chadwick, *The Victorian Church*, 2 vols. L: Black, 1966, 1970. Pp. x, 606; viii, 510. Rev: *EHR* 83, 133ff.

[898] Ford K. Brown, *Fathers of the Victorians: the age of Wilberforce*. CUP: 1961. Pp. 596. Rev: *EHR* 78, 741ff.

[899] David Newsome, *The Parting of Friends: a study of the Wilberforces and Henry Manning*. L: Murray: 1966. Pp. xiii, 486. Rev: *EHR* 83, 415f.; *HJ* 12, 707ff.

altogether solved even today. This first became apparent in
the years after the enactment of Catholic emancipation had
demonstrated the state's decision to enforce total formal toler-
ance, as a study of the early days of the ecclesiastical commissioners makes plain.[900] Questions of patronage often disturbed the relations between the queen and her ministers.[901]
Much less certain is the degree to which the revived Church
penetrated the whole nation: Inglis documents both the efforts
of the clergy to bring the gospel to the ghastly industrialized
towns, and the very limited success they enjoyed.[902] Best
finds popular beliefs hostile to the elevated formalism favoured
by some of the most zealous clerics.[903] Some historians would
actually consider that the masses were, at the height of
Victorian piety, essentially alienated from the Church. Later
in the century, their betters began to follow them,[904] and the
declining authority of the Church was firmly underlined when
those parts of the realm which could not be considered even
technically anglican refused any longer to support its maintenance.[905]

Halévy believed, without offering much proof, that the
nonconformists harvested better, and this may be so; but the
only substantial work on the dissenting Churches concentrates
on politics and on contributions to the solution of social problems.[906] To Machin the activities of these groups seem less

---

[900] Olive J. Brose, *Church and Parliament: the reshaping of the Church of England, 1828 – 1860.* Stanford UP: 1959. Pp. vii, 239. *See also* remarks in Gash, n. 643.

[901] D. W. R. Bahlman, 'The queen, Mr Gladstone, and Church patronage', *VS* 3 (1959 – 60), 349–80.

[902] K. S. Inglis, *Churches and the Working Classes in Victorian England.* L: Routledge: 1963. Pp. viii, 350. Rev: *EHR* 80, 427.; *EcHR*² 17, 169ff.

[903] Geoffrey F. A. Best, 'Popular protestantism in Victorian Britain', *Kitson Clark Ft* (n. 137), 115–42.

[904] P. T. Marsh, *The Victorian Church in Decline: Archbishop Tait and the Church of England 1868 – 1882.* L: Routledge: 1969. Pp. x, 344. Rev: *HJ* 12, 718ff.

[905] P. M. H. Bell, *Disestablishment in Ireland and Wales.* L: SPCK: 1969.

[906] Raymond G. Cowherd, *The Politics of English Dissent: the religious aspects of liberal and humanitarian reform movements from 1815 to 1848.* New York UP: 1956. Pp. 242. Rev: *EHR* 73, 168f.

spontaneous.[907] The things that seemed important to some members of the clergy themselves may be learned from Chadwick's amusing sketch of a rural parish.[908] Even on the larger scene one hears little enough of the masses. A weighty and powerful prelate like Philpotts of Exeter, conservative to his bones, in the end found nothing better to do with his time than to inflict a very anachronistic prosecution for heresy on one of his clergy.[909] The anglo-catholic schism, which often deteriorated into petty squabbles over incense and vestments, evoked at least from R. W. Church an intellectually more positive reaction.[910] The facts of an industrialized society did not remain hidden from everyone, and the 'Christian socialists', among whom F. D. Maurice deserves particular mention, grew so active that at present they are a favourite subject for aspiring doctoral candidates.[911] They have, however, also produced rather more developed work from Vidler, who elegantly reflects on the group,[912] and from Jones who gets away from the leaders to demonstrate the multifariousness and muddleheadedness of this mixture of visionary religion and practical concern.[913] The newly revived roman catholicism of England, too, knew more conflict than unity. A relentless champion of authority like Cardinal Manning[914] found himself

---

[907] G. I. T. Machin, 'The Maynooth grant, the dissenters, and disestablishment, 1845 – 1847', *EHR* 82 (1967), 61–85.

[908] Owen Chadwick, *Victorian Miniature*. L: Hodder & Stoughton: 1960. Pp. 189. Rev: *EHR* 77, 399f.

[909] J. C. S. Nias, *Gorham and the Bishop of Exeter*. L: SPCK: 1951. Pp. 195. – G. C. B. Davies, *Henry Philpotts, Bishop of Exeter, 1778 – 1869*. L: SPCK: 1954. Pp. 415. Rev: *EHR* 71, 336f.

[910] Basil A. Smith, *Dean Church: the anglican response to Newman*. L: OUP: 1958. Pp. xiii, 334. Rev: *EHR* 74, 545f.

[911] E.g. Olive J. Brose, 'F. D. Maurice and the Victorian crisis of belief', *VS* 3 (1959 – 60), 227–48. – Peter R. Allen, 'F. D. Maurice and J. M. Ludlow: a reassessment of the leaders of christian socialism', *VS* 11 (1967 – 8), 461–82.

[912] Alec Vidler, *F. D. Maurice and Company: nineteenth century studies*. L: Students' Christian Movement: 1966. Pp. 287. Rev: *VS* 11, 107f.

[913] Peter d'A. Jones, *The Christian Socialist Revival, 1877 – 1914*. Princeton UP: 1968. Pp. xiii, 504. Rev: *EHR* 85, 196f.; *Hist* 54, 308f.

[914] V. A. McClelland, *Cardinal Manning: his public life and influence*. L: OUP: 1962. Pp. xii, 256. Rev: *EHR* 79, 880f.

opposed by a liberal movement which had the firm support
of Lord Acton.[915] Nor was the fear – unreasoning and passionate – of Rome's intentions yet at an end.[916] One man whom
his study of the history of ideas rendered incapable of continuing in the faith but not of continuing in a post ostensibly
requiring Christian beliefs was Benjamin Jowett, that odd
creature and improbably influential Oxford don.[917]

[915] Joseph L. Altholz, *The Liberal Catholic Movement in England: the
'Rambler' and its contributors, 1848 – 1864*. L: Burns & Oates: 1962.
Pp. x, 251. Rev: *AHR*, 70, 126f.

[916] Edward R. Norman, *Anticatholicism in Victorian England*. L:
Allen & Unwin: 1968. Pp. 240. Rev: *EHR* 85, 196; *VS* 12, 452ff.

[917] Geoffrey Faber, *Jowett: a portrait with background*. L: Faber: 1957.
Pp. 456.

IX

The Twentieth Century (1914 – 1945)

(A) GENERAL

Although, strictly, this period has by now escaped the confines of 'contemporary history', it still labours under the well-known difficulties attending upon that genre, more especially the mixture of enormous mountains of materials on the one hand and inaccessible sources of information on the other. This has not, of course, prevented a perfect flood of writings, and the two wars in particular have breached every dam. Now that the archives are being opened more rapidly, and private papers are being more readily offered, one may expect an ever swelling torrent. All of this makes anything resembling complete coverage even more impossible than it was in the earlier sections, the only consolation being that a great deal of the stuff that pours forth is clearly not going to stand the test of time. I have therefore confined myself essentially to the works of professional historians and especially to those which seem, at least, to avoid the air of evanescence and *parti pris*.

Surprisingly enough, we have no fewer than four highly respectable general surveys, the most remarkable being Taylor's whose book (despite its serious failure to treat of matters economic and scientific, and its occasional lack of balance) scores by wit, penetration and sense.[918] As a work of art it is positively assisted by the author's prejudices; his refusal to take public figures at their own inflated value, and his preferred search for low motives, do nothing but good. The excellent bibliography may be cited to excuse, in part, the brevity of this present section. Taylor's excellence

---

[918] Alan J. P. Taylor, *English History, 1914 – 1945.* O: Clarendon: 1965. Pp. xxvii, 709. Rev: *EHR* 82, 807ff.; *Hist* 53, 266f.

should not, however, make one overlook the other accounts: Mowat's more balanced approach, with its skilful treatment of the crucial socio-economic problems,[919] Medlicott's more conventional but careful and very useful book which succeeds in applying an historical stance to the author's own life-time,[920] and Havighurst's plain, thorough, sympathetic handling of this complex period which shows that such books are often best written from outside the country discussed.[921]

(B) POLITICAL HISTORY

Beaverbrook, press baron and politician, has written an unusual set of books, recording his own time and involvement but applying the mind of a natural, though untrained, historian.[922] The crisis of 1916 he described in an earlier work; now he adds the inner history of the coalition down to 1922; and the books are the more valuable because they rest on unpublished materials in the author's possession of which some are produced. Koss offers further information on the fall of Asquith who is (correctly) made to appear pretty much the author of his own fate.[923] The Asquithian view, which makes Lloyd George solely responsible for the decay of the liberal party, can no longer be maintained; Wilson seeks the cause less in personalities than in social circumstances.[924] He also argues that, contrary to such views as McEwen's, the election of 1918 did not make Lloyd George into a prisoner of the

---

[919] Charles L. Mowat, *Britain between the Wars, 1918 – 1940*. L: Methuen: 1955. Pp. ix, 694. Rev: *EcHR*² 9, 152ff.

[920] W. N. Medlicott, *Contemporary England, 1914 – 1964*. L: Longmans: 1967. Pp. 614. Rev: *EHR* 84, 636f.

[921] Alfred F. Havighurst, *Twentieth Century Britain*, 2nd ed. New York: Harper & Row: 1966. Pp. xiv, 572.

[922] Lord Beaverbrook, *Men and Power, 1917 – 1918*. L: Hutchinson: 1956. Pp. 448. – Idem, *Decline and fall of Lloyd George*. L: Collins: 1963. Pp. 320.

[923] Stephen E. Koss, 'The destruction of Britain's last liberal government', *JMH* 40 (1968), 257–77.

[924] Trevor Wilson, *The Downfall of the Liberal Party, 1914 – 1935*. L: Collins: 1966. Pp. 416. Rev: *Hist* 53, 279f.

tories.[925] Another party in decline, the old I.L.P., is studied by Marwick at the time of the crisis which the growth of communism inflicted on it.[926] The communist party itself is described in all its futility by MacFarlane; the book is awfully dry, but the uproar among the old guard of the party proves it to be essentially truthful.[927] More general and reflective is Pelling's study of the same theme.[928] Bromhead discusses the fate of the house of lords during its declining phase – after the abolition of its veto and before the curious rise of the new life senators.[929] Several episodes have been studied with care. Johnson gives a lot of space to the ultimately futile plans worked out in the first war for the social reconstruction that never came.[930] Lyman analyses the ineffectual first labour government, and Symonds a bit superficially one of the more striking consequences of its collapse.[931] Much has been written about the fatal return to the gold standard in Churchill's chancellorship, but all of it is superseded by Moggeridge's analysis which shows that the fault lay with the very well-intentioned ignorance of the government's advisers.[932] The second labour government and the crisis that swallowed it

[925] J. M. McEwen, 'The coupon election of 1918 and unionist members of parliament', *JMH* 34 (1962), 294–306. – Trevor Wilson, 'The coupon and the British general election of 1918', *ibid.* 36 (1964), 24–42.

[926] A. J. B. Marwick, 'The independent labour party in the nineteen twenties', *BIHR* 35 (1962), 62–74.

[927] L. J. MacFarlane, *The British Communist Party: its origin and development until 1929*. L: MacGibbon & Kee: 1966. Pp. 338. Rev: *Hist* 52, 107f.

[928] Henry Pelling, *The British Communist Party: a historical profile*. L: Black: 1958. Pp. viii, 204. Rev: *EHR* 75, 191f.

[929] P. A. Bromhead, *The House of Lords and Contemporary Politics, 1911 – 1957*. L: Routledge: 1958. Pp. xiii, 283.

[930] [Paul B. Johnson, *Land Fit for Heroes: the planning of British reconstruction, 1916 – 1919*. Chicago: U of Chicago P: 1968. Pp. viii, 540. Rev: *AHR* 75, 126f.]

[931] Richard W. Lyman, *The First Labour Government, 1924*. L: Chapman & Hall: [1957]. Pp. x, 302. – Julian Symonds, *The General Strike*. L: Cresset: 1957. Pp. xi, 259.

[932] Donald E. Moggeridge, *The Return to Gold in 1925*. CUP: 1969. Pp. 119.

have been twice reviewed: Bassett endeavours to rehabilitate Ramsay MacDonald, while Skidelsky efficiently demolishes what was left of his repute and his party's.[933] The first volume of a highly authoritative study of naval policy has appeared.[934]

And once again it is necessary to pursue history through the products of the biographers. The monarchs have been served well. Nicolson has managed to be fair to George V while at the same time impressively unravelling the problems of monarchy in an age of democratization.[935] George VI's biography is too long and a good deal too 'official', but it is highly competent.[936] Edward VIII has taken care of himself.[937] Of the many lives of Lloyd George, not one can be called at all satisfactory; the best of a poor bunch is that by Tom Jones who relies on personal memories rather than archival studies.[938] His autobiographical writings, published both in his life-time and after his death, need very critical treatment (and have not yet received it); however, they do throw a good deal of light behind the scenes of a stage on which dwarfs behaved like giants.[939] As for Churchill, we have had essays galore, but nothing written so far has achieved useful distance, employed the instruments of historical science, or superseded his own writings. Still, one may mention the

---

[933] R. Bassett, *Nineteen Thirty-One: political crisis*. L: Macmillan: 1958. Pp. xvi, 464. Rev: *EHR* 74, 377f. – Robert Skidelsky, *Politicians and the Slump: the labour government of 1929 – 1931*. L: Macmillan: 1967. Pp. xiv, 431. Rev: *EHR* 84, 215f.

[934] Stephen W. Roskill, *Naval Policy between the Wars*, vol. 1: the period of Anglo-American antagonism, 1919 – 1929. L: Collins: 1968. Pp. 639.

[935] Harold Nicholson, *King George the Fifth*. L: Constable: 1952. Pp. xxiii, 520.

[936] John W. Wheeler-Bennett, *King George VI: his life and reign*. L: Macmillan: 1958. Pp. xiv, 891. Rev: *EHR* 75, 374ff.

[937] The Duke of Windsor, *A King's Story*. L: Cassell: 1951. Pp. xvi, 440. – *See also* Brian Inglis, *Abdication*. L: Hodder & Stoughton: 1966. Pp. xiv, 433.

[938] Tom Jones, *Lloyd George*. L: OUP: 1951. Pp. xii, 330.

[939] Tom Jones, *A Diary with Letters, 1930 – 1950*. L: OUP: 1954. Pp. xlv, 582. – Idem, *Whitehall Diary*, 2 vols., ed. Keith Middlemas. L: OUP: 1969. Pp. xxiv, 358; xiii, 309.

contribution of a good friend,[940] the self-advertisement of a good doctor,[941] and the laboured devotion of a good son, interrupted by death but to be carried on by less filial hands.[942] Baldwin, too, had a loyal son who tried to defend his father against his many detractors;[943] a co-operative work, no less determined to prove the man's excellence, scores largely by its positively indecent length in which the facts of history, not always correctly stated, quite overwhelm any impression one might hope to get.[944] Neville Chamberlain enjoyed the services of a professional historian, Lord Halifax those of a professional biographer; both books are solid enough, no more.[945] The politicians of the other side have done rather worse, partly because some still survive. Among the dead, Hugh Dalton enshrined himself, in a book redolent of the man and highly revealing of the strange philosophy of an upper-class socialism which mistook emotion for rationality.[946] A man greatly beloved by all who knew him, but who to the historian must seem particularly misguided, was George Lansbury.[947] One's feelings about these emotional non-thinkers, however, are greatly altered by even one glimpse of the supposedly scientific reasoners: thus Sir Stafford Cripps has inspired two books, the first (written while he was in office) full of starry-eyed adulation

---

[940] Violet Bonham Carter, *Winston Churchill as I Knew Him*. L: Eyre & Spottiswoode: 1965. Pp. 491.

[941] Lord Moran, *Winston Churchill: the struggle for survival*. L: Constable: 1966. Pp. ix, 829.

[942] Randolph S. Churchill, *Winston Churchill*, vols. 1 (youth, 1874 – 1900) and 2 (young statesman). L: Heinemann: 1966, 1967. Pp. xxxvi, 608; 775. Rev: *HJ* 12, 164ff. Also three volumes of original materials.

[943] A. W. Baldwin, *My Father: the true story*. L: Allen & Unwin: 1955. Pp. 360.

[944] Keith Middlemas and John Barnes, *Baldwin: a biography*. L: Weidenfeld: 1969. Pp. xvii, 1149.

[945] Keith Feiling, *The Life of Neville Chamberlain*. L: Macmillan: 1946. Pp. ix, 472. – Lord Birkenhead, *Halifax*. L: Hamilton: 1965. Pp. xiii, 626.

[946] Hugh Dalton, *Memoirs*, 3 vols. L: Muller: 1953, 1957, 1962. Pp. xii, 330; xvi, 493; xiv, 453.

[947] Raymond Postgate, *The Life of George Lansbury*. L: Longmans: 1951. Pp. xiii, 332.

for the most improbable of objects, the second much more suitably critical but written without historical competence.[948] Much more important is Bullock's massive life of the massive Bevin; two volumes have appeared and there is still no end.[949] Equally incomplete is the life of Bevan by his friend and disciple Foot.[950] Butler was commissioned to write on Philip Kerr, that over-valued devotee of Milner and Lloyd George whose success as ambassador to the United States astonished all who knew him.[951] Smuts was as frequently a British statesman as he was a South African politician: he merits mention here, especially as Hancock's book is superior to most of the biographies written about these people.[952] A naval historian has done justice to Jellicoe, the one English admiral to be remembered solely for suffering a major defeat.[953] One must include a selection from the biographies of the many who, though not politicians themselves, tried to play a political part from the side-lines. Northcliffe, in many ways a little man suffering from delusions of grandeur, is very suitably commemorated in a book which is much too long and heavily overestimates him.[954] Harrod does a friend's service to John Maynard Keynes, and very nicely too;[955] he is rather less kind to Churchill's tame scientist, Lindemann, who apparently did not improve on personal acquaintance (and Harrod was per-

---

[948] Eric Estorick, *Stafford Cripps*. L: Heinemann: 1949. Pp. viii, 378. – Colin A. Coote, *The Life of Richard Stafford Cripps*. L: Hodder & Stoughton: 1957. Pp. 415. Rev: *EHR* 73, 740.

[949] Alan Bullock, *The Life and Times of Ernest Bevin*, 2 vols. (so far). L: Heinemann: 1960, 1967. Pp. xiii, 672; xii, 407.

[950] Michael Foot, *Aneurin Bevan*, vol. 1: 1897 – 1945. L: MacGibbon & Kee: 1962. Pp. 536.

[951] J. R. M. Butler, *Lord Lothian, 1882 – 1940*. L: Macmillan: 1960. Pp. xiii, 385.

[952] W. Keith Hancock, *Smuts*, 2 vols. CUP: 1962, 1968. Pp. viii, 619; xiii, 590. Rev: *EHR* 84, 819f.; *HJ* 11, 565ff.

[953] A. Temple Patterson, *Jellicoe: a biography*. L: Macmillan: 1969. Pp. 277. Rev: *Hist* 55, 151f.

[954] Reginald Pound and Geoffrey Harmsworth, *Northcliffe*. L: Cassell: 1959. Pp. xvi, 933.

[955] Roy F. Harrod, *The Life of John Maynard Keynes*. L: Macmillan: 1963. Pp. xvi, 674. Rev: *AHR* 57, 136ff.

sonally acquainted).[956] Thereby provoked, Birkenhead wrote about this fairly unsympathetic climber as though he had really mattered.[957]

(c) GOVERNMENT

Recent and contemporary government structure is being constantly studied – by sociologists, political scientists, and the practitioners themselves. The real value of much of this work is hard to estimate, and I confess to a strong feeling that it hardly belongs in a review of historical studies. I may just draw attention to the many interesting, though sometimes puzzling, articles that appear in the journal *Public Administration*. That same breeding ground has produced a collection which pursues the theme from 1914 into the later fifties.[958] Of particular institutions, the cabinet has aroused the main interest, though it is a subject for which the materials are exceptionally hard to come by. Though Mackintosh's history starts in 1660 (why?), its main concern is with the twentieth century.[959] A book translated from the Dutch deals rather too schematically with reform proposals, most of which came to nothing.[960] Obviously, the two great wars produced crises in this central organization of government: indeed, the first was responsible for the first serious attempt to provide it with an organization whose architect has left behind an excessively discreet description.[961] Earlier gropings and parallel problems

[956] Roy F. Harrod, *The Prof: a personal memoir of Lord Cherwell.* L: Macmillan: 1959. Pp. xv, 282.

[957] Lord Birkenhead, *The Prof in Two Worlds: the official life of Professor F. A. Lindemann, Viscount Cherwell.* L: Collins: 1961. Pp. 383.

[958] D. N. Chester and F. M. G. Willson, eds., *The Organization of British Central Government, 1914 – 1956.* L: Allen & Unwin: 1957. Pp. 457.

[959] John P. Mackintosh, *The British Cabinet.* L: Stevens: 1962. Pp. xi, 546.

[960] Hans Daalder, *Cabinet Reform in Britain, 1914 – 1963.* Stanford UP: 1964. Pp. x, 381. Rev: *EHR* 81, 211.

[961] Lord Hankey, *The Supreme Command, 1914 – 1918,* 2 vols. L: Allen & Unwin: 1961. Pp. xv, 905. Rev: *EHR* 78, 347ff. – Idem, *The Supreme Command at the Paris Peace Conference, 1919. Ibid.*: 1963. Pp. 209.

are reviewed in a book which suffers from the methods of American political science and has too little understanding of the actual realities.[962] Ehrman's comparative study of practice in the two wars, on the other hand, is illuminating and could be wished longer.[963] There have been several studies of the civil service, at present a hot subject. Gladden, writing from inside, thinks it necessary to defend every stage of the service's history over the last hundred years.[964] Fry, on the other hand, espouses the popular charge of the day that 'generalists' are nothing but amateurs; a solidly based historical study (which also has useful things to say about recruitment), his book is burdened with somewhat naïve proposals for reform.[965] Less controversially, Kensall applies methods learned from the sociologists to the higher reaches of the service, at one time the chief pride of the nation and now one of its common aunt sallies.[966] Despite various ephemeral analyses of parties, their structure and power problems, the only book to establish itself – possibly a little too quickly – is still McKenzie's.[967] Using his own experience, which does not quite make up for the absence of a scholar's training, Herbert Morrison, one of labour's Big Three in 1945 – 51, attempts to make plain the necessary relations between any sort of government and the parliamentary party supporting it.[968]

---

[962] Franklyn A. Johnson, *Defence by Committee: the British committee of imperial defence, 1885 – 1959.* L: OUP: 1960. Pp. ix, 416. Rev: *EHR* 77, 580f.

[963] John P. W. Ehrman, *Cabinet Government and War.* CUP: 1958. Pp. xi, 138. Rev: *EHR* 77, 339ff.

[964] E. N. Gladden, *Civil Services in the United Kingdom, 1855 – 1970.* L: Cass: 1967. Pp. xxv, 289.

[965] Geoffrey K. Fry, *Statesmen in Disguise: the changing role of the administrative class of the British Home Civil Service, 1853 – 1966.* L: Macmillan: 1969. Pp. 479.

[966] R. K. Kelsall, *Higher Civil Servants in Britain from 1870 to the Present Day.* L: Routledge: 1955. Pp. xvi, 233.

[967] Robert T. McKenzie, *British Political Parties.* L: Heinemann: 1963 (2nd ed.). Pp. xv, 694.

[968] Herbert Morrison, *Government and Parliament: a survey from inside.* L: OUP: 1954. Pp. xiii, 363.

(D) FOREIGN AFFAIRS

(Well treated in n. 918). The one general diplomatic history attempted tries to juxtapose the realities and the myths of British world power between the wars.[969] Less ambitious, and less useful, is a survey originally intended for the sixth forms in schools.[970] Winkler investigates the various proposals for an international organization, born out of the horror of the first world war;[971] a leading propagandist for the idea receives personal attention.[972] A discursive but remarkable history of British relations with revolutionary Russia has achieved two out of a probable three volumes and covered two and a half years out of four.[973] A pointless occasion in 1919 on which war-weary Britain nearly went to war again is described by Walder in reliance on unpublished materials.[974] Graubard, looking into the special case of the attitude of British labour to the socialist revolutionaries, discovers some tepid sympathies and essentially very cool relations.[975] The labour party, more insular than either of the other two, faced a real problem in coming to terms with the existence of foreign affairs and diplomacy: Winkler sketches the growth of a foreign policy particular to this party, while Miller demonstrates the development of that mystique (composed of pacifist aspirations and deep suspicion of collusion among Europe's upper classes) which labour adopted in the twenties and imposed on all 'advanced' thinking in the thirties – the belief that peace was

---

[969] F. S. Northedge, *The Troubled Giant: Britain among the great powers, 1916 – 1939*. L: Bell: 1966. Pp. xi, 652. Rev: *EHR* 83, 639ff.

[970] Philip A. Reynolds, *British Foreign Policy in the Inter-War Years*. L: Longmans: 1954. Pp. xi, 182.

[971] Henry R. Winkler, *The League of Nations Movement in Great Britain, 1914 – 1919*. New Brunswick N.J.: Rutgers UP: 1952. Pp. xiii, 288.

[972] Maja Bachofen, *Lord Robert Cecil und der Völkerbund*. Zürich: Europa Verlag: 1959. Pp. 138.

[973] Richard H. Ullman, *Intervention and the War: Anglo-Soviet relations, 1917 – 1921*, 2 vols. (so far). Princeton UP: 1961, 1968. Pp. xvi, 310; xix, 395. Rev: *Hist* 54, 326f.

[974] D. Walder, *The Chanak Affair*. L: Hutchinson: 1969. Pp. xv, 380.

[975] Stephen R. Graubard, *British Labour and the Russian Revolution, 1917 – 1924*. C (Mass.): Harvard UP: 1956. Pp. 305.

B H—L

154 *The Twentieth Century (1914 – 1945)*

prevented by capitalism, secret diplomacy, the armament trade and other morally wrong phenomena.[976] The crises of the Hitler era have produced plenty of books some of which deserve mention here. Gilbert's and Gott's somewhat one-sided and rather helter-skelter survey, which also betrays insufficient familiarity with the facts of European life, nevertheless has the virtues of passionate readability.[977] Bassett attempts to defend Britain's far eastern policy; at least it makes a change to have some nice things said about Sir John Simon, an obstinately undeserving recipient.[978] The Austrian *Anschluss* has been covered in a solid doctoral dissertation.[979] Munich remains an active issue. Of all those who have written about it, Wheeler-Bennett remains the most reliable chronicler; the preface to the second edition (1963) reviews the recent literature.[980] Curiously enough, the one attempt to treat the matter dispassionately, by an historian too young to recall it, suffers from being so detached as to get the flavours wrong.[981] For the most incredible actor in the whole business, the blind and conceited Henderson, Strauch does all that is required.[982]

[976] Henry R. Winkler, 'The emergence of a labour foreign policy in Great Britain, 1918 – 1929', *JMH* 28 (1956), 247–58. – Kenneth E. Miller, *Socialism and Foreign Policy: theory and practice to 1931*. The Hague: Nijhoff: 1967. Pp. viii, 301. Rev: *EHR* 84, 442f.

[977] Martin J. Gilbert and Richard Gott, *The Appeasers*. L: Weidenfeld: 1963. Pp. 380. Rev: *EHR* 80, 217f. – *See also* a partial recantation: Martin J. Gilbert, *The Roots of Appeasement*. *Ibid.* 1966. Pp. xvi, 254. Rev: *EHR* 83, 430f.; *HJ* 10, 481f.

[978] R. Bassett, *Democracy and Foreign Policy: the Sino-Japanese dispute 1931 – 1933*. L: Longmans: 1952. Pp. xxiii, 654.

[979] Mary Antonia Walker, *The Policy of England and France towards the 'Anschluss' of 1938*. Washington: Catholic U of America P: 1954. Pp. 224. The review in *Historische Zeitschrift*, 180, 110ff. interestingly documents the survival of a *grossdeutsch* attitude.

[980] John W. Wheeler-Bennett, *Munich: prologue to tragedy*. L: Macmillan: 1948. Pp. xv, 507. Rev: *EHR* 64, 382f.

[981] Keith Robbins, *Munich 1938*. L: Cassell: 1968. Pp. 398.

[982] Rudi Strauch, *Sir Nevile Henderson, britischer Botschafter in Berlin von 1937 bis 1939*. Bonn: Röhrscheid: 1959. Pp. 384.

(E) THE TWO WARS

Though interest in the first world war remains sufficiently alive to call forth numbers of popular, polemical and picture books, historians have not paid a great deal of attention to it. The one general survey, basically a straight military history of those four years, is rendered special and moving by the author's ability to infuse his own experience.[983] The most important piece of historical writing, however, is Marder's multi-volume treatment of the navy and the war at sea; of this magnificent work the projected four volumes have now appeared, but it looks as though another will be needed to complete the story.[984] Siney contributes a study of the other maritime method of warfare.[985] Guinn goes the round of the various theatres of war in order to bring out the close links between the fighting and domestic politics.[986] Moorehead does a fine job on the most controversial of all the campaigns.[987] This was probably the first of England's wars in which public opinion, itself severely under pressure, played an important part in affairs. Crosby usefully assembles the story of peace moves and of protests against continued war,[988] and Hanak demonstrates how strongly the will to fight was influenced by the anti-Austrian propaganda of Slav exiles.[989] Official

[983] E. Llewellyn Woodward, *Great Britain and the War of 1914 – 1918.* L: Methuen: 1967. Pp. xxxiii, 610. Rev: *Hist* 54, 121f.

[984] Arthur J. Marder, *From the Dreadnought to Scapa Flow: the royal navy in the Fisher era, 1909 – 1919,* 4 vols. (so far). L: OUP: 1961, 1965, 1966, 1969. Pp. xii, 459; xxvi, 467; xxiii, 307; xxiv, 364. Rev: *EHR* 78, 748f.; 82, 198f.; 83, 216f. – *See also* Richard Hough, *First Sea Lord: an authorised biography of Admiral Lord Fisher.* L: Allen & Unwin: 1969. Pp. 392.

[985] Marion C. Siney, *The Allied Blockade of Germany, 1914 – 1916.* Ann Arbor: U of Michigan P: 1957. Pp. x, 339. Rev: *EHR* 75, 752f.

[986] Paul Guinn, *British Strategy and Politics, 1914 – 1918.* O: Clarendon: 1965. Pp. xvi, 359. Rev: *EHR* 82, 361ff.

[987] Alan Moorehead, *Gallipoli.* L: Hamilton: 1956. Pp. 384.

[988] Gerda Richards Crosby, *Disarmament and Peace in British Politics, 1914 – 1919.* C (Mass.): Harvard UP: 1957. Pp. viii, 192.

[989] H. Hanak, *Great Britain and Austria-Hungary during the First World War: a study in the formation of public opinion.* L: OUP: 1962. Pp. vi, 312. Rev: *EHR* 80, 640f.

attitudes only are studied in Nelson's book on political war aims.[990] One of the more ominous features of the war years was the manner in which the whole nation had to be organized for the struggle; resistance slowed the process down a lot, but a great many traditions of liberty and individual rights, already under attack, now finally went down before the paternalistic state.[991] The surprisingly small amount of principled socialist opposition to the war is exaggerated by Bünger who concludes that it played a significant part in ensuring the survival of Russia's revolution.[992] He may be right.

There is a different story to tell of the second war – or there would be if there were room to do justice to the mass of publications. From Taylor's perverse attempt to prove that Hitler did not want war in 1939 but had it forced on him by Great Britain (a book which has caused raised eyebrows and raised voices on all sides),[993] to the last military memoirs, real or ghosted, the chain of books runs to infinity. What it may all amount to, and how far the historian will have to consider it, are questions which even the expert finds it hard to resolve and the present non-expert will be wise to avoid. We confine our report to a few exceptional books, to some non-English studies absent from the bibliographies, and to the amazing phalanx of the official history. Further guidance may be sought in Taylor's careful list (n. 918).

No matter what research may do to it, Churchill's personal history will continue to deserve pride of place.[994] Details and essentials will unquestionably be altered; the author's own role

---

[990] Harold I. Nelson, *Land and Power: British and allied policy on Germany's frontiers, 1916 – 1919*. L: Routledge: 1963. Pp. xiv, 402. Rev: *EHR* 80, 641f.

[991] S. J. Hurwitz, *State Intervention in Great Britain: a study of economic control and social response, 1914 – 1919*. New York: Columbia UP: 1949. Pp. x, 321.

[992] Siegfried Bünger, *Die sozialistische Antikriegsbewegung in Grossbritannien, 1914 – 1917*. Berlin: VEB Deutscher Verlag der Wissenschaften: 1967. Pp. 213.

[993] Alan J. P. Taylor, *The Origins of the Second World War*. L: Hamilton: 1961. Pp. 261. Rev: *EHR* 78, 205; *PP* 29, 67ff. and 30, 110ff.

[994] Winston S. Churchill, *The Second World War*, 6 vols. L: Cassell: 1948 – 54. Pp. xv, 640; xvii, 684; x, 818; ix, 917; x, 673; ix, 716.

will cease to appear quite so central or quite so effective; but a work which brings so much source material and faithfully mirrors the mind of one of the great personalities of the conflict (quite apart from its impact as a work of art, in which respect it does not stand very high in the Churchill canon) will continue to matter. So far, by the way, his volumes also remain the best complete account of the event, in English at least. By their side one may place the two volumes which Bryant fashioned out of Alanbrook's fairly self-satisfied diaries.[995] The material included (which often usefully corrects Churchill's account) is more important than the editor's contributions. The battle of Britain has been too frequently described, but one must draw attention to two German contributions about the plan of campaign and its decisive defeat.[996] An American work, which promises more than it performs, also rests on the German sources.[997] One of the domestic battles attending upon the event has recently been renewed in a book which seeks justice for the British commander whom Churchill (or somebody else?) sacked after victory was won.[998]

For the historian, however, everything pales before the serried ranks of the so-called Official History, the *History of the Second World War* commissioned by the government, organized by the cabinet, but controlled by independent professional historians and mainly written by professional historians who enjoyed the advantage of personal experience. It is perfectly plain that if there was pressure of any sort it was very small, and everything except really deep secrets was made accessible. The very fact that the volumes are often extremely critical of the war-time leadership inspires confidence.

---

[995] Arthur Bryant, *The Alanbrook Diaries*, 2 vols. L: Collins: 1957, 1959. Pp. 766; 576.

[996] Karl Klee, *Das Unternehmen 'Seelöwe': die geplante deutsche Landung in England, 1940*, 2 vols. Göttingen: Musterschmidt: 1958 – 9. Pp. 300; 457. – Theo Weber, *Die Luftschlacht um England*. Wiesbaden: Flugwelt Verlag: 1956. Pp. 205.

[997] Walter Ausel, *Hitler Confronts England*. Durham N.C.: Duke UP: 1960. Pp. xx, 348.

[998] [R. Wright, *Dowding and the Battle of Britain*. L: Macdonald: 1969.]

The manner of execution is as admirable as the speed of production. It can be asserted that no other country involved in the war displayed itself in public so freely, so completely, and so fast. One thing alone cannot attract unstinted praise: perhaps inescapably these volumes, produced with the help of government departments and research assistants, are not exactly a pleasure to read.

The enterprise comprises two series, both nearly complete, one military and one civil.[999] The military series is founded on six projected volumes (four have appeared) which deal with the general situation, planning and control.[1000] The western theatre of war, at the start and the end of hostilities, is covered in three volumes,[1001] the war in North Africa so far in four,[1002] the war in the Far East in five altogether.[1003] Lesser occasions are not forgotten: there are thorough works on the military defence of the home country and on the Norwegian fiasco.[1004] The four volumes on the aerial attack on Germany have attracted exceptional attention because of their very

---

[999] All published L: HMSO. J. R. M. (now Sir James) Butler is responsible for the military series, W. K. (now Sir Keith) Hancock for the civil.

[1000] J. R. M. Butler, *Grand Strategy*, vol. 2 (Sept. 1939 – June 1941). 1957. Pp. xix, 603. Rev: *EHR* 74, 509ff.; *HJ* 1, 92f. – J. M. A. Gwyer and J. R. M. Butler, *Grand Strategy*, vol. 3 (2 parts: June 1941 – August 1942). 1964. Pp. xv, 783. – John P. W. Ehrman, *Grand Strategy*, vols. 5 and 6 (Aug. 1943 – Aug. 1945). 1956. Pp. xvii, 634; xvi, 422.

[1001] L. F. Ellis, *The War in France and Flanders, 1939 – 1940*. 1953. Pp. xviii, 425. – Idem, *Victory in the West*, 2 vols. 1962, 1968. Pp. xix, 595; xviii, 455.

[1002] I. S. O. Playfair, *et al.*, *The Mediterranean and the Middle East*, 4 vols. (The early successes against Italy; the Germans come to the aid of their ally; British fortunes reach their lowest ebb; the destruction of the Axis forces in Africa.) 1954, 1956, 1960, 1966. Pp. 506; xi, 392; xvi, 482; xviii, 556. Rev: *EHR* 83, 809ff.

[1003] S. Woodburn, Kirby *et al.*, *The War against Japan*, 5 vols. 1957 – 1969. Pp. xxii, 568; xiv, 541; xix, 559; xxv, 568; xxiii, 599, Rev: *EHR* 74, 512ff.

[1004] Basil Collier, *The Defence of the United Kingdom*. 1957. Pp. xix, 557. – T. K. Derry, *The Campaign in Norway*. 1952. Pp. xvi, 289.

severe criticisms of the methods and strategies employed.[1005] The maritime war, in all the oceans, is also dealt with in four exceptionally authoritative volumes.[1006] So far we have only one volume about the secret war of the European resistance and the English organization supporting it, a theme thoroughly mashed in less official and less trustworthy books.[1007] Finally, three volumes discuss the military administration of occupied territories in Germany, Italy and the far east.[1008]

Three books need to be interposed here; they deal with the same sort of themes as the military series of the Official History and do the job as well or better, but were undertaken apart from that sponsored enterprise. Shepperd fills a gap in the official series where the Italian campaign still awaits treatment.[1009] Gowing tells the fascinating and vitally important story of the atom bomb, so far as the story is a British one.[1010] And Howard disposes of many somewhat self-satisfied accounts of the alleged farsighted policy pursued by Churchill and the British in the teeth of shortsighted American opposition, though he does not by any means in the process lengthen the American vision, either.[1011]

The achievement of the military series is impressive enough,

[1005] Charles K Webster and Noble Frankland, *The Strategic Air Offensive against Germany, 1939 – 1945*, 4 vols. 1961. Pp. viii, 522; ix, 322; ix, 332; xiii, 530. Rev: *EHR* 79, 132ff.

[1006] Stephen W. Roskill, *The War at Sea*, 4 vols. 1954, 1956, 1960, 1961. Pp. xxiii, 664; xvii, 523; xvi, 413; xvii, 502. Rev: *EHR* 77, 413f.; 78, 581f.

[1007] M. R. D. Foot, *S.O.E. in France*. 1966. Pp. xxvii, 550.

[1008] F. S. V. Donnison, *Civil Affairs and Military Government, North-West Europe 1945 – 1946*. 1961. Pp. xviii, 518 – C. R. S. Harris, *Allied Military Administration of Italy, 1943 – 1945*. 1957. Pp. xv, 479. – F. S. V. Donnison, *British Military Administration in the Far East, 1943 – 1946*. 1956. Pp. xviii, 483.

[1009] G. A. Shepperd, *The Italian Campaign, 1943 – 1945: a political and military re-assessment*. L: Barker: 1968. Pp. xiii, 450. Rev: *Hist* 54, 448f.

[1010] Margaret M. Gowing, *Britain and Atomic Energy, 1939 – 1945*. L: Macmillan: 1964. Pp. xvi, 464. Rev: *EHR* 81, 437f.

[1011] Michael E. Howard, *The Mediterranean Strategy in the Second World War*. L: Weidenfeld: 1968. Pp. xii, 83.

but at least a thorough treatment of that side of the war might have been expected. Even more impressive is the even longer civil series which touches on every point of the nation's life and reminds one how much more total British involvement in the war was than that of any other nation. Several books between them amount to a detailed and comprehensive survey of the economy.[1012] Two tackle the problems of defence against air attacks and blockades, problems which only in part were military.[1013] The volumes which treat of particular industrial topics divide into two sections: production for military purposes,[1014] and production for civilian uses.[1015] Financial problems yield two books.[1016] Finally, it is not to be forgotten that the waging of total war was made possible only by an energetic social policy which succeeded on the whole in dis-

---

[1012] W. Keith Hancock and Margaret M. Gowing, *British War Economy.* 1949. Pp. xvii, 583. – M. M. Postan, *British War Production.* 1952. Pp. xvi, 512. – H. M. D. Parker, *Manpower.* 1957. Pp. xviii, 535. Rev: *EHR* 74, 323ff. – E. L. Hargreaves and Margaret M. Gowing, *Civil Industry and Trade.* 1952. Pp. xii, 678. Rev: *EHR* 69, 131ff. – C. A. B. Behrens, *Merchant Shipping and the Demands of War.* 1955. Pp. xix, 494. Rev: *EHR* 72, 138ff.

[1013] Terence H. O'Brien, *Civil Defence.* 1955. Pp. xvii, 729. – W. N. Medlicott, *The Economic Blockade*, 2 vols. 1952, 1959. Pp. xiv, 732; xiv, 727. Rev: *EHR* 75, 703ff.

[1014] Joel Hurstfield, *The Control of Raw Materials.* 1953. Pp. xv, 530. Rev: *EHR* 69, 508f. – Peggy F. Inman, *Labour and the Munition Industries.* 1957. xv, 461. Rev: *EHR* 74, 323ff. – H. Duncan Hall, *North American Supply.* 1955. Pp. xvi, 559. – J. D. Scott and Richard Hughes, *The Administration of War Production.* 1955. Pp. xii, 544. – H. Duncan Hall and C. C. Wrigley, *Studies of Overseas Supply.* 1956. Pp. xi, 535. Rev: *EHR* 72, 549f. – William Hornby, *Factories and Plant.* 1958. Pp. xiii, 421. – M. M. Postan, Denys Hay, J. D. Scott, *Design and Development of Weapons.* 1964. Pp. xiv, 579.

[1015] W. H. B. Court, *Coal.* 1951. Pp. xii, 422. – R. J. Hammond, *Food*, 3 vols. 1951, 1956, 1962. Pp. xii, 436; xiii, 835; xiii, 836. – C. M. Kohan, *Works and Buildings.* 1952. Pp. xvi, 540. – Keith Murray, *Agriculture.* 1955. Pp. xii, 422. – C. I. Savage, *Inland Transport.* 1957. Pp. xvii, 678. Rev: *EHR* 72, 720ff.

[1016] Richard S. Sayers, *Financial Policy 1939 – 1945.* 1956. Pp. xv, 608. – W. Ashworth, *Contracts and Finance.* 1953. Pp. x, 309.

tributing hardships evenly and during the war already prepared the ground for the later social revolution.[1017]

(F) ECONOMIC HISTORY

Many of the books mentioned in the previous section deal also, of course, with this period (e.g. nn. 848, 850, 865, 880). There is little enough to add. Most of the problems have not yet, as it were, achieved historical status by ceasing to be immediately relevant, and they are therefore still subject to the sway of the economist. One such economist has collected his influential articles.[1018] Pollard has attempted a no doubt premature general survey.[1019] How tentative this sort of work must be is shown by Aldcroft's efforts to rescue Britain's economic growth from the charge of being pitifully inadequate, only at once to find his arguments and figures modified in a downward direction by Dowie.[1020] The unexpectedly swift economic recovery after the 1931 crisis – a question still under discussion – is once more considered by Richardson who comes to the conclusion that an earlier long-term development was merely interrupted by the crisis.[1021] (Some interruption.) There have been several good business histories. Wilson has raised the story of soap and margarine to a new level, and Coleman has done the same for that of silk and rayon.[1022] These are massive achievements of a new kind of

---

[1017] Richard M. Titmuss, *Problems of Social Policy*. 1950. Pp. xi, 596. – S. M. Ferguson and H. Fitzgerald, *Studies in the Social Services*. 1954. Pp. ix, 366ff. Rev: *EHR* 69, 690f.

[1018] A. C. Pigou, *Aspects of British Economic History, 1918 – 1925*. L: Macmillan: 1947. Pp. viii, 251.

[1019] Sidney Pollard, *The Development of the British Economy, 1914 – 1950*. L: Arnold: 1962. Pp. ix, 422. Rev: *EHR* 79, 637; *EcHR*² 15, 562f.

[1020] Derek H. Aldcroft, 'Economic Growth in Britain in the inter-war years: a reassessment', *EcHR*² 20 (1967), 311–26. – J. A. Dowie, 'Growth in the inter-war period: some more arithmetic', *ibid*. 21 (1968), 93–112.

[1021] H. W. Richardson, 'The basis of economic recovery in the nineteen-thirties: a review and a new interpretation', *EcHR*² 15 (1962 – 3), 344–63.

[1022] Charles H. Wilson, *A History of Unilever: a study of economic growth*

business history, employing the sophistications of modern economic history and modern institutional financing. A study of a single firm in the metal industry, covering 200 years but mainly concerned with very recent times, is rather more oldfashioned.[1023]

and social change, 2 vols. L: Cassell: 1954. Pp. xx, 335; 480. Rev: *EHR* 70, 300ff. – Donald C. Coleman, *Courtaulds: an economic and social history*, 2 vols. O: Clarendon: 1969. Pp. xxii, 283; xxi, 521.

[1023] Ronald E. Wilson, *Two Hundred Precious Metal Years: a history of the Sheffield Smelting Co. Ltd, 1760 – 1960*. L: Benn: 1960. Pp. xxii, 316.

X

Social History

A good many entries that might have been included here have been scattered elsewhere in the text.

(A) WELFARE

The phenomenon of charitable giving has attracted the attention of two American scholars. Jordan has published several volumes on the period 1480 – 1660.[1024] His work rests in the main on the systematic analysis of thousands of wills and unquestionably presents innumerable important facts about the society studied – in the main the propertied urban classes. Whether, however, the author's large conclusions can be accepted is another matter. He showers extravagant praise on the charity of the people investigated and believes that they purposefully led the way towards practical and secular ways of investing good will towards the poor. Unfortunately, the analysis ignores too many problems of the statistics presented and fails to allow for a strong bias built into the sources, so that despite the author's charming enthusiasm reaction has been more critical than favourable. Owen takes over where Jordan leaves off. His book lacks both the broad statistical basis of the other and its dogmatic point of view: exploring rather more types of sources and employing a more literary

---

[1024] Wilbur Kitchener Jordan, *Philanthropy in England, 1480 – 1660*. L: Allen & Unwin: 1959. Pp. 410. Rev: *EHR* 75, 685ff.; *HJ* 3, 89ff. – Idem, *The Charities of London, 1480 – 1660. Ibid.:* 1960. Pp. 463. – Idem, *The Charities of Rural England, 1480 – 1660. Ibid.:* 1961. Pp. 484. Rev: *EHR* 79, 109ff.; *EcHR²* 15, 155f. – Idem, *Social Institutions of Kent, 1480 – 1660*. Ashford: Kent Archaeol. Society: 1961. Pp. x, 172. Rev: *EcHR²* 15, 376f. – Idem, *The Social Institutions of Lancashire, 1480 – 1660*. Manchester: Chetham Soc.: 1962. Pp. xii, 128. Rev: *EHR* 79, 592f.; *EcHR²* 15, 541.

approach, the author is content with more conventional conclusions.[1025] Between them, Jordan and Owen have, however,
usefully reminded us of the extent and success of private efforts
made in the last 400 years to help ease misery and advance
virtue. Self-help among the working classes did not really
begin before the nineteenth century, with the formation of
bodies to provide some insurance against unemployment and
sickness.[1026] Self-help of another kind showed itself in the frequent utopian experiments whose hopes to solve the problems
of the world by active withdrawal from the world are discussed
in a book which runs from puritan sects to garden suburbs
and artificial new towns.[1027] Fuz employs a clumsier technique, redolent of the dissertation: from many and very various
and often highly naïve writings, he picks and classifies 'ideas
of social welfare' like land reform or guaranteed food supplies.[1028] Mowat describes a society which hoped by charity
to educate the poor to self-reliance.[1029] In the end, of course,
the state took over, an outcome laboriously discussed in yet
another of the books that search for the beginnings of the
welfare state.[1030] Perhaps the second oldest profession to look
after the well-being of mankind is the medical profession: how
they came gradually to accept the fact that public health is a
public concern is explained by Brand.[1031] The history of the

[1025] David Owen, *English Philanthropy, 1660 – 1960*. C (Mass.): Harvard UP: 1965. Pp. xii, 610. Rev: *EHR* 82, 127f.; *HJ* 9, 244ff.

[1026] P. H. J. H. Gosden, *The Friendly Societies in England, 1815 – 1875*.
Manchester UP: 1961. Pp. x, 262. Rev: *EHR* 77, 794f.; *EcHR*² 15,
162f.

[1027] W. H. G. Armytage, *Heaven Below: utopian experiments in England,
1560 – 1960*. L: Routledge: 1961. Pp. vii, 458. Rev: *EHR* 78,
776f.

[1028] J. K. Fuz, *Welfare Economics in English Utopias from Francis Bacon
to Adam Smith*. The Hague: Nijhoff: 1952. Pp. vii, 133.

[1029] Charles L. Mowat, *The Charity Organization Society, 1869 – 1913:
its ideas and work*. L: Methuen: 1961. Pp. xii, 188.

[1030] Bentley B. Gilbert, *The Evolution of National Insurance in Great
Britain: the origins of the welfare state*. L: Joseph: 1966. Pp. 497.
Rev: *HJ* 10, 462ff.

[1031] Jeanne L. Brand, *Doctors and the State: the British medical profession
and government action in public health, 1870 – 1912*. Baltimore: Johns
Hopkins UP: 1965. Pp. xiii, 307. Rev: *HJ* 10, 462ff.

main body of doctors back to Henry VIII is told by Clark in a book which concentrates on the institutional and personal story, but has little to contribute to the history of ideas or of science.[1032] While we are on the subject of professions, we may draw attention to Reader's study of the first century of true professionalism, though he still has to confine himself to the old groups – the Church, medicine and the law.[1033] Another profession, only allowed the title in the twentieth century but active since the sixteenth, is loyally described by Thompson.[1034]

Welfare includes toleration: Henriques shows how long it took, after official encouragement, for this to become generally effective.[1035] It took even longer to include the Jews, partly because they themselves feared that emancipation might mean disappearance.[1036] Another sort of welfare again was created by the Elizabethan statute of artificers, partly designed to protect apprentices but mainly shaped to support an impossible ambition to freeze the social structure. Davies's investigation of the law in operation proves that in the main it was either ignored or insufficiently enforced.[1037] Dyos's look at the operations which made London into its present sprawl ought to be the first step in a really large and varied attack on this dark subject.[1038]

[1032] George N. Clark, *A History of the Royal College of Physicians of London*, 2 vols. O: Clarendon: 1964/6. Pp. xxiii, 800. Rev: *History of Science* 5, 87ff.

[1033] William J. Reader, *Professional Men: the rise of the professional classes in nineteenth-century England*. L: Weidenfeld: 1966. Pp. vii, 248. Rev: *EHR* 83, 208.

[1034] F. M. L. Thompson, *Chartered Surveyors: the growth of a profession*. L: Routledge: 1968. Pp. xvi, 400. Rev: *EcHR²* 22, 122.

[1035] Ursula Henriques, *Religious Toleration in England, 1787 – 1833*. L: Routledge: 1961. Pp. vii, 294. Rev: *EHR* 79, 188f.

[1036] Ursula Henriques, 'The Jewish emancipation controversy in nineteenth-century Britain', *PP* 40 (1968), 126–46.

[1037] Margaret G. Davies, *The Enforcement of English Apprenticeship, 1563 – 1642*. C (Mass.): Harvard UP: 1956. Pp. ix, 319. Rev: *EHR* 72, 170.

[1038] H. J. Dyos, 'The speculative builders and developers of Victorian London', *VS* 11 (1967 – 8), 641–90.

(B) EDUCATION

Armytage offers a general survey which, however, is much too scrappy before the eighteenth century.[1039] Less burdened with the sheer hunt for facts is a study of the humanistic foundations of English education in schools and universities; Scotland and Ireland also make brief appearances.[1040] This system of teaching and learning emerged in the sixteenth century from a veritable educational revolution which has inspired two books. Charlton assembles information which was previously badly scattered, successfully criticizes some historians' commonplaces, and includes the less formal types of education in the family, as for instance travel abroad.[1041] Simon ploughs a deeper furrow and escapes the tyranny of the printed book to manage a successful linkage of educational problems with social developments; contrary to older views, she stresses the sixteenth century's role as innovator and reviver.[1042] True enough for the ascendant party; the troubles of roman catholic education for Englishmen, home and abroad, are chronicled by Beales.[1043] That the principles fought for in the sixteenth century became obstructive conservatism in the seventeenth emerges from Vincent's study of the grammar schools.[1044] At last some serious attention is being given to the question whether one can discover how effective all this education was. However, this is a difficult matter. The careful and necessary principles to be practised in the use of both records and statistics for the study of literacy are set out by

---

[1039] W. H. G. Armytage, *400 Years of English Education*. CUP: 1964. Pp. viii, 353.

[1040] M. L. Clarke, *Classical Education in Britain, 1500 – 1900*. CUP: 1959. Pp. viii, 234. Rev: *EHR* 75, 344.

[1041] Kenneth Charlton, *Education in Renaissance England*. L: Routledge: 1965. Pp. xv, 317. Rev: *HJ* 10, 468ff.

[1042] Joan Simon, *Education and Society in Tudor England*. CUP: 1966. Pp. xi, 452. Rev: *EHR* 82, 384; *HJ* 10, 468ff.

[1043] A. C. F. Beales, *Education under Penalty: English catholic education from the Reformation to the fall of James II, 1547 – 1689*. L: Athlone: 1963. Pp. xiii, 306. Rev: *EHR* 80, 832f.

[1044] W. A. L. Vincent, *The Grammar Schools: their continuing tradition, 1660 – 1714*. L: Murray: 1969. Pp. x, 297. Rev: *Hist* 55, 122f.

Schofield;[1045] they are ignored in Stone's cheerful romp
through nearly three centuries which attempts to establish
some very large conclusions about the phases of effective
education.[1046] Silver falls back on the more conventional
methods: he shows us less what happened to the poor when
their betters decided to educate them, than what their betters
thought the social purposes of education should be.[1047]

At this point, Simon takes over the history of schools; his
answers are necessarily determined by being sought firmly
from a working-class point of view and by means of Marxist
theory.[1048] Newsome, at the opposite end of the spectrum,
instead analyses an ideal of education, compounded of pious
learning and active Christianity which the ruling classes imposed on the rest of society.[1049] Indeed, religious jealousies for
long inhibited the growth of a proper national school system:
the problem, which resulted in duplication and dilution of
quality, is generally rehearsed by Cruickshank, while Sacks
tells the story specifically from the point of view of the
schools.[1050] Religion was not the only political obstacle to the
achievement of a good educational system. Reviewing the era
of 'secondary education for by no means all' (from the Bryce
Report to the Butler Act, 1894 – 1944), Kazamias has to
relate a good few tiresome opinions, but himself, being an

[1045] Roger S. Schofield, 'The measurement of literacy in pre-industrial
England', *Literacy in Traditional Societies* (ed. J. Goody; CUP,
1968), 311–25.
[1046] Lawrence Stone, 'Literacy and Education in England, 1640 –
1900', *PP* 42 (1969), 69–139.
[1047] Harold Silver, *The Concept of Popular Education: a study of ideas
and social movements in the early nineteenth century.* L: MacGibbon &
Kee: 1965. Pp. 284.
[1048] Brian Simon, *Studies in the History of Education, 1780 – 1870.* L:
Lawrence & Wishart: 1960. Pp. 375. Rev: *EHR* 76, 738; *EcHR²*
13, 486ff. – Idem, *Education and the Labour Movement, 1870 – 1920.*
Ibid.: 1965. Rev: *EHR* 82, 196f.; *EcHR²* 19, 672f.
[1049] David Newsome, *Godliness and Good Learning.* L: Murray: 1961.
Pp. xii, 291.
[1050] Marjorie Cruickshank, *Church and State in English Education, 1870
to the present day.* L: Macmillan: 1963. Pp. xvi, 200. – Benjamin
Sacks, *The Religious Issue in the State Schools of England and Wales,
1902 – 1914.* Albuquerque: U of New Mexico P: 1961. Pp. xi, 292.

American used to comprehensive schooling, fails to share the progressives' 'bland beliefs' (his phrase, not mine) in the advantages of that system.[1051] Adult education has always, with justice, been a truly creditable part of English social history; Harrison surveys it in full.[1052] The potential political consequences of education are recognized by Webb in his book on the many self-taught men from the lower orders who graced the nineteenth century.[1053] Altick similarly looks at the common reader, but his book does not get beyond compilation.[1054]

Little systematic work has been done on the English universities. Curtis demonstrates that in the early-modern period Oxford and Cambridge did not deserve the poor reputation which has somehow become attached to them; he also argues that the educational stampede produced a socially disruptive academic proletariat, a thesis which remains at the very least doubtful.[1055] A work which discovers the manner in which the old scholastic curriculum still maintained itself in the seventeenth century in the face of humanist reform lacks quite the weight to clinch its point.[1056] A very different academic theme engages Rex in her study of the universities' members of parliament.[1057] Roach, whose contribution to the *Victoria*

[1051] Andreas M. Kazamias, *Politics, Society and Secondary Education in England*. Philadelphia: U of Pennsylvania P: 1966. Pp. 381.

[1052] J. F. C. Harrison, *Learning and Living, 1790 – 1960: a study of the English adult education movement*. L: Routledge: 1961. Pp. xvi, 404. Rev: *EHR* 78, 803f.

[1053] Robert K. Webb, *The British Working Class Reader, 1790 – 1848: literacy and social tension*. L: Allen & Unwin: 1955. Pp. 192. Rev: *EHR* 70, 499f.

[1054] Richard D. Altick, *The English Public Reader: a social history of the mass reading public, 1800 – 1900*. Chicago: U of Chicago P: 1957. Pp. ix, 430.

[1055] Mark H. Curtis, *Oxford and Cambridge in Transition, 1558 – 1642*. O: Clarendon: 1959. Pp. ix, 314. Rev: *EHR*, 76, 102ff.; *HJ* 3, 197ff. – Idem, 'The alienated intellectuals of early Stuart England', *PP* 23 (1962), 25–43.

[1056] William T. Costello, *The Scholastic Curriculum at early 17th century Cambridge*. C (Mass.): Harvard UP: 1958. Pp. 221. Rev: *EHR* 75, 350ff.

[1057] Millicent B. Rex, *University Representation in England, 1604 – 1690*. L: Allen & Unwin: 1954. Pp. 408. Rev: *EHR* 70, 488ff.

County History now forms the best comprehensive account of Cambridge, also contributes an interesting article about the social role of both universities at a time when the leaders of learning rarely bothered to have contact with them.[1058] How a new academic generation changed this at Cambridge is the subject of Rothblatt's fascinating study of the first age of academic professionalism.[1059] At Oxford, reform encountered more, and more personal, opposition, as Green's and Sparrow's accounts of one of the great (and impossible) men on that small stage well show.[1060] Winstanley concluded his history of Cambridge with a volume starting at the next reforms in 1882.[1061] Ward, while lacking Winstanley's charm, similarly treats Oxford from inside and as an isolated theme.[1062] Two good historians allowed themselves to be distracted from their proper concerns into celebrating the long glories of Glasgow and Edinburgh in anniversary volumes which are distinctly better than one expects from the genre.[1063] Of the newer universities, on the other hand, only Belfast has received a sound and serious history.[1064]

[1058] John P. C. Roach, 'The University of Cambridge', *History of the County of Cambridge and the Isle of Ely*, vol. 3, 150–321. L: OUP: 1959. – Idem, 'Victorian universities and the national intelligentsia', *VS* 3 (1959 – 60), 131–50.

[1059] Sheldon Rothblatt, *The Revolution of the Dons.* L: Faber: 1968. Pp. 319. Rev: *Hist* 54, 305f.

[1060] V. H. H. Green, *Oxford Common Room: a study of Lincoln College and Mark Pattison.* L: Arnold: 1957. Pp. 336. – John Sparrow, *Mark Pattison and the Idea of a University.* CUP: 1967. Pp. x, 148. Rev: *EHR* 83, 630; *VS* 11, 549f.

[1061] D. A. Winstanley, *Later Victorian Cambridge.* CUP: 1947. Pp. xii, 367.

[1062] W. R. Ward, *Georgian Oxford: University politics in the 18th century.* O: Clarendon: 1958. Pp. x, 296. – Idem, *Victorian Oxford.* L: Cass: 1965. Pp. xv, 431.

[1063] J. D. Mackie, *The University of Glasgow, 1451 – 1951.* Glasgow: Jackson: 1954. Pp. xi, 341. – D. B. Horn, *A Short History of the University of Edinburgh, 1556 – 1889.* Edinburgh UP: 1967. Pp. xiii, 228.

[1064] T. W. Moody and J. C. Beckett, *Queen's, Belfast, 1845 – 1949: the history of a university*, 2 vols. L: Faber: 1959. Pp. lxvii, 983.

(c) PRINTING

A very mixed bag. Blagden wrote the history of the body which for centuries controlled book-publishing in England.[1065] Bennett links his description of printing's early days with an interesting analysis of the audience for whom the printers worked.[1066] The collection of one such member of the audience is well described by Watson: this is a book that tells more about seventeenth-century intellectual attitudes than one might guess from the title.[1067] Wiles shows how early serial publication, always popular in this country, became quite customary.[1068] Two leading printers and publishers of the eighteenth century have been attended to – the first thoroughly, the second pretty superficially.[1069] The two university presses went through crises in this age: McKenzie at length investigates Cambridge in the age of Bentley's reforms,[1070] while Philip briefly (and mostly by printing documents) demonstrates the effect that Blackstone procured at Oxford.[1071] The first genuine newspapers – too genuine for some – made their appearance in the political upheavals of the seventeenth

[1065] Cyprian Blagden, *The Stationers' Company: a history, 1403 – 1959*. L: Allen & Unwin: 1960. Pp. 321.

[1066] H. S. Bennett, *English Books and Readers, 1475 – 1603*, 2 vols. CUP: 1952, 1965. Pp. xiv, 327; xviii, 320. Rev: *EHR* 68, 222ff.; 83, 160f.

[1067] Andrew G. Watson, *The Library of Sir Simonds D'Ewes*. L: Trustees of the British Museum: 1966. Pp. xiv, 379. Rev: *EHR* 82, 836f.

[1068] R. M. Wiles, *Serial Publication in England before 1750*. CUP: 1957. Pp. xv, 391. Rev: *EHR* 73, 356f.

[1069] William M. Sale, *Samuel Richardson, Master Printer*. Ithaca: Cornell UP: 1950. Pp. vii, 389. – J. A. Cochrane, *Dr Johnson's Printer: the life of William Strachan*. L: Routledge: 1964. Pp. xiv, 225.

[1070] D. F. McKenzie, *The Cambridge University Press, 1696 – 1712*, 2 vols. CUP: 1966. Pp. xv, 436; ix, 381. Rev: *EHR* 83, 357ff.; *EcHR*² 20, 172f.

[1071] I. G. Philip, *William Blackstone and the Reform of the Oxford University Press in the Eighteenth Century*. O: Oxford Bibliographical Soc. Publications, new ser. 7: 1957 (for 1955). Pp. 130. Rev: *EHR* 73, 359f.

century, and Frank's thorough investigation of the technical process of production and distribution has at last made this material properly usable.[1072] In the eighteenth century, the centre of gravity temporarily moved into the provinces.[1073] Munter supplies the information on the parallel developments in Ireland.[1074] Rea investigates the part the press played in the politics of the upheavals caused by George III's accession and personality.[1075] For the nineteenth century, one must not overlook the *History of the Times* which in its general concern with the nation spares time for the particulars of that newspaper, too (n. 669). Clive's discussion of a famous slayer of the (intellectual) heathen contains much illumination beyond the theme as stated.[1076] A potentially most valuable attempt is made by Dalziel in her look at Victorian romances, books of edification, and similar low-level literature; but while this ought to throw floods of light on general and commonplace attitudes, the author writes from too far away, physically and in the spirit.[1077] The greatest news agency of all has also received its history, to remind us that printing is no longer the last word in communications.[1078]

[1072] Joseph Frank, *The Beginnings of the English Newspapers, 1620 – 1660.* C (Mass.) Harvard UP: 1961. Pp. x, 384 Rev: *EHR* 78, 780f.

[1073] G. A. Cranfield, *A Hand-List of English Provincial Newspapers and Periodicals, 1700 – 1760.* C: Bowes & Bowes: 1952. Pp. viii, 31. – Idem, *The Development of the Provincial Newspaper, 1700 – 1760.* O: Clarendon: 1962. Pp. xiv, 287. Rev: *EHR* 79, 853f.; *HJ* 7, 336ff. – R. M. Wiles, *Freshest Advice: earliest provincial newspapers in England.* Columbus: Ohio State UP: 1965. Pp. xv, 555.

[1074] R. Munter, *The History of the Irish Newspaper, 1685 – 1760.* CUP: 1967. Pp. xiii, 217. Rev: *EHR* 83, 842; *EcHR²* 20, 398f.

[1075] Robert R. Rea, *The English Press in Politics, 1760 – 1774.* Lincoln, Neb.: U of Nebraska P.: 1963. Pp. xi, 272.

[1076] John Clive, *Scotch Reviewers: the Edinburgh Review, 1802 – 1815.* L: Faber: 1957. Pp. 224. Rev: *EcHR²* 11, 527.

[1077] Margaret Dalziel, *Popular Fiction 100 Years Ago: an unexplored tract of literary history.* L: Cohen & West: 1967. Pp. vii, 188.

[1078] Graham Storey, *Reuter's Centenary, 1851 – 1951.* L: Parrish: 1951. Pp. xii, 276.

(D) LAW

For the post-medieval period, the history of law, law courts
and justice remains something of a cinderella, though some of
the constitutional and institutional studies referred to elsewhere have their relevance here. However, while one may
rightly call with some urgency for more particular studies and
general interpretations by historians who understand the law
(or those rarer birds still, lawyers who can think historically),
a little more life can be reported here, too, than would have
been possible twenty-five years ago. Holdsworth's gigantic
history of English law from the death of Edward I, begun
some seventy years ago, was in fact brought down by him to
1875, that year of revolution, though publication had in part
to be posthumous.[1079] The sheer magnitude of the work and
of the labour naturally causes awe; whether the result is all it
should be is another matter. Perhaps it never could have been,
but the fact remains that even on the law the work can be
quite wrong, while on institutions and more general history
it is more usually misleading than reliable. One of Holdsworth's lesser books has been replaced by Simpson who offers
secure guidance through the central mystery of English law.[1080]
By way of a general introduction into everything connected
with the law, its administration, and its social role, one may
mention Harding's concise treatise; here, at last, matters of
the law are treated in a manner familiar to historians from
the study of other social themes.[1081] Dawson has written a
rather original and very civilized book which, in the course of
reviewing lay adjudication from ancient Rome to modern
America, explains some of the peculiarities of the English
system both convincingly and without the customary senti-

[1079] William G. Holdsworth, *A History of English Law*, vols. 13–16.
L: Methuen: 1952, 1964, 1965, 1966. Pp. xlviii, 803; xxx, 403;
xxviii, 577; xxviii, 196. Rev: *EHR* 69, 113ff.; *LQR* 70, 121ff., and
82, 253ff.

[1080] A. W. B. Simpson, *An Introduction to the History of the Land Law*.
L: OUP: 1961. Pp. xx, 276.

[1081] Alan Harding, *A Social History of English Law*. Harmondsworth:
Penguin Books: 1966. Pp. 503.

mentality.[1082] And criminal law, usually neglected, has found its worthy spokesman: in three massive volumes, Radzinowicz deals with all that concerns it – law, police, social attitudes, etc.[1083]

Particular institutions: Yale expounds the history of chancery during the seventeenth century, the period of final settlement.[1084] Squibb attends learnedly to the more obscure of the two courts which, in England, used the law of Rome;[1085] the other (admiralty) still waits sleeping for its prince, though there are rumours that he is on the way. The creation of a modern system of appeals is discussed in an article which shows that the preservation in this function of the house of lords (however changed) resulted from the need to compensate their lordships for the loss of political influence.[1086]

Particular legal problems: Holden covers the history of bills of exchange and cheques from 1200 to 1955.[1087] Gray has written an example of that important genre – a study of legal history for the purpose of social analysis; he argues that historical conditions plus judicial pronouncements succeeded in getting the unfree and customary law of copyhold incorporated in the king's courts and the common law, and thus belatedly helped to end the distinction between free and unfree.[1088] While there is point in his demonstration of the part played

---

[1082] John P. Dawson, *A History of Lay Judges*. C (Mass.): Harvard UP: 1960. Pp. x, 310. Rev: *Hist* 47, 104f.

[1083] Leo Radzinowicz, *A History of English Criminal Law and its Administration, from 1750*, 3 vols. L: Stevens: 1948, 1956. P. xxiv, 853; xvii, 761; xvii, 688. Rev: *EHR* 72, 709ff.; *EcHR*² 11, 168ff.

[1084] D. E. C. Yale, *Lord Nottingham's Chancery Cases*, 2 vols. L: Quaritch, Selden Soc.: 1957, 1961. Pp. cxxxi, 1039. – Idem, *Lord Nottingham's 'Manual of Chancery Practice' and 'Prolegomena of Chancery and Equity'*. CUP: 1965. Pp. xv, 301.

[1085] G. C. Squibb, *The High Court of Chivalry: a study of the civil law in England*. L: OUP: 1959. Pp. xxvi, 301.

[1086] Robert Stevens, 'The final appeal: reform of the house of lords and privy council, 1867 – 1876', *LQR* 80 (1964), 343–69.

[1087] J. Milnes Holden, *A History of Negotiable Instruments in English Law*. L: Athlone: 1955. Pp. xxxix, 350. Rev: *EHR* 71, 331ff.

[1088] Charles M. Gray, *Copyhold, Equity, and Common Law*. C (Mass.): Harvard UP: 1963. Pp. 254. Rev: *EHR* 80, 393f.

by chancery, he has clearly overlooked the earlier interest of the common law in manorial custom, a point rightly stressed by Kerridge (n. 263). Jones's history of one area of the law of trusts is a thorough, learned, distinguished piece of work of the kind which relieves the subject for ever from the need to be studied again.[1089] McGregor, by contrast, brings the mind and training of a sociologist to the study of the law of divorce: perhaps divorce is a strictly social problem, while charity is one of law?[1090]

The legal profession: Ives describes the means and ways of advance in an age in which the numbers of lawyers increased greatly in the wake of fast increasing profits.[1091] Legal education is a subject on which we could do with more knowledge; Prest looks only at the special problem of the experience of those who in the main did not want to be trained as lawyers, despite their presence at the inns of court.[1092] The lower level of the profession enjoyed a sordid reputation in the eighteenth century; whether this was deserved is not a question – among others – that Robson's rather slight book enables one to answer.[1093] A good deal slighter still is another book on this theme, if only because it covers a longer span in time.[1094] Even the age of the smuggest self-satisfaction harboured plans for reform.[1095] A few judges – too few, compared with bishops – have found biographers. Two well-known seventeenth-century figures appear in Hurst's article, which somewhat depreciates the long over-valued Matthew Hale, and in Keeton's

[1089] Gareth Jones, *History of the Law of Charity, 1532 – 1827*. CUP: 1969. Pp. xxiii, 270.

[1090] Oliver R. McGregor, *Divorce in England: a centenary study*. L: Heinemann: 1957. Pp. xi, 220.

[1091] E. W. Ives, 'Promotion in the legal profession of Yorkist and early Tudor England', *LQR* 75 (1959), 348–63.

[1092] Wilfrid Prest, 'Legal education of the gentry at the inns of court, 1560 – 1640', *PP* 38 (1967), 20–39.

[1093] Robert Robson, *The Attorney in Eighteenth Century England*. CUP: 1959. Pp. xii, 182.

[1094] Michael Birks, *Gentlemen of the Law*. L: Stevens: 1960. Pp. xi, 304. Rev: *EHR* 77, 147f.

[1095] Paul Lucas, 'Blackstone and the reform of the legal profession', *EHR* 77 (1962), 456–89.

book which distinctly overpraises the long hated Jeffreys.[1096] Heuston, in Lord Campbell's footsteps, presents a collection of extended biographical sketches of what are in effect nowadays the heads of the English judiciary.[1097]

[1096] Gerald Hurst, 'Sir Matthew Hale', *LQR* 70 (1954), 342–52. – G. W. Keeton, *Lord Chancellor Jeffreys and the Stuart Cause*. L: MacDonald: 1965. Pp. xv, 553.

[1097] R. F. V. Heuston, *Lives of the Lord Chancellors, 1885 – 1940*. O: Clarendon: 1964. Pp. xxiii, 632. Rev: *EHR* 82, 355ff.

XI
History of Ideas

(A) POLITICAL THOUGHT

The study of political theory has long been a preoccupation among English historians, and one is therefore entitled to expect solid contributions also from the new generation. They do not disappoint, though people seem to be less ready to undertake the large surveys which were once so fashionable. However, Morris provides a good concise introduction to sixteenth-century thinking.[1098] Mostly, individual thinkers have been tackled, and only a few historians have tried their hand at the markedly more fruitful enterprise of investigating a theme as treated by a succession of writers. This is what Ferguson does in a book which shows that humanism fundamentally altered men's beliefs about the state, about the possibility of selfconscious reform, and about active participation in the business of government.[1099] These points are supported by Lehmberg, who finds English thinkers debating the question of counselling monarchs,[1100] and by Elton who identifies Thomas Cromwell as the deliberate leader of an active reform group using constitutional means, and Thomas Starkey as the central figure among Cromwell's men of ideas.[1101] Hexter's excellent analysis of *Utopia* concentrates on the conflict be-

---

[1098] Christopher Morris, *Political Thought in England: Tyndale to Hooker*. L: OUP: 1953. Pp. x, 320. Rev: *EHR* 70, 324f.

[1099] Arthur B. Ferguson, *The Articulate Citizen and the English Renaissance*. Durham N.C.: Duke UP: 1965. Pp. xvii, 429. Rev: *EHR* 82, 121ff.

[1100] Stanford E. Lehmberg, 'English humanists, the Reformation, and the problem of counsel', *Archiv für Reformationsgeschichte*, 52 (1961), 74–91.

[1101] G. R. Elton, 'Reform by statute: Thomas Starkey's *Dialogue* and Thomas Cromwell's policy', *Proceedings of the British Academy* 54 (1970 for 1968), 165–88.

tween scholarship and public service.[1102] The old notion that
More should be seen as a premature socialist was still alive
enough to mislead Ames entirely.[1103] The other great thinker
of the century, Richard Hooker, also receives his due tribute.
Davies concisely sums up his ideas;[1104] Shirley places him
within his own time.[1105] Munz tries to make him no more
than the heir of ancient and medieval traditions.[1106] It looks
as though Hooker's famed judiciousness deprives those who
study him not only of passion but of life.

Salmon leads us over into the troubles of the seventeenth
century by tracing the influence of French theories of resistance to authority.[1107] Filmer, champion of patriarchal despotism, receives from Laslett the kiss of life, after long neglect
and contempt.[1108] Greenleaf even makes Filmer's historical
thinking appear sensible in the context of contemporary ideas,
however peculiarly silly it may seem to a later age.[1109] The
influence of Italy has not been forgotten. Raab pursues the
fortunes of Machiavelli in English sixteenth- and seventeenth-
century thought in a book which provides many insights but
also some bad slips;[1110] Fink's study of the influence which

---

[1102] J. H. Hexter, *More's 'Utopia': the biography of an idea.* Princeton
UP 1952. Pp. xii, 171. Rev: *AHR* 58, 346ff. Hexter continued
the working out of the problem in his introduction to the Yale
edition of *Utopia* (n. 73).

[1103] Russell Ames, *Citizen More and his Utopia.* Princeton UP: 1040.
Pp. viii, 230. Rev: *EHR* 65, 114ff.

[1104] E. T. Davies, *The Political Ideas of Richard Hooker.* L: SPCK:
1946. Pp. xii, 98.

[1105] F. J. Shirley, *Richard Hooker and Contemporary Political Ideas.* L:
SPCK: 1949. Pp. 274.

[1106] Peter Munz, *The Place of Hooker in the History of Thought.* L:
Routledge: 1952. Pp. x, 217.

[1107] J. H. M. Salmon, *The French Religious Wars in English Political
Thought.* O: Clarendon: 1959. Pp. vii, 202. Rev: *EHR* 75, 725f.

[1108] Robert Filmer, *Patriarcha and other Political Works*, ed. Peter Laslett. O: Blackwell: 1949. Pp. 326.

[1109] W. H. Greenleaf, 'Filmer's patriarchal history', *HJ* 9 (1966),
157–71.

[1110] Felix Raab, *The English Face of Machiavelli.* L: Routledge: 1964.
Pp. xii, 306. Rev: *EHR* 81, 356ff.; *Il Politico*, 39 (1966), 127ff.
(S. Anglo).

Roman and Venetian examples had on the English republicans is simpler and more convincing.[1111] These republicans themselves are represented in a careful edition of two of their writings and, less straightforwardly, in a subtle study of the thought of Andrew Marvell whose changes of mind are not unconvincingly portrayed as a form of consistent loyalty.[1112] Macpherson employs another instrument of analysis again, a socially conditioned enquiry dominated by Marxism. Applying this to the writers who, after the collapse of the old organic concept of the political commonwealth, tried to discover a new synthesis, he finds their essence in the notion of the individual with its entitlement to property. The book is weighty, though the thesis is overstated and too conveniently simple.[1113] It is now rivalled, not very successfully, by another attempt to find the comprehensive answer by the methods of political science: Gunn's treatment of all these writers as searchers for the common good.[1114] The writer who best supports Macpherson was Harrington (on whom indeed Marxist interpretations of the century have always had to rely too exclusively); Blitzer supplies us with a good straight analysis.[1115]

Hobbes is a mystery still some way from solution, as the contributors to a collection of essays succeed in proving.[1116] Goldsmith treats him systematically as a fully systematic man, a possible approach in this case.[1117] Warrener attempts to

[1111] Z. S. Fink, *The Classical Republicans*. Evanston: Northwestern UP: 1945 (2nd ed. 1962). Pp. xii, 229.

[1112] Caroline Robbins, ed., *Two English Republican Tracts*. CUP: 1969. Pp. ix, 275. – John M. Wallace, *Destiny his Choice: the loyalties of Andrew Marvell*. CUP: 1968. Pp. x, 265. Rev: *EHR* 84, 613.

[1113] C. B. Macpherson, *The Political Theory of Possessive Individualism, Hobbes to Locke*. O: Clarendon: 1962. Pp. xi, 310. Rev: *EHR* 79, 607f.; *HJ* 7, 150ff.; *PP* 24, 86ff.

[1114] J. A. W. Gunn, *Politics and the Public Interest in the Seventeenth Century*. L: Routledge: 1969. Pp. viii, 355.

[1115] C. Blitzer, *The Immortal Commonwealth: the political thought of James Harrington*. New Haven: Yale UP: 1960. Pp. xv, 344. Rev: *EHR* 78, 174f.

[1116] K. C. Brown, ed., *Hobbes Studies*. O: Blackwell: 1965. Pp. xv, 300. Rev: *EHR* 82, 123ff.

[1117] M. M. Goldsmith, *Hobbes's Science of Politics*. New York: Columbia UP: 1966. Pp. xv, 274. Rev: *EHR* 83, 612f.

present him as a pure moralist who in no sense regarded duty
as equal to self-interest.[1118] Hood takes this sort of rehabilitation further still by finding nothing but religious inspiration
in his thought.[1119] Watkins very justly finds this absurd and
returns to much of the traditional Hobbes;[1120] he is, in a
manner, assisted by McNeilly who confines himself to plod-
ding exegesis.[1121] Skinner breaks new ground by proving that
even Hobbes was not an isolated phenomenon but fits his
own time both at home and abroad.[1122] It may be suggested
that Hobbes is one case where innovation does not work; the
further from tradition interpretation moves, the less probable
does it seem to be. However, misunderstanding Hobbes is a
game with a long tradition behind it, as books about contemporary and later opponents make plain.[1123] Locke causes less
furore. Cranston supplies a sober biography, to which may be
added a new edition of some of Locke's diaries.[1124] His general
political philosophy has been reviewed no less than three times.
Gough groups it neatly for the student in eight independent
essays;[1125] Seliger provides a systematic – much too neatly
systematic – exegesis which discovers liberalism in every

[1118] Howard Warrender, *The Political Philosophy of Hobbes*. O: Clarendon: 1957. Pp. xii, 346. Rev: *EHR* 73, 492ff.

[1119] F. C. Hood, *The Divine Politics of Thomas Hobbes: an interpretation
of Leviathan*. O: Clarendon: 1964. Pp. xii, 263. Rev: *HJ* 7, 321ff.

[1120] John W. N. Watkins, *Hobbes's System of Ideas: a study in the political
significance of philosophical theories*. L: Hutchinson: 1965. Pp. 192.
Rev: *EHR* 81, 830.

[1121] F. S. McNeilly, *The Anatomy of Leviathan*. L: Macmillan: 1968.
Pp. vii, 264.

[1122] Quentin Skinner, 'The ideological context of Hobbes's political
thought', *HJ* 9 (1966), 286–317; 'Thomas Hobbes and his disciples in France and England', *Comparative Studies in Society and
History*, 8 (1965 – 6), 153–68.

[1123] Samuel H. Mintz, *The Hunting of Leviathan*. CUP: 1962. Pp. x,
189. Rev: *HJ* 7, 321ff. – John Bowle, *Hobbes and his Critics*. L:
Cape: 1951. Pp. 215.

[1124] Maurice Cranston, *John Locke*. L: Longmans: 1957. Pp. xvi, 496.
– John Lough, ed., *Locke's Travels in France, 1675, 1679*. CUP:
1953. Pp. lxvi, 309. Rev: *EHR* 69, 320f.

[1125] J. W. Gough, *John Locke's Political Philosophy*. O: Clarendon:
1950. Pp. viii, 204.

compromise;[1126] Dunn, who rightly reacts against some recent anachronisms, sees perhaps most clearly but by his language too often prevents his reader from doing so.[1127] Cox concentrates on Locke's ideas about relations between states and concludes that he identified the law of nature with the law of nations; this is improbable.[1128] Locke's works are being continuously edited anew. The most important piece here is Laslett's edition of the masterpiece: at last a definitive text and also at last a reliable history of its origin.[1129] Von Leyden has brought out a lesser but important piece;[1130] Abrams contributes the edition of two early works with an important introduction which demonstrates that Locke was a great deal less consistent through life than used to be supposed.[1131] Yolton traces Locke's influence on his contemporaries, and Bonno his influence on France.[1132] That the new editions and all this work may well have succeeded in moving Locke, too, from the agreed to the controversial sector would appear to be the message of a recent collection of essays on him.[1133]

This may be the place to mention an unusual book which, though it studies tradition, hardly fits into the tradition of

---

[1126] Martin Seliger, *The Liberal Politics of John Locke*. L: Allen & Unwin: 1968. Pp. 387. Rev: *EHR* 85, 174f.

[1127] John W. Dunn, *The Political Thought of John Locke*. CUP: 1969. Pp. xiii, 290.

[1128] Richard H. Cox, *Locke on War and Peace*. O: Clarendon: 1960. Pp. xx, 220.

[1129] John Locke, *Two Treatises of Government*, ed. Peter Laslett. CUP: 1960. Pp. xiii, 521. Rev: *EHR* 76, 686ff.; *HJ* 5, 97ff.

[1130] John Locke, *Essays on the Law of Nature*, ed. W. von Leyden. O: Clarendon: 1954. Pp. xi, 292.

[1131] John Locke, *Two Tracts on Government*, ed. P. Abrams. CUP: 1967. Pp. x, 264. Rev: *EHR* 83, 613f.

[1132] John W. Yolton, *John Locke and the Way of Ideas*. L: OUP: 1956. Pp. xi, 235. – Gabriel Bonno, *Les relations intellectuelles de Locke avec la France*. Berkeley: U of California P (Univ. of California Publications in Modern Philosophy, vol. 38, part 2): 1955. Pp. vi, 228.

[1133] John W. Yolton, ed., *John Locke: Problems and Perspectives*. CUP: 1969. Pp. vii, 278.

these studies. Using the help of 'literary' writers, Greenleaf discerns two very different lines in English political thought before Locke of which that relying on a mechanistic empiricism survived, while that confident in the existence of organic development disappeared for a long time.[1134]

However, Locke certainly brought peace. Every effort to make more of Bolingbroke than a purveyor of mostly tedious commonplaces encounters the subject's lack of co-operation, but Kramnick scores a measure of success where Hart and Jackman cannot be said to have got very far.[1135] On Hume, whose ideas and mind were so much more original, we have no serious study in English, though Mossner supplies a usefully complete biography (with too many lapses into solemnity and roguishness),[1136] while Bongie amusingly describes the uses to which the French counter-revolutionaries could put Hume's mixture of scepticism and loyalty to the Stuarts.[1137] The only attempt to study his ideas which is worthy of the man was made by an Italian scholar.[1138] Burke, on the other hand, has proved devastatingly popular, and the bibliographical report by Bryant is already quite insufficient.[1139] The chief reason for all this is the opening of the Burke archive which Cone, for instance, has energetically exploited to write

---

[1134] W. H. Greenleaf, *Order, Empiricism and Politics: two traditions of English political thought, 1500 – 1700*. L: OUP: 1964. Pp. vii, 299. Rev: *HJ* 9, 136ff; *AHR* 72, 715f.

[1135] Isaac Kramnick, *Bolingbroke and his Circle: the politics of nostalgia in the age of Walpole*. C (Mass.): Harvard UP: 1968. Pp. xvi, 321. Rev: *Hist* 54, 284f. – Jeffrey Hart, *Viscount Bolingbroke – Tory Humanist*. L: Routledge: 1965. Pp. xi, 169. – Sydney W. Jackman, *Man of Mercury: an appreciation of the mind of Henry St John, Viscount Bolingbroke*. L: Pall Mall Press: 1965. Pp. xi, 166. Rev: *EHR* 84, 396f.

[1136] Ernest C. Mossner, *The Life of David Hume*. Edinburgh: Nelson: 1954. Pp. xx, 683.

[1137] Lawrence L. Bongie, *David Hume: prophet of the counter-revolution*. O: Clarendon: 1965. Pp. xvii, 182. Rev: *EHR* 82, 389f.

[1138] G. Giarizzo, *David Hume politico e storico*. Turin: Einaudi: 1962. Pp. 277.

[1139] Donald C. Bryant, 'Edmund Burke: a generation of scholarship and discovery', *JBS* 2 (1963), 91–114.

the first really thorough biography.[1140] Admittedly he is a less satisfactory guide to Burke's philosophy. On this, Parkin's little volume, discovering the consistent moral background to all Burke's thought, is more helpful.[1141] Stanlis certainly exaggerates in this search for consistency: he will have it that Burke held to an ancient and 'correct' view of natural law which rationalism perverted, but forgets how flexibly Burke adapted himself to the common parlance of the day.[1142] Canavan, too, would forward the revisionist concept of Burke as a systematic thinker.[1143] But the reaction has been swift, and Chapman, endeavouring to rescue Burke from the systems and systematizers, brings back the old empiricist that we grew up with.[1144] Wilkins finds Burke burdened with a sort of natural law theory (conservative and a bit like Canavan's), while Lucas firmly shows him to have been hostile to any mere prescription, whether in natural or common law.[1145] This looks to be one argument that the outsider would be wise to leave alone, at least until the combatants have arrived at more agreed points. Meanwhile, a German dissertation collects all Burke's sayings on law and justice;[1146] Mahoney discourses upon his relations with his native country, never forgotten and never escaped from;[1147] and Skalweit shows that Burke's

---

[1140] Carl B. Cone, *Burke and the Nature of Politics*, 2 vols. Lexington: U of Kentucky P: 1957, 1964. Pp. xv, 415; xi, 527. Rev: *AHR* 64, 367ff.; 70, 1089f.

[1141] Charles W. Parkin, *The Moral Basis of Burke's Political Thought*. CUP: 1956. Pp. viii, 145. Rev: *EHR* 72, 551f.

[1142] Peter J. Stanlis, *Edmund Burke and the Natural Law*. Ann Arbor: U of Michigan P: 1958. Pp. xv, 311.

[1143] Francis P. Canavan, S. J., *The Political Reason of Edmund Burke*. Durham N.C.: Duke UP: 1960. Pp. xvi, 222.

[1144] Gerald W. Chapman, *Edmund Burke: the practical imagination*. C (Mass.): Harvard UP: 1967. Pp. x, 350. Rev: *Hist* 53, 259f.

[1145] Burleigh Taylor Wilkins, *The Problem of Burke's Political Philosophy*. O: Clarendon: 1967. Pp. ix, 262. Rev: *HJ* 11, 555ff. – Paul Lucas, 'Burke's doctrine of prescription; or an appeal from the new to the old lawyers', *HJ* 11 (1968), 35–63.

[1146] [Gisela Schell, *Englischer Rechtsgedanke im Werke Edmund Burkes*. Frankfurt: Selbstverlag: 1955. Pp. 132.]

[1147] Thomas H. D. Mahoney, *Edmund Burke and Ireland*. C (Mass.): Harvard UP: 1960. Pp. xiv, 413. Rev: *AHR* 65, 886f.

quarrel with the French Revolution arose from disagreements with Rousseau that provide a deeper root for Burke's feelings than had been assumed.[1148] On this last point, Fennessy seems to suggest that Burke and Paine quite agreed about the meaning of the French Revolution and differed only in their feelings: Paine, conventional supporter of eighteenth-century rationalism, welcomed it, while Burke, the rebel in ideas, rejected it.[1149] There is certainly far more in this than mere paradox.

As distance increases, the Utilitarians are beginning to be more attractive. They form the mainstay of a book which draws in also Hume and Beatrice Webb (!) as examples of a form of political thought which is rooted in practicality.[1150] A comprehensive edition of Bentham's writings is in the making; no doubt it will lead to much more work. A start has been made: of Mack's biography, intended also to review his ideas, the first volume has appeared.[1151] Baumgardt, somewhat improbably, treats him as a deeply ethical philosopher.[1152] James Mill, his favourite pupil, has twice been looked at from the point of view of his political strategy and influence.[1153] The younger Mill merits and receives more, for instance a straight and simple biography.[1154] More important is Cowling's savage attack on his reputation as a liberal philosopher and reformer: he describes him as often hypocritical and always ineffective, a man who never understood

---

[1148] Stephan Skalweit, *Edmund Burke und Frankreich*. Köln/Opladen, Westdeutscher Verlag: 1956. Pp. 75.

[1149] R. R. Fennessy, *Burke, Paine and the Rights of Man: a difference of political opinion*. The Hague: Nijhoff: 1963. Pp. xiii, 274. *EHR* 80, 850f.; *HJ* 10, 293ff.

[1150] Shirley R. Letwin, *The Pursuit of Certainty*. CUP: 1965. Pp. viii, 391. Rev: *EHR* 82, 576ff.

[1151] Mary P. Mack, *Jeremy Bentham*, vol. 1: 1748 – 1792. L: Heinemann: 1962. Pp. xii, 482. Rev: *EHR* 79, 857.

[1152] David Baumgardt, *Bentham and the Ethics of Today*. Princeton UP: 1952. Pp. xiv, 594.

[1153] Joseph Hamburger, *James Mill and the Art of Revolution*, New Haven: Yale UP: 1963. Pp. xiii, 289 – William Thomas, 'James Mill's politics: the "Essay on Government" and the movement for reform', *HJ* 12 (1969), 249–84.

[1154] Michael St J. Packe, *The Life of John Stuart Mill*. L: Secker & Warburg. 1954. Pp. xvi, 567.

the realities of living in politics.[1155] Since for academic liberals Mill remains something of a prophet, and since Cowling's language can be unrestrained, his book has met with predictable resistance; but it should be said that Hamburger's more sympathetic study of the severe disappointment which befell Mill and his friends in their parliamentary activities really arrives at much the same conclusions.[1156] Mueller and Drescher illuminate the contacts between these English radicals and French men and ideas.[1157] Stokes links the history of ideas with what actually happened when he expounds the effects which the Utilitarians had upon imperial policy.[1158] Richter reminds us that that tradition did not remain unquestioned;[1159] and Pinto-Duschinsky tries with moderate success (he fails to take account of the man's neurotic personality) to present the thought of a practising politician who rebelled against the radical commonplaces.[1160] Less readily forgotten has been the inescapable Acton whose ideas Fasnacht describes as political philosophy;[1161] Himmelfarb writes his intellectual biography, while Mathew confines himself to a pretty inadequate account of his early days.[1162]

[1155] Maurice Cowling, *Mill and Liberalism*. CUP: 1963. Pp. xviii, 161. Rev: *EHR* 80, 851f.

[1156] Joseph Hamburger, *Intellectuals in Politics: John Stuart Mill and the philosophic radicals*. New Haven: Yale UP: 1965. Pp. xi, 308. Rev: *EHR* 82, 415f.

[1157] Iris Wessel Mueller, *John Stuart Mill and French Thought*. Urbana: U of Illinois P: 1956. Pp. xi, 275. – Seymour Drescher, *Tocqueville in England*. C (Mass.): Harvard UP: 1964. Pp. xi, 263. Rev: *EHR* 80, 861.

[1158] Eric T. Stokes, *The English Utilitarians and India*. O: Clarendon: 1959. Pp. xvi, 350. Rev: *EHR* 75, 532.

[1159] Melvin Richter, *The Politics of Conscience: T. H. Green and his age*. C (Mass.): Harvard UP: 1964. Pp. 415.

[1160] Michael Pinto-Duschinsky, *The Political Thought of Lord Salisbury, 1854 – 1868*. L: Constable: 1967. Pp. 214. Rev: *VS* 11, 552f.

[1161] G. F. Fasnacht, *Acton's Political Philosophy: an analysis*, L: Hollis Carter: 1958. Pp. xiv, 265. Rev: *EHR* 68, 108ff.

[1162] Gertrude Himmelfarb, *Lord Acton: a study in conscience and politics*. L: Routledge: 1952. Pp. x, 260. Rev: *EHR* 68, 292f. – David Mathew, *Acton: the formative years*. L: Eyre & Spottiswoode: 1946. Pp. viii, 196. Rev: *EHR* 61, 412ff.

Political thought should, one supposes, include the imperialism of the later nineteenth century. Koebner and Schmidt help to explain the concept by explaining the word and making history out of semantics.[1163] Thornton, who to the scholar's buckler adds the lance of true wit, analyses the passionate defenders and attackers who gathered around the whole idea.[1164] Milner was a sufficiently classical example of the intellectual who, in spite of his bodily insufficiencies, wishes to be a man of action: hence his imperialism. Stokes discusses the peculiar form which the concept took in that overestimated mind; Halpérin, on the same theme, is much too kind.[1165]

(B) SOCIAL THOUGHT

Ferguson's book (n. 1099) is supplemented by McConica's which describes the part played by humanist writers in the social and political renewal of the commonweal which was associated with the Reformation.[1166] This study's importance is not much affected by the author's overestimation of the intellectuals and in particular of Erasmus. Less original is Caspari's treatment of some familiar figures as makers of a humanistic programme of education.[1167] Originality cannot be denied to Esler who seeks to explain Elizabethan intellectual and cultural conflicts by means of the modern conflict of the generations; it is doubtful whether there is anything in this, but the author's habitual inaccuracy as to fact and inference

---

[1163] Richard Koebner and Helmut D. Schmidt, *Imperialism: the story and significance of a political word, 1840 – 1960*. CUP: 1964. Pp. xxv, 432. Rev: *EHR* 81, 127ff.

[1164] A. P. Thornton, *The Imperial Idea and its Enemies*. L: Macmillan: 1959. Pp. xiv, 370. Rev: *EHR* 75, 549f.

[1165] Eric T. Stokes, 'Milnerism', *HJ* 5 (1962), 47–60. – Vladimir Halpérin, *Lord Milner and the Empire: the evolution of British imperialism*. L: Odham: n.d. Pp. 256 *See also* n. 694.

[1166] James K. McConica, *English Humanists and Reformation Politics*. O: Clarendon: 1965. Pp. xii, 340. Rev: *EHR* 82, 608f.; *HJ* 10, 137f.; *Hist* 52, 77f.

[1167] Fritz Caspari, *Humanism and the Social Order in Tudor England*. Chicago: U of Chicago P: 1954. Pp. ix, 293. Rev: *EHR* 70, 481f.

makes the book an oddity only.[1168] Investigating that gentle communist of the civil wars, Gerald Winstanley, Hudson not surprisingly finds him to have been an oldfashioned prophet, not a premature disciple of Marx.[1169] Of Locke's social thinking, his writings on education are possibly the most representative.[1170] A jump into the nineteenth century. Houghton uses belletristic writings in order to discover the emotional, intellectual and moral tenets of the middle and upper layers of Victorian society.[1171] Burrow, more precisely and very successfully, analyses the socio-political consequences of Darwinism.[1172] Here, too, biography has made its inroads, and five books on opinion-makers of the day shall be cited: on the insufferable Cobbett, propagandist and journalist of genius;[1173] on the radical blue-stocking Harriet Martineau, no more bearable;[1174] on the delightful Bagehot, whose opinions, so well expressed, have been the more enduringly influential because of their lack of depth;[1175] on the explosive essayist Leslie Stephen who sired both the *D.N.B.* and Virginia Woolf;[1176]

[1168] Anthony Esler, *The Aspiring Mind of the Elizabethan Younger Generation*. Durham N.C.: Duke UP: 1966. Pp. xxiv, 266. Rev: *Hist* 53, 100f.

[1169] Winthrop S. Hudson, 'The economic and social thought of Gerrard Winstanley', *JMH* 18 (1946), 1–21.

[1170] J. L. Axtell, ed., *The Educational Writings of John Locke*. CUP: 1968. Pp. xvi, 442. Rev: *Hist* 54, 103f.

[1171] W. E. Houghton, *The Victorian Frame of Mind*. New Haven: Yale UP: 1957. Pp. xvii, 467. Rev: *EHR* 74, 135ff.

[1172] John W. Burrow, *Evolution and Society: a study in Victorian social thought*. CUP: 1966. Pp. xvii, 295. Rev: *EHR* 83, 418f.

[1173] John W. Osborne, *William Cobbett: his thought and his time*. New Brunswick N.J.: Rutgers UP: 1966. Pp. x, 272. Rev: *EHR* 83, 629.

[1174] Robert K. Webb, *Harriet Martineau: a radical Victorian*. L: Heinemann: 1960. Pp. xiii, 385. Rev: *EHR* 77, 395f.; *HJ* 3, 199ff.

[1175] Norman St John Stevas, *Walter Bagehot: a study of his life and thought, together with a selection from his political writings*. L: Eyre & Spottiswoode: 1959. Pp. xvi, 485.

[1176] Noel Annan, *Leslie Stephen: his thought and character in relation to his time*. L: MacGibbon & Kee: 1951. Pp. viii, 342.

and on Kipling, a much misunderstood prophet of an imperialism that never was.[1177]

Lastly, two works may be mentioned which cannot be classified. Hale has had the excellent idea of tracing England's love affair with the Italian Renaissance through the centuries.[1178] Gauger, too, had a good idea, namely to analyse the art of rhetoric in England where politics for so long have been dominated by the orators; but though she nobly plods from Pym to Churchill, her muse of speech, analysing style and explaining phrases, crawls relentlessly upon her belly.[1179]

(c) HISTORIOGRAPHY

It is only quite recently that English historians have begun to treat their own kind as subjects for serious study, and that the writing of history has been investigated as an intellectual activity closely linked with history itself. Butterfield's contribution consists in the main in the stimulus he has provided for others and in his definition of the necessary methods.[1180] Hay shows how English historical writing round about 1500 was revived by direct fertilization from Italy.[1181] Levy's brilliant general account of Tudor historiography suffers a little from his reluctance to allow the reader to see how hard his task had been.[1182] For the Reformation, history became an armoury of weapons; this was particularly true in England where the whole upheaval was defended on historical

---

[1177] Charles Carrington, *Rudyard Kipling: his life and work*. L: Macmillan: 1955. Pp. xxiii, 549.

[1178] John R. Hale, *England and the Italian Renaissance: the growth of interest in its history and art*. L: Faber: 1954. Pp. 216. Rev: *EHR* 70, 532f.

[1179] Hildegard Gauger, *Die Kunst der politischen Rede in England*. Tübingen: Niemeyer: 1952. Pp. viii, 259.

[1180] Herbert Butterfield, *Man on his Past*. CUP: 1955. Pp. xvii, 238.

[1181] Denys Hay, *Polydore Vergil: Renaissance historian and man of letters*. O: Clarendon: 1952. Pp. xiii, 223. Rev: *EHR* 67, 573ff.

[1182] Fritz J. Levy, *Tudor Historical Thought*. San Marino, Cal.: Huntington Library: 1967. Pp. xii, 305. Rev: *Hist* 54, 92f.

grounds.[1183] As the century progressed, historical writing became more self-conscious; there grew up the conviction, which
was to endure for two centuries, that the historian's duty
consisted in explaining God's will to men and to teach
philosophy by example. Even though Fussner was probably
rash to speak of a revolution, he nevertheless manages to show
how swiftly such practices were developed in the century after
Elizabeth's accession.[1184] More modestly, the contributors to
a colloquium arrive at the same conclusion, though they were
more concerned with the deeply learned antiquarians of the
day than with the pretentious 'true' historians.[1185] A new
awareness of the past as history can also be seen in the first
phase of autobiographical writing, in the seventeenth cen-
turn.[1186] Pocock has gone further than this: by studying the
relationship between historical investigation, constitutional
ideas, and the century's general ideology, he hoped to create
a sociology of thought for the leaders of political strife, and
in great measure he also succeeded.[1187] Only Skinner has so
far ventured to follow him onto this pretty treacherous
ground.[1188]

The students of particular historians have led easier lives.
Perhaps it causes astonishment to find Newton in this section,
but Manuel demonstrates the great scientist's preoccupation
with chronology and often mythical history.[1189] More typical
(though untypically intelligent) was a worthy eighteenth-

[1183] Rainer Pineas, 'William Tyndale's influence on John Bale's
polemical use of history', *Archiv für Reformationsgeschichte* 53 (1962),
79–96.

[1184] F. Smith Fussner, *The Historical Revolution.* L: Routledge: 1962.
Pp. xxiv, 343. Rev: *EHR*, 79, 411.

[1185] Levi Fox, ed., *English Historical Scholarship in the 16th and 17th
centuries.* L: OUP: 1956. Pp. ix, 153. Rev: *CHJ* 13, 190ff.

[1186] Paul Delany, *British Autobiography in the Seventeenth Century.* L:
Routledge: 1969. Pp. ix, 198. Rev: *Hist* 55, 119f.

[1187] John G. A. Pocock, *The Ancient Constitution and the Fundamental
Law.* CUP: 1957. Pp. ix, 262. Rev: *EHR* 73, 352f.

[1188] Quentin Skinner, 'History and ideology in the English revolution', *HJ* 8 (1965), 151–78.

[1189] Frank E. Manuel, *Isaac Newton, Historian.* CUP: 1963. Pp. x, 328.
Rev: *AHR* 69, 111f.

century antiquary.[1190] Dissertations have to seek their subjects where they may, but Schütt's seemingly far-fetched study of the attitude adopted by eighteenth-century Englishmen to the ancient Teutons actually contributes something to the understanding of a period which, despite its insistence on the rational, could be extraordinarily naïve and romantic.[1191] Some true romantics – who very nearly were also true historians – appear in a book published in Germany by an American student of English, which deserve its place for its rarity value.[1192]

However, eighteenth-century historiography means mainly Gibbon. In gloomy Norway, Fuglum extracts from his view of history the conviction that everything always gets worse;[1193] in courteous Italy, Giarizzo accords him the leading position in European culture which he always wanted to fill;[1194] in America, they write his life (one wishes one could read the great man's review of this superficial book);[1195] in England, they study his style.[1196] It is also in England, quite properly, that the only attempt is made to treat him in the round and no more solemnly than he would have approved.[1197] Since Gibbon, the legitimate succession has never been interrupted. Among the historians of the early nineteenth century, one

---

[1190] Stuart Piggott, *William Stukeley, an eighteenth-century antiquary*. O: Clarendon: 1950. Pp. xvi, 228.

[1191] Marie Schütt, *Das Germanenproblem in der englischen Geschichtsschreibung des 18. Jahrhunderts*. Hamburg: de Gruyter: 1960. Pp. 70.

[1192] Robert Preyer, *Bentham, Coleridge and the Science of History*. Bochum-Langendreer: Pöppinghans: 1958. Pp. ix, 105. Rev: *EHR* 75, 360f.

[1193] Per Fuglum, *Edward Gibbon: his view of life and conception of history*. Oslo: Akademisk Forlag: 1953. Pp. 176. Rev: *EHR* 71, 335f.

[1194] G. Giarizzo, *Edward Gibbon e la cultura europea del settecento*. Naples: Istituto Italiano per gli studi storici: 1954. Pp. 534. Rev: *EHR* 71, 655ff.

[1195] Joseph Ward Swain, *Edward Gibbon the Historian*. L: Macmillan: 1966. Pp. xii, 161. Rev: *History & Theory* 7, 144ff.

[1196] Harold K. Bond, *The Literary Art of Edward Gibbon*. O: Clarendon: 1960. Pp. 167.

[1197] Gavin de Beer, *Gibbon and his World*. L: Thames & Hudson: 1968. Pp. 144. Rev: *EHR* 84, 401.

particular group deserves attention (Grote, Milman, Arnold, Thirlwall): they sought, and of course found, in history the foundations for their own liberal and christian beliefs, but nevertheless wrote some good history.[1198] Grote has merited an individual study, which tells more of the man than of his work.[1199] Soon after this, German historicism (whatever it may have been) reached England, an invasion described in tones of needless superiority by Dockhorn.[1200] Dockhorn's other book, in which he presumes to recommend to his German readers both American and English achievements in the history of ideas, is even more remarkably and insufferably patronizing.[1201] A curious by-product of romanticism and historicism – the cult of anglo-saxon origins and contempt for the celtic element which were so widespread in Victorian England – is reviewed by Curtis in a book that could be a good deal better: like a good Freudian, he can see no difference between the wildest prejudice and the mildest joke, nor does he observe the chronological niceties necessary to historians.[1202] Burrow shows something of the growth of true scholarship which was so marked in that age; this is a theme worth pursuing further.[1203] Shannon, on the other hand, shows how the desire to put history to practical uses led to tedious, and dangerous, absurdities in Sir John Seeley's second-rate mind.[1204] A very much better historian – the English historian's patron saint – proves rather too much for

---

[1198] Duncan Forbes, *The Liberal Anglican Idea of History*. CUP: 1952. Pp. x, 208.

[1199] M. L. Clarke, *George Grote, a biography*. L: Athlone: 1962. Pp. x, 196. Rev: *EHR* 79, 621f.

[1200] Klaus Dockhorn, *Der deutsche Historismus in England*. Göttingen: Vandenhock & Ruprecht: 1950. Pp. 230.

[1201] Klaus Dockhorn, *Deutscher Geist und angelsächische Geistesgeschichte*. Göttingen: Musterschmidt: 1954. Pp. 85.

[1202] Lewis P. Curtis, *Anglo-Saxons and Celts: a study of anti-Irish prejudice in Victorian England*. Bridgeport: New York UP: 1968. Pp. ix, 162. Rev: *VS* 12, 452ff.

[1203] John W. Burrow, 'The uses of philology in Victorian England', *Kitson Clark Ft* (n. 137), 180–204.

[1204] R. T. Shannon, 'John Robert Seeley and the idea of a national Church', *Kitson Clark Ft* (n. 137), 236–67.

Bell's critical skill.[1205] And then there is Acton whose failure ever to produce a sizable piece of historical writing never inhibited him from offering advice to others. Kochan almost performs the miracle of constructing out of his notes and annotations an actual historian.[1206]

Three books stand by themselves because they treat of the manner in which particular historical problems have been handled by historians whom nothing else connects. Ben-Israel casts her eye over those English historians from Aloysius to Acton who have tried to write about the French Revolution; she has much of interest to say about individuals, but no particularly useful general intellectual picture emerges.[1207] Schenk considers the German historians who before the first war wrote about England; with the exception of the sane Marxist Bernstein, he finds them all – such giants as Weber, Oncken, Marcks and Delbrück included – bemused by chauvinism, bogus notions of Darwinism in history, false prophecies and darkling talk of destiny.[1208] A very revealing book. Less drastic are the results of an investigation the other way on in which English historians from Hallam to A. J. P. Taylor are asked their opinion of Germany; here the ominous tends to be replaced by the trivial.[1209] One fears the effect may be no less revealing – but perhaps the question is at fault.

(D) SCIENCE

There is now an increasing interest in the history of science, medicine and technology, though the best English work is not

[1205] H. E. Bell, *Maitland: a critical examination and assessment*. L: Black: 1965. Pp. 150. Rev: *EHR* 82, 221f.

[1206] Lionel Kochan, *Acton on History*. L: Deutsch: 1954. Pp. 184. Rev: *EHR* 74, 127f.

[1207] Hedva Ben-Israel, *English Historians on the French Revolution*. CUP: 1968. Pp. xii, 312. Rev: *VS* 12, 476f.

[1208] W. Schenk, *Die deutsch-englische Rivalität vor dem ersten Weltkrieg in der Sicht deutscher Historiker: Missverstehen oder Machtstreben?* Aarau: Keller Verlag: 1967. Pp. 173. Rev: *Hist* 53, 163.

[1209] Manfred Messerschmidt, *Deutschland in englischer Sicht: die Wandlungen des Deutschlandbildes in der englischen Geschichtsschreibung*. Düsseldorf: Triltsch: 1955. Pp. vi, 191.

necessarily done on the fortunes of these phenomena in England. There have so far been more articles than books, and it is clear that a good deal more in the way of sources should be published, or at least be made accessible. In general, I may draw attention to two periodicals in which important relevant studies are occasionally found: *British Journal of the History of Science*, and *Journal of Medical History*. *History of Science* is an annual which has room for longer pieces.

Here, too, Butterfield has pointed the way.[1210] Debus has described the English disciples of Paracelsus, the scientist, mystic and magician.[1211] More typical of his day was Digby, a dilettante of something like genius as well as a member of the greater gentry; he was interested in everything about nature, supported and imitated the researchers, and managed to find time on the side to take part in diplomacy and politics.[1212] His day also witnessed the first argument about the conflict between religious dogma and the discoveries of the physicists.[1213] In a way, science may be said to have won with the foundation of the Royal Society, though the point did not become clear till two centuries after. The Society itself commissioned a set of historical essays which are respectable and conventional, and may well be perfectly accurate about those early scientists; but no one will be blamed too much for omitting to read the volume.[1214] By contrast, Purver is almost certainly wrong in trying to recapture the origins of the Society for Oxford and for formal Baconianism, but the book is quite exciting and may help to secure a more serious treatment of these questions than has been habitual while they remained the preserve of scientists taking time off to write

---

[1210] H. Butterfield, *The Origins of Modern Science*. L: Bell: 1949. Pp. x, 217.

[1211] Allen G. Debus, *The English Paracelsians*. L: Oldbourne: 1965. Pp. 222.

[1212] R. T. Peterson, *Sir Kenelm Digby: the ornament of England, 1603 – 1665*. L: Cape: 1956. Pp. 366. Rev: *EHR* 72, 746f.

[1213] Richard S. Westfall, *Science and Religion in 17th Century England*. New Haven: Yale UP: 1958. Pp. 235.

[1214] Harold Hartley, ed., *The Royal Society: its origins and founders*. L: Royal Society: 1960. Pp. ix, 275.

chronicles.[1215] Skinner casts doubt upon the notion that from the first the Society specialized in 'real' scientists: he shows that Hobbes was excluded on personal grounds, not because he practised the wrong discipline.[1216]

Quite apart from the Royal Society, the seventeenth century witnessed the first appearance of the great man of science in England. Boas writes an important book on Robert Boyle, universal genius and father of chemistry.[1217] 'Espinasse offers a book that is nearly as good on the versatile Robert Hooke.[1218] Much less impressive is a little book on the leading astronomer Halley.[1219] William Harvey, discoverer of the major circulation of the blood, receives a large and solid volume which in great part assembles the fruits of bibliographical research;[1220] his anatomical lectures have been magnificently edited with a translation (very necessary).[1221] As was said above (n. 340), Hill has provoked a major discussion of the question whether this increasing activity had anything to do with political and more generally intellectual events. Not only have his reviewers undermined a thesis erected on some provisional work done in the 1930's, but Greaves and Shapiro, who both endeavour to rescue something of the thesis by showing that such links as there were had nothing to do with the puritanism which Hill advanced by way of explanation, make one even

---

[1215] Margery Purver, *The Royal Society: concept and creation*. L: Routledge: 1967. Pp xviii, 246. Rev: *EHR* 83, 568ff.; *History of Science* 6, 106ff. (highly critical).

[1216] Quentin Skinner, 'Thomas Hobbes and the nature of the early Royal Society', *HJ* 12 (1969), 217–39.

[1217] Marie Boas, *Robert Boyle and 17th Century Chemistry*. CUP: 1958. Pp. viii, 240.

[1218] Margaret P. M. 'Espinasse, *Robert Hooke*. L: Heinemann: 1956. Pp. vii, 192.

[1219] Angus Armytage, *Edmond Halley*. Edinburgh: Nelson: 1960. Pp. xii, 220.

[1220] Geoffrey Keynes, *The Life of William Harvey*. O: Clarendon: 1966. Pp. xviii, 483. Rev: *Hist* 52, 328f.

[1221] Gweneth Whitteridge, ed., *The Anatomical Lectures of William Harvey: Prelectiones Anatomie Universalis De Musculis*. Edinburgh: Livingstone (for Royal College of Physicians): 1964. Pp. lxvi, 504. Rev: *EHR* 80, 837f.; *History of Science* 4, 103ff.

more sceptical of all these attempts at finding a single comprehensive explanation for all form of intellectual activity.[1222]

The massive edition of Newton's letters (n. 39) has not yet been exploited, but work has been done on him nevertheless. Bell has tried to explain the 'Newton chapter' in the history of natural science within the framework of history in general: this sort of thing needs more room and more references.[1223] In a strictly technical study, Herival investigates the prehistory of the *Principia*, that is to say, the development of Newton's ideas.[1224] Cohen's treatise on the further development of Newtonian science forms a real model of the kind of history that should be written; he rests an imaginative general thesis on the specific study of Benjamin Franklin's electrical experiments.[1225] A book about the influence of Newton's optics on the poets of the eighteenth century stands out as something of an oddity.[1226] Several well known scientists discuss several sides of that towering genius in the collection with which the Royal Society celebrated his 300th birthday.[1227]

There is little to report on the eighteenth century. Hoskin has published Herschel's most important astronomical treatise, with a notable introduction.[1228] Gibbs contributes a useful but brief life of Priestley, the chemist and intellectual.[1229] Le Fanu

---

[1222] Richard L. Greaves, 'Puritanism and science: the anatomy of a controversy', *Journal of the History of Ideas* 30 (1969), 345–68. – B. J. Shapiro, 'Latitudinarianism and science in seventeenth-century England', *PP* 40 (1968), 16–41.

[1223] Arthur E. Bell, *Newtonian Science*. L: Arnold: 1961. Pp. 176.

[1224] John Herival, *The Background to Newton's 'Principia': a study of Newton's dynamical researches in the years 1664 – 1684*. O: Clarendon: 1965. Pp. xvi, 337.

[1225] I. Bernard Cohen, *Franklin and Newton*. Philadelphia: Amer. Philosophical Soc.: 1956. Pp. xxvi, 657.

[1226] Marjorie Hope Nicolson, *Newton Demands the Muse*. Hamden, Conn.: Anchor Books: 2nd ed. 1963. Pp. xi, 178.

[1227] Royal Society, *Newton Tercentenary Celebrations*. CUP: 1947. Pp. xv, 92.

[1228] Michael A. Hoskin, *William Herschel and the Construction of the Heavens*. L: Oldbourne: 1963. Pp. 199.

[1229] F. W. Gibbs, *Joseph Priestley*. Edinburgh: Nelson: 1965. Pp. xii, 258.

collects all the material left behind by Jenner, medical man and essentially the inventor of vaccination.[1230]

With respect to the nineteenth century, it looks as though historians have been unable to work up an interest in anything except the biological discoveries and their effects in the general history of ideas. Gillispie investigates a pre-Darwinian controversy – the conflict between science and revelation which arose as fossil finds called forth the first grave doubts about biblical dating.[1231] The real storm, of course, broke only with the publication of Darwin's *Origin of Species*. Himmelfarb employs a biographical method to describe the reception of his ideas and the fortunes of his book.[1232] Another book pursues much the same theme, but confines itself to the newspapers in which, no doubt, popular reaction was most reliably reflected.[1233] How immediately that watershed of 1859 produced its effects also in anthropological studies is shown by Burrow.[1234]

(E) RELIGIOUS THOUGHT

This is eminently a theme which has had to be treated throughout the chronological sections of this survey; the present section confines itself to works very specifically concerned

[1230] W. R. Le Fanu, *A Bio-Bibliography of Edward Jenner, 1749 – 1822*. L: Harvey & Blythe: 1951. Pp. xx, 176. Rev: *History of Science* 1, 115ff.
[1231] Charles C. Gillispie, *Genesis and Geology: a study in the relations of scientific thought, natural theology, and social opinion in Great Britain, 1790 – 1850*. C (Mass.): Harvard UP: 1951. Pp. xv, 315. Rev: *EHR* 67, 420f.
[1232] Gertrude Himmelfarb, *Darwin and the Darwinian Revolution*. L: Chatto & Windus: 1959. Pp. ix, 422. Rev: *EHR* 76, 173f.
[1233] Alvar Ellegård, *Darwin and the General Reader: the reception of Darwin's theory of evolution in the British periodical press, 1859 – 1872*. Göteborg: Acta Universitatis Gothoburgensis 64: 1958. Pp. 394. Rev: *EHR* 75, 544f.
[1234] John W. Burrow, 'Evolution and anthropology in the 1860s: the Anthropological Society of London, 1863 – 1871', *VS* 8 (1965 – 1966), 137–54.

with religion rather than history or society. Pineas has analysed Thomas More's polemical methods against heretics; he brings few surprises but also no comfort to those who worship More the plaster-saint.[1235] How very confused the spiritual state of men was round about 1600, as new knowledge 'called all in doubt', is brought out by Harris in a book which uses another quotation from the same hackneyed poem for its title; it must be said that this is a literary critic's production which knows too little of historical method or concerns.[1236] How well the theme, on the other hand, deserves serious study is shown also in Walzer's demonstration that a serious collapse of social philosophy lay behind at least some forms of puritan apocalyptic thinking (n. 372). Mosse, who like Hall has made a somewhat desperate attempt to find an accurate definition for the term 'puritan',[1237] has also very interestingly described the protestant casuistry which resulted among some more active puritans from the attempt to bring reason of state in accord with christian principles.[1238] Orr discusses the ideas of one of Hooker's disciples who in the end could see no reason for rejecting Rome.[1239] Anti-puritan ideas are also investigated in a study of some intellectual contacts between England and Holland in the early seventeenth century.[1240] As fanaticism weakened and the speculations of natural science clamoured to be heard, a new state of uncertainty developed once more which induced in the characteristic members of the Church

---

[1235] Rainer Pineas, *Thomas More and Tudor Polemics*. Bloomington: Indiana UP: 1968. Pp. xi, 262. Rev: *Hist* 54, 421f.

[1236] Victor I. Harris, *All Coherence Gone*. Chicago: U of Chicago P: 1949. Pp. x, 255. Rev: *AHR* 55, 354f.

[1237] George L. Mosse, 'Puritanism reconsidered', *Archiv für Reformationsgeschichte*, 55 (1964), 37–48. – Basil Hall, 'Puritanism: the problem of definition', *Studies in Church History* 2 (1965), 283–96.

[1238] George L. Mosse, *The Holy Pretence: a study of christianity and reason of state from William Perkins to John Winthrop*. O: Blackwell: 1957. Pp. 159.

[1239] Robert R. Orr, *Reason and Authority: the thought of William Chillingworth*. O: Clarendon: 1967. Pp. xi, 217. Rev: *EHR* 84, 393.

[1240] Rosalie L. Colie, *Light and Enlightenment: a study of the Cambridge Platonists and the Dutch Arminians*. CUP: 1957. Pp. xiii, 162.

of England their equally characteristic trust in common sense.[1241]

But common sense does not satisfy for long: the first reaction against a peace that was thought to be a sign of spiritual death came with Wesley on whom Green has lavished a piety which arises from Wesley's membership of Green's own Oxford college rather than from any community of faith or ideas.[1242] Among the other reactions, the Oxford Movement of ritualism has long been familiar, but White directs attention to a Cambridge movement which, animated by a perversely Gothic passion, exercised an influence on church architecture and forms of worship which is not yet dead.[1243] Elliott-Binns, a bit drily, runs over the second half of the century.[1244] A work on the beginnings of that particular English phenomenon, christian socialism, which treats it firmly by the methods of intellectual history, should be included here.[1245]

[1241] Henry G. van Leeuwen, *The Problem of Certainty in English Thought, 1630 – 1690*. The Hague: Nijhoff: 1963. Pp. xvii, 159. Rev: *EHR* 81, 167f.

[1242] V. H. H. Green, *The Young Mr Wesley*. L: Arnold: 1961. Pp. viii, 342. Rev: *EHR* 77, 780f. – Idem, *John Wesley*. L: Nelson: 1964. Pp. 168.

[1243] James F. White, *The Cambridge Movement: the ecclesiologists and the Gothic revival*. CUP: 1962. Pp. xii, 365. Rev. *EHR* 79, 624ff.

[1244] L. E. Elliott-Binns, *English Thought, 1860 – 1900: the theological aspect*. L: Longmans: 1956. Pp. ix, 388.

[1245] Torben Christensen, *Origin and History of Christian Socialism, 1848 – 1854*. Aarhus: Universitetsforlaget: 1962. Pp. 369. Rev: *EHR* 79, 567ff.

XII

Scotland

(A) GENERAL

The Scots, it is said, love their history but do not study it – perhaps love it the more easily because they do not permit study to interfere with preconceptions. There is less truth in this opinion than once there was, but it has to be confessed that the number of writings to be recorded is disappointingly small: it is only in the last few years, perhaps in the last decade, that the sort of professional work commonplace in English and Welsh history has become at all prominent in the northern kingdom. An older tradition of lively narrative, little analysis, and doubtful accuracy survives still in Mackie's brief introduction,[1246] while signs of improvement appear in the more generously planned two-volume general history produced by Dickinson and Pryde.[1247] These works all follow tradition by concentrating on the history of politics and the Church. In view of the dearth of really detailed investigation, it is surprising to find that a multi-volume general history is also in the making; indeed, its modern section is complete in two volumes of which Donaldson's on the sixteenth and seventeenth centuries is the more impressive.[1248] Campbell's

---

[1246] J. D. Mackie, *History of Scotland*, Harmondsworth: Penguin Books: 1964. Pp. 406. Rev: *Scottish History Review*, 45, 203f.

[1247] W. Croft Dickinson, *Scotland from the Earliest Times to 1603*. Edinburgh: Nelson: 1961. Pp. viii, 408. – George S. Pryde, *Scotland from 1603 to the Present Day. Ibid.:* 1962. Pp. viii, 359. Rev: *EHR* 79, 173ff.

[1248] Gordon Donaldson, *Scotland: James V to James VII*. Edinburgh: Oliver & Boyd: 1965. Pp. x, 449. Rev: *EHR* 82, 571ff. – William Ferguson, *Scotland: 1689 to the Present. Ibid.:* 1968. Pp. ix, 464. Rev: *Hist* 54, 426ff. (These are vols, 3 and 4 of the *Edinburgh History of Scotland*.)

attempt to add the dimension of economic history is particularly welcome, though the treatment is impressionistic,
there is a striking dearth of statistical material, and we still
do not move quite in the later twentieth century.[1249] These
strictures cannot be at all applied to Smout's very fine social
history of early-modern Scotland, a well-planned, sensible
and fascinating work with excellent bibliographies.[1250] At the
same time, it must strike one as significant that what in any
country would have been regarded as good and most welcome,
was in this case received with extremes of rejoicing or dis-
approbation, provoked by the destruction of comfortable
legends, thus underlining the relative backwardness of this historiography. His American nationality did not save Notestein's
readable survey of Scotland's historical role from the characteristic sentimentality which Smout so entirely avoids.[1251]
Burleigh's survey of Scotland's ecclesiastical history has not
always made use of recent findings.[1252] A very small part of
Scottish christianity has been separately chronicled.[1253] A
somewhat antiquarian book on Scotland's parliamentary
peers at Westminster yet supplies a quantity of useful information.[1254] Coupland's brief history of nationalism in Wales and
Scotland really begins only in 1700, but since it came too
early to take account of the serious revival of active nationalism in the last ten years it is less useful than it might be.[1255]

[1249] R. H. Campbell, *Scotland since 1707: the rise of an industrial society*.
O: Blackwell: 1965. Pp. xii, 354. Rev: *EHR* 81, 599.

[1250] T. C. Smout, *A History of the Scottish People, 1560 – 1830*. L:
Collins: 1969. Pp. 576.

[1251] Wallace Notestein, *The Scot in History: a study of the interplay of
character and history*. New Haven: Yale UP: 1946. Pp. xviii, 371.
Rev: *AHR* 52, 501f.

[1252] J. H. S. Burleigh, *A Church History of Scotland*. L: OUP: 1960.
Pp. x, 456. Rev: *EHR* 77, 151f.

[1253] H. Escott, *A History of Scottish Congregationalism*. Glasgow Congre-
gational Union of Scotland: 1960. Pp. xv, 400.

[1254] James Fergusson, *The Sixteen Peers of Scotland: an account of the
elections of the representative peers of Scotland, 1707 – 1959*. O: Clarendon: 1960. Pp. viii, 175.

[1255] Reginald Coupland, *Welsh and Scottish Nationalism*. L: Collins:
1954. Pp. xii, 426.

Here Hanham's much better book fills an important gap.[1256]
One thing that Scottish historians do handle well is the story
of buildings.[1257]

(B) THE SIXTEENTH CENTURY

The last strictly medieval king of Scotland has received a
biography;[1258] his moderately Renaissance successor has been
studied with a view to discovering what he felt about Church
reform (he was not against it).[1259] Englishmen usually forget
that the notorious problem of England's northern frontier was
also Scotland's notorious problem of a southern frontier; Rae's
book at last deprives them of excuses for such one-sidedness.[1260]
But the main part of the story in this century, in Scotland
even more than elsewhere, must be the Reformation. Dickinson's excellent edition of John Knox's own account gives that
powerful document a fresh chance to dominate the scene;[1261]
but Donaldson's researches have shown that the truth differs
quite markedly from the presbyterian tradition, a piece of
iconoclasm which exposed the scholar to the expected fury of
entrenched convictions.[1262] Less contemptuous of traditions
is Ridley's life of Knox, a massive production which sorts out
many facts and may not be particularly misleading in making
its hero (intentionally?) a most unpleasant man.[1263] Donaldson further adds some new information on the prehistory of

[1256] H. J. Hanham, *Scottish Nationalism*. L: Faber: 1969. Pp. 250.

[1257] John G. Dunbar, *The Historical Architecture of Scotland*. L: Batsford: 1966. Pp. 268.

[1258] R. L. Mackie, *King James IV of Scotland*. Edinburgh: Oliver &
Boyd: 1958. Pp. 300. Rev: *EHR* 74, 153.

[1259] J. Wilson Ferguson, 'James V and the Scottish Church', *Harbison Ft* (n. 128), 52–76.

[1260] Thomas I. Rae, *The Administration of the Scottish Frontier, 1513–
1603*. Edinburgh UP: 1966. Pp. vii, 294. Rev: *EHR* 83, 392.

[1261] William Croft Dickinson, ed., *John Knox's History of the Reformation in Scotland*, 2 vols. Edinburgh: Nelson: 1949. Pp. cix, 374; 498.

[1262] Gordon Donaldson, *The Scottish Reformation*. CUP: 1960. Pp.
viii, 242. Rev: *EHR* 76, 715ff. – Idem, 'The Scottish episcopate
and the Reformation', *EHR* 60 (1945), 349–64.

[1263] Jasper Ridley, *John Knox*. O: Clarendon: 1968. Pp. vii, 596.

the personal union produced when James VI succeeded Elizabeth I in England.[1264] Shaw's study of the reformed church in the rest of the century helps to establish the new conviction that reform came to Scotland by stages and not like a thunderclap at the behest of Knox.[1265] Lee's highly competent studies of three leading politicians offer much assistance to a better understanding of Queen Mary's reign.[1266] Scotland's backward economy is well described by Lythe.[1267]

(C) THE SEVENTEENTH CENTURY

This is the century when the fate of both realms was most manifestly tied up with the fortunes of a Scottish dynasty and its Scottish policy. It is therefore sad to have virtually nothing to report. Nobbs' brief introduction at least brings out the problems to which research ought to be attending.[1268] Mathew's social history is superficial.[1269] Trevor-Roper's long article, on the other hand, which could profitably have become a book, offers many striking insights into the society and the affairs of a country much torn by tradition and religion at a time of deepest humiliation.[1270] Two works assist

---

[1264] Gordon Donaldson, 'Foundations of Anglo-Scottish Union', *Neale Ft* (n. 125), 282–314.

[1265] Duncan Shaw, *The General Assemblies of the Church of Scotland*. Edinburgh: St Andrew Press: 1964. Pp. xii, 261.

[1266] Maurice Lee, *James Steward, Earl of Moray: a political study of the Reformation in Scotland*. New York: Columbia UP: 1953. Pp. xi, 320. Rev: *AHR* 59, 105f. – Idem, *John Maitland of Thirlestane and the Foundations of Stuart Despotism in Scotland*. Princeton UP: 1959. Pp. xii, 314. Rev: *EHR* 76, 147ff. – Idem, 'The fall of the regent Morton: a problem in satellite diplomacy', *JMH* 28 (1956), 111–29.

[1267] S. G. E. Lythe, *The Economy of Scotland in its European Setting, 1550 – 1625*. Edinburgh: Oliver & Boyd: 1960. Pp. viii, 277. Rev: *EHR* 77, 152f.

[1268] Douglas Nobbs, *England and Scotland, 1560 – 1707*. L: Hutchinson: 1952. Pp. xxi, 173.

[1269] David Mathew, *Scotland under Charles I*. L: Eyre & Spottiswoode: 1955. Pp. xiv, 320.

[1270] Hugh R. Trevor-Roper, 'Scotland and the Puritan Revolution', *Ogg Ft* (n. 129), 78–130.

to a better understanding of the Church of Scotland in this century: alternating between an episcopal and a presbyterian organization, it finally did away with bishops for good in 1688, but again this was a more complex story than tradition used to suppose.[1271]

(D) SINCE 1707

After the Union, the history of Scotland becomes in many ways absorbed into that of Great Britain, but it is not to pander to nationalist prejudice if one deplores the readiness with which differences in history and development are so often forgotten. True enough, the Union gave Scotsmen a bigger stage on which to distinguish themselves, and in the life of the united kingdoms the men of Scotland have always played a markedly larger role than their numbers justify. Still, Scottish history as such also continued, a fact which offers some justification for modern nationalism. The Union itself has, of course, attracted work. Smout's investigation of Scottish trade with Scandinavia before the Union is especially important because the economic consequences have been particularly in dispute.[1272] In co-operation with Campbell, Smout has also put the Union itself through the mangle: extreme opinions are soberly corrected and the need for further research is well brought out.[1273] The political issues are firmly clarified by Pryde in his introduction to a good edition of the actual treaty.[1274] Riley shows the manner in which, during the first generation of a United Kingdom, English ministers attempted to rule the distant and little known north all the way from

---

[1271] W. G. Sinclair Snow, *The Times, Life and Thought of Patrick Forbes, Bishop of Aberdeen, 1618 – 1635*. L: SPCK: 1952. Pp. xi, 207. – Walter R. Foster, *Bishop and Presbytery: the Church of Scotland, 1661 – 1688. Ibid.*: 1958. Pp. 182. Rev: *EHR* 74, 354f.

[1272] T. C. Smout, *Scottish Trade on the Eve of the Union, 1660 – 1707*. Edinburgh: Oliver & Boyd: 1963. Pp. 320. Rev: *EHR* 80, 563f.; *EcHR*² 17, 158.

[1273] T. C. Smout and R. H. Campbell, 'The Anglo-Scottish Union of 1707', *EcHR*² 16 (1963 – 4), 455–77.

[1274] George S. Pryde, *The Treaty of Union of Scotland and England, 1707.* Edinburgh: Nelson: 1950. Pp. viii, 120.

Whitehall.[1275] The fatal venture to Darien, in search of rapid wealth, is romantically described by Prebble; a serious work on this episode would be welcome.[1276] Some useful work has been done in the economic history of the eighteenth century – that age when, thanks to the industrial revolution, Scotland suddenly jumped to the fore-front of progressive nations. Hamilton's general history and Handley's accounts of agriculture are still rather impressionistic and, so to speak, unprofessional, but they help to introduce the story.[1277] Fay similarly produced a nice but not very incisive old man's book on the situation in which Adam Smith could happen and become influential, while Kettler competently reviews the influential thinking of Smith's chief rival for the title of the first leading sociological thinker.[1278] The odd survival of a form of serfdom in Scottish mining is dug out by Duckham.[1279] And a real start on 'modern' economic history is made in Gray's careful analysis of the causes and course of Highland decline (and progress): decline in the north-west, progress elsewhere, are seen to result from the customary economic circumstances and not from the wickednesses and follies beloved by traditional sentimentalists.[1280]

Scotland's chief pride has for long been its system of education which quite early on was more democratic than most and remained at a high level down to about the middle of the

[1275] P. W. J. Riley, *The English Ministers and Scotland, 1707 – 1727*. L: Athlone: 1964. Pp. xiv, 326.

[1276] J. Prebble, *The Darien Disaster*. L: Secker & Warburg: 1968. Pp. x, 366.

[1277] H. Hamilton, *An Economic History of Scotland in the Eighteenth Century*. O: Clarendon: 1963. Pp. xviii, 452. Rev: *EHR* 80, 357ff. – J. E. Handley, *Scottish Farming in the Eighteenth Century*. L: Faber: 1953. Pp. 314. Rev: *EHR* 69, 340f. – Idem, *The Agricultural Revolution in Scotland*. Glasgow: Burns: 1963. Pp. vii, 317.

[1278] C. R. Fay, *Adam Smith and the Scotland of his Day*. CUP: 1956. Pp. viii, 174. – David Kettler, *The Social and Political Thought of Adam Ferguson*. Ohio State UP: 1965. Pp. 325.

[1279] Baron F. Duckham, 'Serfdom in eighteenth-century Scotland', *Hist* 54 (1969), 178–97.

[1280] Malcolm Gray, *The Highland Economy, 1750 – 1850*. Edinburgh: Oliver & Boyd: 1957. Pp. viii, 280.

nineteenth century. (His scepticism in the face of certain shibboleths on this subject has caused Smout (n. 1250) most trouble, though many Scotsmen are well aware, however reluctant they are to admit it, that since about 1860 even England has been ahead of Scotland in schools and universities.) Pride has, quite rightly, led to some good work. Perhaps Craig a little exaggerates the democratic and popular elements in Scotland's eighteenth-century literature, but essentially he is right:[1281] after all, this was the element which Sir Walter Scott added to the literature of Europe. Law drily discusses the intellectual excellences of Edinburgh in an age when the university, at any rate, enjoyed a justly high European reputation.[1282] That the new demands of the nineteenth century – more general education, but also more new specialisms – did not at once overwhelm these ancient universities emerges from Davie's loving account.[1283] Saunders tackles an allied theme with the weapons of the sociologist; though the result strikes one as a trifle abstract, it is nevertheless very useful to have these problems of education linked with a background of social themes such as urban expansion or the better provision of welfare.[1284] Some of the problems of a newly industrialized society appear in Wright's reminder that chartism had its far northern branch.[1285] Mechie finds the church anxious to do something about these miseries.[1286] Macmillan, on the other hand, shows that the real solution as often as not lay outside Scotland, whether it was found in going else-

---

[1281] David M. Craig, *Scottish Literature and the Scottish People, 1680 – 1830*. L: Chatto & Windus: 1961. Pp. 340. Rev: *EHR* 78, 383f.

[1282] A. Law, *Education in Edinburgh in the Eighteenth Century*. L: U of London P: 1965. Pp. 239.

[1283] G. E. Davie, *The Democratic Intellect: Scotland and her universities in the nineteenth century*. Edinburgh UP: 1961. Pp. xx, 352.

[1284] Lawrence J. Saunders, *Scottish Democracy, 1815 – 1840: the social and intellectual background*. Edinburgh: Oliver & Boyd: 1950. Pp. 444. Rev: *EHR*, 66, 421ff.

[1285] L. C. Wright, *Scottish Chartism*. Edinburgh: Oliver & Boyd: 1953. Pp. vii, 242. Rev: *EHR* 69, 170f.

[1286] Stewart Mechie, *The Church and Scottish Social Development, 1780 – 1870*. L: OUP: 1960. Pp. xi, 181. Rev: *EHR* 77, 389f.

where or in seeking wealth from elsewhere.[1287] The north-western highlands had special reasons for discontent which at times led to potentially violent movements rather reminiscent of Irish peasant rebellions.[1288]

All this was some cry away from the beauty of that reconstruction which the later eighteenth century imposed so wisely upon Scotland's still medieval capital.[1289]

[1287] David S. Macmillan, *Scotland and Australia, 1788 – 1850: emigration, commerce, and investment.* O: Clarendon: 1967. Pp. xviii, 434. Rev: *EHR* 84, 126f.

[1288] H. J. Hanham, 'The problem of Highland discontent, 1880 – 1885', *TRHS* (1969), 21–65.

[1289] A. J. Youngson, *The Making of Classical Edinburgh, 1750 – 1840.* Edinburgh UP: 1966. Pp. xvi, 338. Rev: *EHR* 83, 849f.

Ireland

The effects of national independence are at long last showing in Ireland. Until recently, few countries were less able to face the truths of history and more firmly convinced of its legends, but the natural feelings of a long suppressed and oppressed nation – feelings too readily enshrined in post-liberation politics – have of late begun to abate sufficiently for serious historical writing to become the rule rather than the exception. Most of this writing is, in consequence, revisionary and still very much in the stage of producing scattered results which have not yet reached the ordinary textbooks or the larger consciousness; there the flattering legend may still be more influential than the sometimes uncomfortable truth towards which, to their great credit, Irish historians are nowadays working. However, there is a good recent introduction to Ireland's modern history in Beckett's textbook.[1290]

(A) BEFORE THE UNION

Tudor Ireland needs a lot of new work on it before Bagley's ancient history is displaced. Meanwhile, Quinn has done his best: in an important article, he reinterprets Henry VIII's policy, while in a short book he puts Elizabeth's policy in a less favourable light than is obtained, for instance, from Fall's study of the conquest, in itself a useful contribution to the story (n. 178).[1291] Gwynn assists to an understanding of the

---

[1290] James C. Beckett, *The Making of Modern Ireland, 1603 – 1922*. L: Faber: 1966. Pp. 496. Rev: *EHR* 82, 836; *HJ* 9, 391ff.

[1291] David B. Quinn, 'Henry VIII and Ireland, 1509 – 1534', *IHS* 12 (1961), 318–44. – Idem, *The Elizabethans and the Irish*. Ithaca:

late-medieval Church,[1292] and Edwards fruitfully continues his earlier labours on the impact of the Reformation.[1293] Some reasons for the failure of Henrician policy, with its dire consequences in Elizabeth's reign, are brought out in White's study of the intervening period.[1294] A somewhat exceptional enterprise in this period is McCracken's excursus into a problem of the economy.[1295] All this work, however, amounts so far really to beginnings that one would like to see more energetically pursued.

Seventeenth-century studies are not all that more plentiful, but they look rather more penetrative. Thus we have some very illuminating enquiries into the critical years of Charles I's reign when a serious attempt was made to transform conquest and colonization into the genuine establishment of a new order – an attempt, admittedly, which led to the rebellion of 1641, indirectly to the English civil wars, and thus in the end to the disaster of a permanent state of enmity between the kingdoms. Mayes shows up the failure of a foolish policy which tried to buy off opposition by bestowing honours on men too poor to sustain the position consequent upon them.[1296] Kearney's powerful investigation of Strafford's rule demonstrates the effect of the struggle for power in Ireland upon a royal policy which the parties were forever frustrating, but also how clumsily Strafford handled the parties.[1297] The contribution of Strafford's greed to his political failure emerges in an

---

Cornell UP (for Folger Library): 1966. Pp. ix, 204. Rev: *EHR* 83, 834f.

[1292] Aubrey Gwynn, S.J., *The Medieval Province of Armagh, 1417 – 1545*. Dundalk: Dundalgan Press: 1946. Pp. xi, 287.

[1293] R. Dudley Edwards, 'Ireland, Elizabeth and the Counter-Reformation', *Neale Ft* (n. 125), 315–39.

[1294] Dean G. White, 'The reign of Edward VI in Ireland: some political, social and economic aspects', *IHS* 14 (1964 – 5), 197–211.

[1295] Eileen McCracken, 'The woodlands of Ireland circa 1600', *IHS* 11 (1958 – 9), 271–96.

[1296] Charles Mayes, 'The early Stuarts and the Irish peerage', *EHR* 73 (1958), 227–51.

[1297] Hugh P. Kearney, *Strafford in Ireland, 1633 – 1641*. Manchester UP: 1959. Pp. xviii, 294. Rev: *EHR* 76, 106ff.

exchange between Ranger and Cooper.[1298] Clarke tackles much the same theme from the other side: he explains why the rebellion found the Old English (those settled before the recent plantations) allied with the Wild Irish.[1299] This alliance, which confirmed the failure of Stuart policy, produced, thanks to the intervention of religion, a movement of support for the Stuarts;[1300] the attempted treaty, however, came too late to help the king.[1301] No significant work has yet been done on the era of Oliver's conquest, but Simms has concerned himself with the next stage in Ireland's calvary, the reorganization by William III. He has discussed the making of the imposed peace and also shown that the victorious protestants' redistribution of the lands (once regarded as making a fundamental transformation) made little difference: by and large, the king simply confirmed a situation left behind by Cromwell and undisturbed by the Restoration.[1302] Some very well entrenched legends fall under Cullen's axe: he demonstrates that the notorious control which England exercised over Irish trade in the era of the 'old colonial system' really enabled Ireland to prosper and maintain an export trade which also assisted internal growth.[1303]

Ireland remained unexpectedly quiescent till close to the end of the eighteenth century; one man who did make a noise is studied in his relation to the country in a book which shows that even Swift could not rouse England to a sense of Irish

---

[1298] Terence Ranger, 'Strafford in Ireland: a revaluation', *PP* 19 (1961), 24–45. – John P. Cooper, 'Strafford and the Byrnes' country', *IHS* 15 (1966 – 7), 1–20.

[1299] Aidan Clarke, *The Old Irish in Ireland, 1625 – 1642*. L: MacGibbon & Kee: 1966. Pp. 288. Rev: *Hist* 52, 209ff.

[1300] Thomas L. Coonan, *The Irish Catholic Confederacy and the Puritan Revolution*. New York: Columbia UP: 1954. Pp. xviii, 402.

[1301] John Lowe, 'Charles I and the Confederation of Kilkenny', *IHS* 14 (1964 – 5), 1–19.

[1302] J. G. Simms, 'Williamite peace tactics, 1690 – 1691', *IHS* 8 (1952 – 3), 303–23. – Idem, *The Williamite Confiscation in Ireland, 1690 – 1703*. L: Faber: 1956. Pp. 207. – Idem, *Jacobite Ireland, 1685–91*. L: Routledge: 1969. Pp. xii, 297.

[1303] Louis M. Cullen, *Anglo-Irish Trade, 1660 – 1800*. Manchester UP: 1968. Pp. viii, 252. Rev: *EcHR²* 22, 562.

grievances.[1304] The country's problems in the main closely resembled those of England: thus the protestant sects managed to grow strong in a system which, officially repressive, was in practice almost tolerant.[1305] How very normal and orderly everything appeared to be, on the surface at least, is explained in a study of government and electioneering methods.[1306] Not until the American revolution did an aggressively disaffected upper class manage to score some radical successes.[1307] Then the French Revolution altered the situation by once more turning Ireland into England's endangered backdoor, as in the days of Philip II and Louis XIV. Although the one French attempt at invasion came to nothing,[1308] Pitt's government resolved upon the policy of union; and since promises of emancipation given to the catholics were at once broken under pressure from the king, the Union led only to a century-long struggle for independence, waged by an Ireland that had changed profoundly. The Union itself has been thoroughly studied; the political motives and manœuvres involved have been explained.[1309] We have also been usefully reminded that the revival of a vigorous nationalism with catholic propensities at once provoked an equally determined counter-movement from the other side.[1310] Behind these politics Ireland still remained prosperous, though once again economic history awaits further study; meanwhile, Cullen has cast doubt upon

[1304] Oliver W. Ferguson, *Jonathan Swift and Ireland*. Urbana: U of Illinois P: 1962. Pp. xii, 217. Rev: *EHR* 79, 419f.

[1305] James C. Beckett, *Protestant Dissent in Ireland, 1687 – 1780*. L: Faber: 1948. Pp. 161.

[1306] Edith M. Johnston, *Great Britain and Ireland, 1760 – 1800: a study in political administration*. Edinburgh: Oliver & Boyd: 1963. Pp. xi, 431. Rev: *EHR* 80, 610f.

[1307] Maurice R. O'Connell, *Irish Politics and Social Conflict in the Age of the American Revolution*. Philadelphia: U of Pennsylvania P: 1965. Pp. 444. Rev: *Hist* 53, 128f.

[1308] E. H. Stuart Jones, *An Invasion that Failed: the French expedition to Ireland, 1796*. O: Blackwell: 1950. Pp. xvi, 256. Rev: *EHR* 66, 273ff.

[1309] G. C. Bolton, *The Passing of the Irish Act of Union*. L: OUP: 1966. Pp. viii, 239.

[1310] Hereward Senior, *Orangeism in Ireland and Britain, 1795 – 1836*. L: Routledge: 1966. Pp. x, 314. Rev: *HJ* 10, 475ff.

the notion that everything can be explained by the potato,[1311] and Large has raised some fundamental questions about the position of the landed classes, absentee or resident, who have usually been rather execrated than studied.[1312]

(B) AFTER THE UNION

Two valuable surveys do not quite replace the missing comprehensive history of Ireland from Union to Free State. McCaffrey judiciously reviews a century of Irish nationalism in a book which oddly enough copies the title of Mansergh's more searching study; this, however, does not start till 1840.[1313] Running over the years, McDowell has described the governmental machinery,[1314] and Black has attempted to elucidate the effect of English economic thinking upon England's Irish policy.[1315] Since the only weapon left to oppressed patriots were the tongue and pen (ready weapons ever in Ireland, anyway) it is perhaps not surprising that we seem to know more about public opinion in that country than in England, though the work done concentrates on the first half of the century.[1316] However, the main thread of Irish history in this age consists of a succession of crises, expressing themselves in ever renewed movements of political and irredentist protest; government reacted with a policy oscillating between repression and con-

[1311] Louis M. Cullen, 'Irish history without the potato', *PP* 40 (1968), 72–83.

[1312] David Large, 'The wealth of the greater Irish landowners, 1750 – 1815', *IHS* 15 (1966 – 7), 21–45.

[1313] Lawrence McCaffrey, *The Irish Question, 1800 – 1922*. U of Kentucky P: 1968. Pp. ix, 202. – P. N. S. Mansergh, *The Irish Question, 1840 – 1921*. L: Allen & Unwin: 1965. Pp. 316. Rev: *Hist* 52, 229f. This is an entirely revised version of the book, *Ireland in the Age of Reform and Revolution* (1940).

[1314] R. B. McDowell, *The Irish Administration, 1801 – 1914*. L: Routledge: 1964. Pp. xi, 328. Rev: *EHR* 81, 186f.

[1315] R. D. C. Black, *Economic Thought and the Irish Question, 1817 – 1870*. CUP: 1960. Pp. xiv, 299. Rev: *EHR* 77, 176f.; *HJ* 5, 208ff.

[1316] R. B. McDowell, *Public Opinion and Government Policy in Ireland, 1801 – 1846*. L: Faber: 1952. Pp. 303. – Brian St John Inglis, *The Freedom of the Press in Ireland, 1784 – 1841*. L: Faber: 1954. Pp. 256.

ciliation, but usually produced its positive proposals too late. A whole series of excellent studies now enables us to follow this fatal story almost continuously.

Broecker opens the tale with a short discussion of the difficulties caused by the need to maintain order during the French wars.[1317] Reynolds analyses the first well-organized crisis, that of catholic emancipation.[1318] His demonstration that success owed most to purely political skills is also borne out by Jupp's conclusion that even the unreformed vote could be successfully mobilized in a good cause by competent tacticians.[1319] O'Connell's triumph in this issue made him Ireland's hero and in the first Irish party in the imperial parliament supplied a weapon which he managed at times to use successfully. Nowlan investigates his aims (repeal of the Union);[1320] Macintyre describes the instrument (the organization, methods, and ultimate dissolution of a party which only O'Connell could hold together);[1321] rather more peripherally, Holl shows how his successes impressed German movements of resistance to absolutism.[1322] The links did exist: Ireland, like the rest of Europe, harboured its romantic rebels who, again like their opposite numbers elsewhere, suffered defeat in 1848.[1323] After O'Connell's death, the Irish party reached its

---

[1317] Galen Broecker, 'Robert Peel and the Peace Preservation Force', *JMH* 33 (1961), 363–73.

[1318] J. A. Reynolds, *The Catholic Emancipation Crisis in Ireland, 1823 – 1829.* New Haven: Yale UP: 1954. Pp. xi, 204. Rev: *EHR* 71, 701f.

[1319] P. J. Jupp, 'Irish parliamentary elections and the influence of the catholic vote', *HJ* 10 (1967), 183–96.

[1320] Kevin B. Nowlan, *The Politics of Repeal: a study in the relations between Great Britain and Ireland, 1841 – 1850.* L: Routledge: 1965. Pp. viii, 248. Rev: *EHR* 81, 867f.

[1321] Angus Macintyre, *The Liberator: Daniel O'Connell and the Irish Party, 1830 – 1847.* L: Hamilton: 1965. Pp. vi, 348. Rev: *HJ* 10, 310ff.

[1322] [K. Holl, *Die irische Frage in der Ära D. O'Connells und ihre Beurteilung in der politischen Publizistik des deutschen Vormärzes.* Mainz Dissertation (1958).]

[1323] Denis Gwynne, *Young Ireland and 1848.* O: Blackwell: 1949. Pp. 325.

lowest levels of meandering incompetence; into these dark corners, Whyte has thrown sufficient light.[1324] As the politicians were proving their sterility, another organization took over the leadership of the cause: in the age of Pius IX, the Church became the mainstay of resistance and supported a conduct which, according to taste, one may call heroic resistance or criminal ruthlessness.[1325] The influence of the clergy declined steadily and expired by about 1895.[1326] Of course, reform, at one time likely, was unhappily held up by the Irish landlord interest in the house of lords.[1327] Thus the Church found itself supporting Fenianism, still probably the most violent movement that even Ireland has known.[1328] The next wave of reform, associated with Gladstone, oddly enough owed a good deal to experience in India, a useful reminder how 'colonial' the whole Irish problem appeared to the Westminster government.[1329] Isaac Butt's attempt to achieve self-determination by constitutional means remained futile while violence in Ireland alienated English opinion.[1330] Then, just as Gladstone's combination of police action and reform was beginning to get the better of the Fenians, Parnell revived the Irish party, and parliamentary agitation reached new heights. O'Brien's account, however marked by the author's involve-

---

[1324] John H. Whyte, *The Independent Irish Party, 1850 – 1859*. L: OUP: 1958. Pp. xiii, 201. Rev: *EHR* 75, 365f.

[1325] Edward R. Norman, *The Catholic Church in Ireland in the Age of Rebellion, 1859 – 1873*. L: Longmans: 1965. Pp. xi, 485. Rev: *EHR* 81, 572ff.; *HJ* 9, 144ff.

[1326] John H. Whyte, 'The influence of the catholic clergy on elections in nineteenth-century Ireland', *EHR* 75 (1960), 239–59.

[1327] David Large, 'The house of lords and Ireland in the age of Peel', *IHS* 9 (1954 – 5), 367–99.

[1328] T. W. Moody, ed., *The Fenian Movement*. Cork: Mercier Press: 1968. Pp. 126 – Desmond Ryan (completed by Owen Dudley Edwards), *The Fenian Chief: a biography of James Stephen*. Dublin: Gill & Son: 1967. Pp. xxv, 390. Rev: *Hist* 53, 458f.

[1329] E. D. Steele, 'Ireland and the empire in the 1860s: imperial precedents for Gladstone's first Irish Land Act', *HJ* 11 (1968), 64–83.

[1330] David A. Thornley, *Isaac Butt and Home Rule*. L: MacGibbon & Kee: 1964. Pp 413. Rev: *EHR* 81, 869f.

ment, is a great deal better than Hurst's inadequately based attempt to see Parnell stripped of hagiographical trappings.[1331] Hurst does, however, demonstrate that the story of Parnell's dependence on the secret ballot is another legend.[1332] Another totally unnecessary tragedy, commonplace in a situation in which young men were roused to a violence which their elders for ever hoped to be able to use for their own political purposes, ended Gladstone's hopes of peace.[1333] While this persuaded him of the need for home rule, his conversion moved others to futile schemes of compromise.[1334] Then Parnell fell, an event that belongs to the history of England; what remained of his party for a time lost touch with the Irish nation and dwindled into an ineffectual faction in the house of commons (nn. 662, 750). The conservative's government's policy – a vigorous restoration of order combined with efficient economic reforms – appeared to be successful and looked likely to give Ireland the fact of home rule without the form.[1335] The question of how agitation revived after ten years of peace remains still far from answered, especially as this is a problem close to the one area which legend still dominates – the beginnings of the final struggle for independence. One ominous development was the growth of an organized unionist party, based on Ulster, under the conservative aegis;[1336] another the lack of interest in Ireland which marked the liberal

---

[1331] Conor Cruise O'Brien, *Parnell and his Party, 1880 – 1890*. O: Clarendon: 1957. Pp. xiii, 373. Rev: *EHR* 74, 139ff.; *HJ* 1, 83ff. – Michael C. Hurst, *Parnell and Irish Nationalism*. L: Routledge: 1968. Pp. ix, 117. Rev: *EHR* 84, 870f.

[1332] Michael C. Hurst, 'Ireland and the Ballot Act of 1872', *HJ* 8 (1965), 326–52.

[1333] Tom Corfe, *The Phoenix Park Murders: conflict, compromise and tragedy in Ireland, 1879 – 1882*. L: Hodder & Stoughton: 1968. Pp. 286.

[1334] Christopher H. D. Howard, 'Joseph Chamberlain, Parnell, and the Irish "Central Board" scheme, 1884 – 1885', *IHS* 8 (1952–3), 324–61.

[1335] Lewis P. Curtis, *Coercion and Conciliation, 1880 – 1892*. Princeton UP: 1963. Pp. xvi, 460. Rev: *EHR* 81, 868f.

[1336] D. C. Savage, 'The origins of the Ulster Unionist party, 1885 – 1886', *IHS* 12 (1960 – 1), 185–208.

administration of 1906 – 10 and caused it to miss some useful chances of settlement.[1337]

Crisis returned to Ireland in the wake of the political troubles in England. The battle over the house of lords grew swiftly into the Ulster crisis, the Easter rebellion of 1916, the bloody attempt at suppression in 1919 – 22, and the even bloodier civil war that followed. On this a great deal has been written – memoirs, propaganda, legend, literature, even some history – but very little of it appears to escape an essentially unhistorical attitude. Passions and party politics predominate: the matter is too recent. However, one may cite Gwynn's book not as the last word but as the most balanced review of the whole tragic decade so far available,[1338] Lyons's life of one of the leading rebels,[1339] and a collection of essays on 1916 which manages to achieve a measure of distance.[1340] Irish independence owed much to Irish Americans (very probably, the revival of the struggle should be investigated there rather than in Ireland itself), nor did the Treaty end the hostility felt in the United States for the oppressor of the fatherland; but 1921 nevertheless marked a very real stage in the influence which this one problem exercised on Anglo-American relations.[1341]

There remains one great crisis which was for long the preserve of legend: the great famine of 1845 – 6, the watershed between Ireland's earlier and later history. Overpopulation became chronic underpopulation; an economy too dependent on one product, the potato, met its nemesis. Much recent research has gone into indicating that the comforting notion, which placed the responsibility for both the famine itself and

[1337] Ronan Fanning, 'The unionist party and Ireland, 1906 – 1910', *IHS* 15 (1966 – 7), 147–71.

[1338] Denis Gwynne, *The History of Partition, 1912 – 1925*. Dublin: Browne & Nolan: 1950. Pp. 244.

[1339] F. S. L. Lyons, *John Dillon: a biography*. L: Routledge: 1968. Pp. xi, 516.

[1340] Kevin B. Nowlan, ed., *Making of 1916: studies in the history of the rising*. Dublin: Stationery Office: 1969. Pp. xiii, 338.

[1341] Alan T. Ward, *Ireland and Anglo-American Relations, 1899 – 1921*. L: Weidenfeld: 1969. Pp. xii, 291.

for the failure to provide adequate relief solely on England, cannot be maintained. A tradition-ridden peasant economy, and the highly inflexible and unchanging society insisted upon by the Church: these were decisive elements in a story of disastrous errors and inability to respond to need when it arose. The revision, largely the work of Irish historians, did not touch the brilliant but by now rather unreliable book on the theme written by an Englishwoman.[1342] Against this, Freeman describes a situation even before the disaster which in itself could hardly continue and offered determined resistance to every effort at improvement.[1343] Connell's important population studies heavily underscore such conclusions: early marriage and a high birth rate produced an 'explosion' which the country could not handle.[1344] The new view, resting on scholarly investigation, gains a hearing in a collection of essays tackling the problem from various sides.[1345] Connell has also studied the history of peasant marriage since 1846 and found a total revolution: now people married late and the population stagnated.[1346] Four essays from his pen throw a soberly lurid light upon the realities of that society, with its illicit stills, ether drinkers, heavy illegitimacy before the famine and enforced celibacy after.[1347] The decline of the population was, of course, assisted by the great emigration to America, an

---

[1342] Cecil Woodham-Smith, *The Great Hunger: Ireland, 1845 – 1849*. L: Hamilton: 1962. Pp. 510.

[1343] T. W. Freeman, *Pre-Famine Ireland: a study in historical geography*. Manchester UP: 1957. Pp. viii, 352. Rev: *EHR* 74, 541f.

[1344] K. H. Connell, 'The population of Ireland in the eighteenth century', *EcHR*² 16 (1963 – 4), 111–24. – Idem, *The Population of Ireland, 1750 – 1845*. O: Clarendon: 1950. Pp. xi, 293. – Idem, 'The colonization of waste land in Ireland, 1780 – 1845', *EcHR*² 3 (1950 – 1), 44–71.

[1345] R. Dudley Edwards and Desmond Williams, eds., *The Great Famine: studies in Irish history, 1845 – 1852*. Dublin: Browne & Nolan: 1956. Pp. xx, 517. Rev: *EHR* 73, 316ff.

[1346] K. H. Connell, 'Peasant marriage after the great famine', *PP* 12 (1957), 76–91; 'Peasant marriage in Ireland: the structure and development since the famine', *EcHR*² 14 (1960 – 1), 502–23.

[1347] K. H. Connell, *Irish Peasant Society: four historical essays*. O: Clarendon: 1968. Pp. xiii, 167. Rev: *Hist* 54, 432f.

event of incalculable consequences for both Ireland and
America.[1348] The demographic and economic features of
modern Ireland – or perhaps those which really modern
Ireland is at last beginning to alter – emerged clearly in the
1850's.

Ireland since independence has somehow lost a good deal
of interest; and historians' interest seems to have declined as
well. McCracken does a good job analysing the parliament of
the Irish Republic,[1349] and Harkness thumps a lot of tubs
in his determination to prove that the new Free State was
mainly responsible for the events which turned the old empire
into the new (and even shorter-lived) commonwealth.[1350]
But it seems more appropriate and more just to end with a
reference to one of Ireland's major contributions to universal
culture – the brewing of a unique beer. Here Lynch and
Vaizey have produced a piece of business history in which
personal experience finds agreeable reflection.[1351]

[1348] S. H. Cousens, 'Emigration and demographic change in Ireland,
1851 – 1861', *EcHR*[2] 14 (1960 – 1), 275–88. – Arnold Schrier,
Ireland and the American Emigration, 1850 – 1900. Minneapolis: U of
Minnesota P: 1958. Pp. xi, 210. Rev: *EHR* 75, 364f.

[1349] J. L. McCracken, *Representative Government in Ireland: a study of
Dáil Éireann, 1919 – 1948*. L: OUP: 1958. Pp. ix, 229. Rev: *EHR*
74, 753.

[1350] D. W. Harkness, *The Restless Dominion: the Irish Free State and the
British Commonwealth of Nations, 1921 – 1931*. L: Macmillan: 1969.
Pp. xviii, 312.

[1351] Patrick Lynch and John Vaizey, *Guinness Brewery in the Irish
Economy, 1759 – 1876*. CUP: 1960. Pp. viii, 274.

Indexes

All references are to numbers of footnotes

(A) AUTHORS AND EDITORS

Abel-Smith, Brian, 865
Abernathy, George R., 377
Abrams, P., 1131
Abramsky, Chimen, 747
Addis, John P., 873
Aldcroft, Derek H., 114, 876, 1020
Allen, Harry C., 110
Allen, Peter R., 911
Altholz, Joseph L., 915
Altick, Richard D., 1054
Alvarez, Manuel F., 173
Amery, Julian, 684
Ames, Russell, 1103
Anderson, Olive, 655
Andrews, Kenneth R., 283-4
Anglo, Sydney, 291
Annan, Noel, 1176
Anstruther, Godfrey, 252
Appleton, William W., 630
Armstrong, Elizabeth, 287
Armytage, Angus, 1219
Armytage, W. H. G., 868, 1027, 1039
Arnstein, Walter L., 661
Ashley, Maurice, 80, 303, 355-6, 436
Ashton, Robert, 321, 328
Ashton, Thomas S., 572-3
Ashworth, W., 850, 1016
Aspinall, A., 22, 44-5, 63, 500, 557

Åström, Sven-Erik, 449
Auerbach, Erica, 289
Ausel, Walter, 997
Ausubel, Herman, 656, 678
Aveling, Hugh, 112
Axtell, J. L., 1170
Aydelotte, William O., 703
Aylmer, Gerald E., 303, 336

Bachofen, Maja, 972
Bahlmann, D. W. R., 901
Baldwin, A. W., 943
Ball, J. N., 315
Barbour, Hugh, 382
Barié, Ottavio, 789, 824
Barlow, Richard B., 570
Barnes, John, 944
Barnes, Thomas G., 337
Bartlett, C. J., 842
Bassett, R., 933, 978
Batho, G. R., 69
Baugh, Daniel A., 563
Baumgardt, David, 1152
Baxter, Stephen B., 396, 411
Bayer, Theodor A., 798
Bayne, C. G., 27
Beales, A. C. F., 1043
Beales, Derek E. D., 632, 700, 785
Bealey, F. W., 736
Beasley, William G., 804
Beattie, John M., 478, 562

Beaverbrook, Lord, 922
Beckett, J. C., 1064, 1290, 1305
Beckingsale, B. W., 165
Beddard, Robert, 400
Behrens, C. A. B., 1012
Bell, Arthur E., 1223
Bell, H. E., 129, 187, 1205
Bell, P. M. H., 905
Ben-Israel, Hedva, 1207
Bennett, G. V., 132, 426
Bennett, H. S., 1066
Beresford, Maurice, 440
Best, Geoffrey F. A., 565, 903
Bindoff, S. T., 125, 142
Binney, J. E. D., 560
Birch, Alan, 872
Birkenhead, Lord, 945, 957
Birks, Michael, 1094
Black, Eugene C., 519
Black, R. D. C., 1315
Blagden, Cyprian, 57, 1065
Blake, Robert, 681, 695
Blanke, Gustav H., 297
Blench, J. W., 293
Blewett, Neal, 664, 704
Blitzer, C., 1115
Bloch, Charles, 794
Bloomfield, Paul, 818
Boahen, A., Adu, 826
Boas, Marie, 1217
Bohatec, Joseph, 307
Bolton, G. C., 1309
Bond, Harold K., 1196
Bongie, Lawrence L., 1137
Bonham Carter, Violet, 940
Bonno, Gabriel, 1132
Bonsall, Brian, 508
Booty, John E., 239
Bosher, R. S., 421
Bossy, John A., 250
Boucher, C. T. G., 610
Bourde, André J., 623
Bourne, Kenneth, 138, 781
Bowden, Peter J., 275
Bowen, Desmond, 896

Bowker, Margaret, 208
Bowle, John, 1123
Boynton, Lindsay, 176, 332
Brand, Jeanne L., 1031
Bridges, Lord, 693
Briggs, Asa, 117, 631, 637, 648,
    866, 868, 888
Brockett, A., 116
Brodie, D. M., 74
Broecker, Galen, 1317
Bromhead, P. A., 929
Bromley, J. S., 131
Brooke, John, 85, 487, 514
Brooks, E. St John, 166
Brooks, Peter, 238
Brose, Olive J., 900, 911
Brown, Ford K., 898
Brown, Gerald S., 489
Brown, K. C., 1116
Brown, Lucy, 771
Brown, Peter, 494
Brown, R. G., 596
Browning, Andrew, 22, 389
Bruce, Maurice, 863
Brunton, D., 345
Bryant, Arthur, 995
Bryant, Donald C., 1139
Bullock, Alan, 949
Bünger, S., 748, 992
Burleigh, J. H. S., 1252
Burn, W. L., 634
Burrow, John W., 1172, 1203,
    1234
Burton, Ann M., 770
Burwash, Dorothy, 277
Bury, J. P. T., 35
Busch, Briton C., 808
Butler, James R. M., 951, 1000
Butler, Jeffrey, 731
Butler, Rohan, 35
Butterfield, Herbert, 481, 510,
    1180, 1210
Butterworth, C. C., 235
Bythell, Duncan, 871
Cairncross, A. K., 882

Campbell, A. E., 811
Campbell, Charles S., 811
Campbell, R. H., 1249, 1273
Canavan, Francis P., 1143
Cannon, John, 515
Cantor, Norman F., 81
Caraman, Philip, 249
Carlson, A. J., 230
Carlson, Leland H., 77
Carpenter, Edward F., 426
Carpenter, S. C., 564
Carrington, Charles, 1177
Carswell, John P., 476, 518
Carter, Charles H., 127, 313
Carter, Jennifer, 413
Carus-Wilson, E. M., 107
Caspari, Fritz, 1167
Chadwick, Owen, 897, 908
Chalklin, C. W., 456
Challis, C. E., 258
Chambers, D. S., 28, 172
Chambers, J. D., 588, 600, 624, 848
Chapman, Gerald W., 1144
Chapman, James K., 830
Chapman, Maybelle K., 810
Charlton, Kenneth, 1041
Chaudhuri, K. N., 443
Checkland, Sidney G., 849
Chester, Allan G., 235
Chester, D. N., 958
Chilston, Viscount, 687-8
Christensen, Torben, 1245
Christie, Ian R., 514, 520
Church, Roy A., 855
Churchill, Randolph S., 942
Churchill, Winston S., 994
Clancy, Thomas H., 253
Clapham, John, 94
Clark, Dora Mae, 556
Clark, George Kitson, 633, 651, 765
Clark, George N., 1032
Clarke, Aidan, 1299
Clarke, M. L. 1040, 1199

Clarkson, L. A., 279
Clebsch, William A., 236
Clegg, H. A., 738
Cliffe, J. T., 260
Clive, John, 1076
Close, David, 702
Coate, Mary, 38
Coats, A. W., 622
Cobban, Alfred B., 42, 529
Cochrane, J. A., 1069
Cohen, I. Bernard, 1225
Cole, Margaret, 66, 744
Cole, W. A., 18
Coleman, Donald C., 104, 451-2, 1022
Colie, Rosalie L., 1240
Collier, Basil, 1004
Collier, Francis, 587
Collins, Doreen, 761
Collins, Henry, 747
Collinson, Patrick, 242-3
Colvin, H. M., 19
Conacher, James B., 654, 713, 719
Cone, Carl B., 1140
Connell, K. II., 1344, 1346-7
Connell-Smith, Gordon, 282
Constable, Robert, 189
Conzemius, Victor, 49
Coombs, Douglas C., 432, 827
Coonan, Thomas L., 1300
Cooper, John P., 150, 224, 1298
Coote, Colin, A., 948
Copeland, T., 42
Corfe, Tom, 1333
Cornford, James P., 723-4
Costello, William T., 1056
Costin, W. C., 23
Cotterell, Mary, 462
Coupland, Reginald, 1255
Court, W. H. B., 94, 851, 1015
Cousens, S. H., 1348
Cowherd, Raymond G., 906
Cowling, Maurice, 658, 1155
Cox, Richard H., 1128
Cragg, Gerald C., 385, 463, 571

Craig, David M., 1281
Craig, John, 87
Cranfield, G. A., 1073
Cranston, Maurice, 1124
Cremeans, C. D., 213
Creswell, John, 399
Cromwell, Valerie, 701, 757, 777
Crosby, Gerda Richards, 988
Cross, Claire, 200, 233
Crouzet, François M. J., 618
Cruickshank, Charles G., 175
Cruickshank, Marjorie, 1050
Cullen, Louis M., 1303, 1311
Curtis, Lewis P., 1202, 1335
Curtis, Lionel, 834
Curtis, Mark H., 335, 1055

Daalder, Hans, 960
Dakin, D., 35
Dalton, Hugh, 946
Dalziel, Margaret, 1077
Davie, G. E., 1283
Davies, C. S. L., 155, 176
Davies, E. T., 212, 1104
Davies, G. C. B., 567
Davies, Godfrey, 365
Davies, K. G., 447
Davies, Margaret G., 1037
Davies, Rupert, 566
Davis, Dorothy, 123
Davis, Ralph, 446, 450, 612–13
Dawley, Powell Mills, 240
Dawson, John P., 1082
Deane, Phyllis W., 18, 577
De Beer, Esmond S., 61
De Beer, Gavin, 1197
Debus, Allen G., 1211
Delany, Paul, 1186
De Roover, Raymond, 276
Derry, John W., 482, 636
Derry, T. K., 1004
Dessain, Charles S., 47
De Villiers, Elizabeth, 333
Dewar, Mary, 198
Dickens, A. G., 163, 211, 220

Dickinson, William Croft, 1247, 1261
Dickson, P. M. G., 412
Dilks, David, 837
Dockhorn, Klaus, 1200–1
Dodd, A. H., 459
Donaldson, Gordon, 1248, 1262, 1264
Donnison, F. S. V., 1008
Donoughue, Bernard, 514
Douglas, D. C., 22
Dowrie, J. A., 1020
Dowse, Robert E., 743
Drescher, Seymour, 1157
Driver, Cecil H., 671
Drus, Ethel, 50, 65, 832
Duckham, Baron F., 1279
Dudley, Edmund, 74
Dugmore, C. W., 238
Dunbabin, J. P. D., 776
Dunbar, John G., 1257
Dunham, W. H., 27
Dunn, John W., 1127
Dunn, Mary M., 398
Dyos, H. J., 114, 1038

Eagleston, A. J., 181
Eddy, J. J., 819
Edgar, F. T. R., 363
Edwards, Francis, 168
Edwards, Michael M., 617
Edwards, Owen Dudley, 1328
Edwards, R. Dudley, 11, 1293, 1345
Ehrman, John P. W., 431, 496, 528, 963, 1000
Ellegård, Alvar, 1233
Elliott, Charles, M., 611
Elliott-Binns, L. E., 1244
Ellis, Kenneth L., 561
Ellis, L. F., 1001
Elton, Geoffrey R., 21, 24, 144–5, 150–1, 154, 163, 183, 190, 195–6, 201, 203, 205, 224, 278, 329, 1101

Emmison, F. E., 199
Erickson, Arvel, B., 674
Erickson, Charlotte, 742
Escott, H., 1253
Esler, Anthony, 1168
'Espinasse, Margaret P. M., 1218
Estorick, Eric, 948
Eusden, John D., 341
Evans, Joan, 469
Everitt, Alan M., 280, 352-3
Eversley, D. E. C., 109, 620
Every, George, 424
Eyck, Frank, 676

Faber, Geoffrey, 917
Fairlie, Susan, 860
Falls, Cyril, 178, 693
Fanning, Ronan, 1337
Farnell, James A., 358
Fasnacht, G. F., 1161
Fay, C. R., 640, 1278
Feiling, Keith, 79, 552, 945
Fennessy, R. R., 1149
Ferguson, Arthur B., 1099
Ferguson, J. Wilson, 1259
Ferguson, Oliver W., 1304
Ferguson, S. M., 1017
Ferguson, William, 1248
Fergusson, James, 1254
Ferns, H. S., 780
Feuchtwanger, E. J., 720-1
Fieldhouse, D. K., 821
Fifoot, C. H. S., 52
Filmer, Robert, 1108
Finch, Mary, 260
Finer, S. E., 759
Fink, Z. S., 1111
Fisher, F. J., 126, 267
Fitton, R. S., 605
Fitzgerald, H., 1017
Flinn, M. W., 607
Foakes, R. A., 54
Foord, Archibald S., 506
Foot, Michael, 950
Foot, M. R. D., 64, 792, 1007

Forbes, Duncan, 1198
Foster, Elizabeth R., 32
Foster, Stephen, 374
Foster, Walter R., 1271
Fox, A., 738
Fox, Levi, 1185
Francis, A. D., 435
Frank, Joseph, 378, 1072
Frankland, Noel, 1005
Fraser, Peter, 414, 664, 686, 699
Freeman, T. W., 1343
Freund, Michael, 342
Fry, Geoffrey K., 965
Fryde, E. B., 20
Fuglum, Per, 1193
Furber, Elizabeth C., 1
Furber, Holden, 42, 615
Fussell, G. E., 98
Fussell, K. R., 98
Fussner, F. Smith, 1184
Fuz, J. K., 1028

Galbraith, J. S., 816, 833
Gallagher, John, 823
Gartner, Lloyd P., 894
Gash, Norman, 643, 672, 712, 718
Gauger, Hildegard, 1179
Genner, Lotti, 812
George, Charles H., 371
George, Katherine, 371
George, M. Dorothy, 502
Giarizzo, G., 1138, 1194
Gibbs, F. W., 1229
Gilbert, Bentley, B., 1030
Gill, Conrad, 117, 614
Gillard, D. R., 828
Gillesen, Günther, 788
Gillispie, Charles C., 1231
Gipson, L. H., 5, 548
Gladden, E. N., 964
Glasgow, E., 650
Glass, D. V., 70, 109, 455
Gleason, John H., 193, 786
Glover, Michael, 539

Glover, Richard, 538
Glow, Lotte, 347
Goldsmith, M. M., 1117
Gollin, A. M., 694
Gosden, P. H. J. H., 1026
Gosses, F., 768
Gough, J. W., 304, 1125
Gowing, Margaret M., 1010, 1012
Graham, Gerald S., 551, 817
Graham, R., 802
Grampp, W. D., 862
Graubard, Stephen R., 975
Gray, Charles M., 1088
Gray, Denis, 498
Gray, Malcolm, 1280
Greaves, Richard L., 1222
Greaves, Rose L., 808
Green, V. H. H., 1060, 1242
Greenberg, Michael, 885
Greenleaf, W. H., 1109, 1134
Gregg, Pauline, 369
Gregory, John S., 803
Grenville, John A. S., 797
Grigg, D., 589
Grosheide, D., 360
Guinn, Paul, 986
Gunn, J. A. W., 1114
Gupta, P. S., 741
Guttridge, G. H., 42, 488
Guttsman, W. L., 638
Gwyer, J. M. A., 1000
Gwyn, William B., 715
Gwynn, Aubrey, 1292
Gwynne, Denis, 1323, 1338

Haas, James M., 543
Habakkuk, Hrothgar J., 268, 439, 442, 572, 593, 595, 852
Haigh, Christopher, 218
Hale, John R., 1178
Haley, K. H. D., 390, 394
Halifax, Marquess of, 78
Hall, Basil, 1237
Hall, G. D. G., 320

Hall, H. Duncan, 1014
Haller, William, 298, 370
Halpérin, Vladimir, 1165
Hamburger, Joseph, 1153, 1156
Hamer, David A., 792
Hamilton, Bernice, 628
Hamilton, Elizabeth, 406
Hamilton, H., 1277
Hammersley, George, 441
Hammond, R. J., 1015
Hanak, H., 989
Hancock, P. D., 10
Hancock, W., Keith, 51, 952, 1012
Handcock, W. O., 22
Handley, J. E., 1277
Hanham, H. J., 24, 714, 1256, 1288
Hankey, Lord, 961
Hanson, L. W., 6
Hannay, R. K., 37
Hardacre, P. H., 362
Harding, Alan, 1081
Hargreaves, E. L., 1012
Harkness, D. W., 1350
Harlow, Vincent T., 549
Harmsworth, Geoffrey, 954
Harris, C. R. S., 1008
Harris, G. G., 118
Harris, J. D., 887
Harris, Victor I., 1236
Harrison, A. E., 878
Harrison, Brian, 642
Harrison, J. F. C., 644, 1052
Harrison, Royden, 734
Harriss, G. L., 145
Harrod, Roy F., 955-6
Hart, A. Tindal, 426
Hart, Jeffrey, 1135
Hart, Jennifer, 756, 775
Hartley, Harold, 1214
Hartwell, R. Max, 578, 584
Hatton, Ragnhild, 131, 526
Haugaard, William P., 230
Hauser, Oswald, 809

Havighurst, Alfred, 415, 921
Havran, Martin J., 335
Hay, Denys, 37, 72, 1014, 1181
Hayek, F. A., 582
Heath, George D., 359
Hecht, J. Jean, 627
Heinze, Rudolph W., 196
Helleiner, Karl, 531
Hembry, Phyllis M., 222
Henriques, Ursula, 1035–6
Herbrüggen, Hubertus S., 36
Herival, John, 1224
Herrick, Francis H., 722
Heuston, R. F. V., 1097
Hexter, J. H., 73, 124, 259, 1102
Hiddy, Ralph W., 881
Hill, Christopher, 303, 316, 334, 340
Hill, L. M., 195
Himmelfarb, Gertrude, 659, 1162, 1232
Hinton, R. W. K., 324, 445
Hjelholt, Holger, 789
Hobshawm, Eric J., 105, 584, 647, 740, 892
Hodgett, Gerald A. J., 219
Hodgson, Norma, 57
Hoff, B. van 't., 40
Hoffmann, Ross J. S., 43
Hoffmann, W. G., 103
Holden, J. Milnes, 1087
Holdsworth, William S., 1079
Hole, Christina, 464
Holl, K., 1322
Hollingsworth, T. H., 121
Holmes, Geoffrey S., 402, 405, 409, 419
Hood, F. C., 1119
Hopf, Constantine, 216
Horn, D. B., 22, 522–3, 1063
Hornby, William, 1014
Horsefield, J. Keith, 453
Horwitz, Henry, 403, 410
Hoskin, Michael A., 1228
Hoskins, W. G., 101, 268

Hough, Richard, 984
Houghton, W. E., 1171
Howard, Christopher H. D., 685, 1334
Howard, Michael E., 1011
Howell, Roger, 354
Howse, Ernest M., 567
Hudson, Winthrop S., 1169
Hughes, Edward, 626, 764
Hughes, J. R. T., 853
Hughes, Paul L., 29
Hughes, Philip, 209
Hughes, Richard, 1014
Hulme, Harold, 315
Hume, L. J., 755
Hunt, Norman C., 568
Hunter, Richard, 486
Hurst, Gerald, 1096
Hurst, Michael C., 729, 1332
Hurstfield, Joel, 125, 157, 161, 188, 206, 1014
Hurwitz, S. J., 991
Huzel, James P., 864
Hyam, Ronald, 838
Hyamson, Albert M., 115
Hyde, Francis E., 887

Illick, Joseph E., 398
Imlah, Albert H., 883
Imlah, Ann G., 791
Inglis, Brian St John, 1316
Inglis, K. S., 902
Inman, Peggy F., 1014
Ives, E. W., 194, 1091

Jackman, Sydney W., 1135
Jacob, Ilse, 525
James, Robert V. R., 689
Jenkins, Roy, 665
Jennings, Ivor, 711
John, A. H., 580, 591, 619
Johnson, Franklyn A., 962
Johnson, Paul B., 930
Johnston, Edith M., 1306
Jones, E. L., 134, 590

Jones, Gareth, 1089
Jones, G. F. Trevallyn, 397
Jones, G. H., 477
Jones, J. R., 391
Jones, P. E., 14
Jones, Peter d'A., 913
Jones, Tom, 938–9
Jones, Wilbur D., 673, 683
Jones, William J., 192
Jordan, Wilbur K., 147, 1024
Joslin, David M., 575
Josten, C. H., 55
Jowitt, Earl, 693
Judd, Denis, 836
Judson, Margaret A., 323
Jupp, P. J., 1319

Kaplan, Lawrence, 375
Kaufmann, William W., 783
Kazamias, Andreas M., 1051
Kazemzadeh, Firuz, 808
Kearney, Hugh P., 1297
Keeler, Mary Freer, 346
Keeton, G. W., 1096
Kelsall, R. K., 966
Kelly, John Barrett, 808
Kelly, Michael J., 224
Kemp, Betty, 83, 491
Kendrick, T. F. J., 505
Kennedy, A. L., 691
Kenny, Robert W., 331
Kenyon, John P., 24, 78, 393
Kerridge, Eric, 100, 263–4
Kettler, David, 1278
Keynes, Geoffrey, 1220
King, Preston, 139
Kirby, S. Woodburn, 1003
Klee, Karl, 996
Kluxen, Kurt, 507
Knachel, Philip A., 368
Knaplund, Paul, 815
Knowles, David, 217
Knox, S. J., 243
Kochan, Lionel, 1206
Koebner, Richard, 207, 1163

Kohan, C. M., 1015
Koss, Stephen E., 692–3, 923
Kramnick, Isaac, 1135
Krause, J. T., 596, 599
Kressner, Helmut, 214
Kriegel, Abraham D., 725
Kurat, A. N., 34

Lachs, Phyllis S., 429
Lambert, M. E., 35
Lambert, Royston, 760, 774
Lambert, Sheila, 17, 503, 777
Lamont, William M., 369
Landes, David S., 579
Lane, Jane, 468
Large, David, 504, 1312, 1327
Larkin, James F., 29
Laslett, Peter, 1108, 1129
Latham, R. C., 333
Law, A., 1282
Leconfield, Lord, 457
Lee, Maurice, 388, 1266
Leeuwen, Henry G. van, 1241
Le Fanu, W. R., 1230
Lefranc, Pierre, 296
Lehmberg, Stanford E., 199, 294, 1100
Letwin, Shirley R., 1150
Letwin, William, 97
Levine, Mortimer, 3, 160
Levy, Fritz J., 1182
Lewis, Clyde J., 682
Lewis, Michael A., 92, 541, 840
Lewis, Richard A., 759
Lewis, W. S., 41
Leyden, W., von, 1130
Lillywhite, Bryant, 467
Lipmann, V. P., 115
Lloyd, Christopher, 841
Lloyd, Howell, A., 260
Lloyd, Trevor, 709
Loades, David M., 76, 156
Locke, John, 1129–31
Lockwood, John F., 693
Loomie, Albert J., 169

Lough, John, 1124
Lowe, Cedric J., 795, 805
Lowe, John, 1301
Lowe, Peter, 801
Lucas, Paul, 1095, 1145
Lutnick, Solomon, 554
Luvaas, Jay, 844
Lyman, Richard W., 931
Lynch, Patrick 1351
Lyons, F. S. L., 662, 750, 1339
Lythe, S. G. E., 1267

Macalpine, Ida, 486
McBriar, A. M., 744
McCaffrey, Lawrence J., 728, 1313
MacCaffrey, Wallace T., 149, 159, 182
McClelland, V. A., 914
Maccoby, S., 733
McConica, James K., 1166
McCord, Norman, 652
McCracken, Eileen, 1295
McCracken, J. L., 1349
McCready, H. W., 732
MacDonagh, Oliver, 751-3
McDowell, R. B., 717, 1314, 1316
McEwen, J. M., 925
MacFarlane, L. J., 927
McGill, Barry, 727
McGinn, Donald J., 246-7
McGrath, Patrick, 232
McGregor, Oliver R., 1090
Machin, G. I. T., 641, 907
McInnes, Angus, 407-8
Macintyre, Angus, 1321
Mack, Mary P., 1151
McKay, Ruddock F., 542
McKendrick, Neil, 603
Mackenzie, D. F., 1070
McKenzie, Robert T., 967
McKeown, T., 596
Mackesy, Piers, 544, 547
Mackie, J. D., 141, 1063, 1246

Mackie, R. L., 37, 1258
Mackintosh, John P., 959
McLachlan, H. J., 381
Maclure, Millar, 254
Macmillan, David S., 1287
McNeilly, F. S., 1121
Macpherson, C. B., 1113
Madden, A. F. McC., 555
Maehl, W. H., 728
Magnus Philip, 680
Mahoney, Thomas H. D., 1147
Manning, B. L., 568
Mansergh, P. N. S., 1313
Manuel, Frank E., 1189
Marchant, Ronald A., 231, 244
Marcus, G. J., 91
Marder, Arthur J., 984
Marshall, Dorothy, 471-2, 625
Marshall, J. D., 58
Marshall, Leon S., 501
Marshall, Peter J., 42, 552-3
Marriner, Sheila, 886
Marsh, P. T., 904
Martin, E. W., 895
Marwick, A. J. B., 926
Masterman, Neville C., 746
Mather, F. C., 773
Mathew, David, 306, 1162, 1269
Mathews, R. C. O., 853
Mathias, Peter, 106, 609, 889
Mattingly, Garrett, 180
Mayes, Charles, 1296
Mechie, Stewart, 1286
Medley, D. J., 4
Medlicott, W. N., 35, 793, 920, 1013
Mendenhall, T. C., 275
Merk, Frederick, 781
Messerschmidt, Manfred, 1209
Meyer, Markus, 524
Michael, Wolfgang, 473
Middlemas, Keith, 939, 944
Miller, Amos C., 179
Miller, Helen, 203
Miller, Kenneth E., 977

Miller, Naomi C., 521
Millman, R., 793
Milne, A. Taylor, 7
Minchinton, Walter E., 71, 108, 608
Mingay, G. E., 134, 588, 591–2
Ming-Hsun, Li, 454
Mintz, Samuel H., 1123
Mitchell, Austin, 725
Mitchell, B. R., 18
Mitchell, William, 327
Moggeridge, Donald E., 932
Moir, T. L., 326
Monger, G. W., 799
Moody, T. W., 1064, 1328
Moore, D. C., 859
Moorehead, Alan, 987
Moran, Lord, 941
More, Thomas, 73
Morgan, I., 317
Morgan, Kenneth O., 668
Morris, Christopher, 1098
Morris, J. H., 873
Morrison, Herbert, 968
Mosse, George L., 325, 1237–8
Mosse, Werner E., 790
Mossner, Ernest C., 1136
Mowat, Charles L., 919, 1029
Mueller, Iris Wessel, 1157
Muggeridge, Kitty, 697
Mulligan, *see* Glow
Mullins, E. L. C., 8–9
Munter, R., 1074
Munz, Peter, 1106
Murray, John J., 525
Murray, Keith, 1015
Murray, Marischal, 887
Musson, A. E., 621, 874, 876

Namier, Lewis B., 85, 487, 509
Neale, John E., 158, 202, 229
Neale, R. S., 585
Nelson, Harold I., 990
New, Chester W., 671
New, John F. H., 234

Newman, Aubrey N., 59, 113, 512
Newsome, David, 899, 1049
Nias, J. C. S., 909
Nicholas, Douglas, 318
Nicolson, Harold, 935
Nicolson, Marjorie Hope, 1226
Nikiforov, L. A., 525
Nish, Ian H., 800
Nobbs, Douglas, 1267
Norman, Edward R., 916, 1325
Norris, John, 493
Norris, John A., 820
Northedge, F. S., 969
Notestein, Wallace, 1251
Nowland, Kevin B., 1320, 1340
Nuttall, Geoffrey F., 384

O'Brien, Conor Cruise, 1331
O'Brien, Terence, 1013
O'Connell, Maurice, 1307
Ogg, David, 309
Ogle, Arthur, 223
O'Gormon, Francis, 516
O'Leary, Cornelius, 716
Ollard, Richard L., 129, 430
Olsen, Alison G., 492
Oman, Carola, 539, 542
Orr, Robert R., 1239
Osborn, James M., 53, 62
Osborne, John W., 1173
Ottley, George, 12
Outhwaite, R. B., 257
Owen, David, 1025
Owen, John, 511
Oxley, J. E., 221

Packe, Michael St J., 1154
Parekh, B. C., 139
Pares, Richard, 135, 513
Pargellis, Stanley, 4
Parker, H. M. D., 1012
Parker, John, 285
Parker, Thomas M., 210
Parkin, Charles W., 1141

Parkinson, C. Northcote, 547
Parmiter, G. de C., 153
Parreaux, André, 581
Parris, Henry, 646, 754, 762
Patterson, A. Temple, 546, 624, 953
Paul, Robert S., 355
Payne, P. L., 890
Pearl, Valerie, 344, 348, 376
Peel, Albert, 77
Pelling, Henry, 708, 735-7, 928
Pennington, Donald H., 345, 351-2
Perham, Margery, 829
Perkin, Harold, 635
Perkins, Bradford, 530
Perry, Thomas W., 499
Peterson, R. T., 1212
Philip, I. G., 1071
Piggott, Stuart, 1190
Pigou, A. C., 1018
Pineas, Rainer, 1183, 1235
Pinkham, Lucille, 395
Pinto-Duschinsky, Michael, 1160
Plass, Jens B., 808
Platt, D. C. M., 779
Playfair, I. S. O., 1002
Plumb, John H., 133, 310, 404, 413, 470, 484
Pocock, John G. A., 1187
Poirier, Philip P., 735
Pollard, Sidney, 574, 602, 604, 893, 1019
Pope-Hennessy, James, 698
Porter, Bernard, 825
Porter, Harry C., 241
Postan, M. M., 1012, 1014
Postgate, Raymond, 947
Pound, Reginald, 954
Powell, J. R., 367
Powicke, F. M., 20
Prall, Stuart E., 461
Prebble, J., 1276
Presnell, L. S., 136, 575-6
Prest, Wilfred, 1092

Prestwich, Menna, 320
Preyer, Robert, 1192
Primus, John H., 245
Prouty, Roger, 771
Pryde, George S., 1247, 1274
Purver, Margery, 1215
Pyrah, G. B., 835

Quinn, David B., 11, 284, 1291

Raab, Felix, 1110
Rabb, Theodore K., 128, 274, 328
Radzinowicz, Leo, 1083
Rae, Thomas I., 1260
Raistrick, Arthur, 606
Ramm, Agatha, 48
Ramsay, G. D., 102
Ramsey, Peter H., 256
Ranger, Terence, 1298
Ransome, Mary, 22
Razzell, P. E., 597-8
Rea, Robert R., 1075
Read, Conyers, 2, 164
Read, Donald, 639, 650, 676
Reader, W. J., 1037
Redford, A., 884
Reid, Loren, 495
Reitan, E. A., 478
Rex, Millicent, 1057
Reynolds, J. A., 1318
Reynolds, Philip A., 970
Richardson, H. W., 1021
Richardson, Walter C., 184-5
Richmond, Herbert, 93
Richter, Melvin, 1159
Rickert, R. T., 54
Ridley, Jasper G., 237, 1263
Riley, P. W. J., 433, 1275
Rimmer, W. G., 870
Ritcheson, Charles R., 480
Ritchie, C. I. A., 231
Ritter, Gerhard A., 327
Roach, John P. C., 1058
Robbins, Caroline, 517, 1112

Robbins, Keith, 981
Roberts, Benjamin C., 739
Roberts, Clayton, 305
Roberts, David, 758
Robinson, E., 621
Robinson, Howard, 88
Robinson, R. E., 823
Robson, Eric, 535
Robson, Maureen M., 814
Robson, Robert, 137, 1093
Robson, Robert J., 508
Robson-Scott, W. D., 466
Rogers, Elizabeth F., 36
Rogers, P. R., 383
Rolo, P. J. V., 670
Rolt, L. C. T., 867
Römer, Klaus, 796
Roos, Carl, 540
Roots, Ivan, 338, 352
Rosenberg, Eleanor, 288
Roseveare, Henry, 86
Roskill, Stephen W., 934, 1006
Rosselli, John, 533
Rosselli, Nello, 784
Rostow, Walt W., 847
Rothblatt, Sheldon, 1059
Routledge, F. J., 428
Rover, Constance, 667
Rowe, John, 580
Rowland, Peter, 663
Rowse, A. Leslie, 148, 167
Roy, Ian, 33
Rubini, Denis, 405
Ruddock, Alwyn A., 271
Rudé, George, 479, 647
Ruffmann, Karl Heinz, 301
Rupp, E. Gordon, 566
Russell, Jocelyne G., 292
Ryan, A. P., 547
Ryan, Desmond, 1328
Ryan, Lawrence V., 295

Sachse, William L., 56, 401
Sacks, Benjamin, 1050
Sainty, J., 416

Sale, William M., 1069
Salmon, J. H. M., 1107
Saunderson, G. N., 806
Saul, S. B., 875, 883
Saunders, Lawrence J., 1284
Savage, C. I., 1015
Savage, D. C., 1336
Savory, Reginald, 536
Sayers, Richard S., 848, 880-1, 1016
Scammell, Geoffrey V., 277
Scarisbrick, J. J., 152, 226
Schell, Gisela, 1146
Schenk, W. (of Oxford), 248, 460
Schenk, W., 1208
Schlatter, Richard, 384
Schlenke, Manfred, 527
Schlote, W., 103
Schmidt, Helmut D., 1163
Schoenfeld, Maxwell P., 386
Schofield, Robert E., 629
Schofield, Roger S., 1045
Schoyen, A., 649
Schreuder, D. M., 831
Schrier, Arnold, 1348
Schubert, H. R., 104
Schulin, Ernst, 96
Schurman, Don M., 845
Schütt, Marie, 1191
Schuyler, Robert L., 854
Scott, J. D., 1014
Scott, J. F., 39
Scouller, R. E., 434
Seigel, J. E., 128
Seliger, Martin, 1126
Semmell, Bernard, 846
Senior, Hereward, 1310
Shannon, R. T., 660, 1204
Shapiro, B. J., 1222
Shaw, Duncan, 1265
Shelby, L. R., 177
Shepperd, G. A., 1009
Sheridan, R. B., 616
Sherwig, John M., 532
Shirley, F. J., 1105

Siebert, Frederick S., 119
Sigworth, E. M., 870
Silver, Arthur W., 869
Silver, Harold, 1047
Simms, J. G., 1302
Simon, Brian, 1048
Simon, Joan, 1042
Simon, Walter G., 423
Simpson, Alan, 260
Simpson, A. W. B., 1080
Siney, Marion C., 985
Skalweit, Stephen, 1148
Skidelsky, Robert, 933
Skinner, Quentin, 1122, 1188, 1216
Slavin, Arthur J., 197
Smedt, Oscar de, 272
Smellie, K. B., 80
Smit, H. J., 68
Smith, Alan G. R., 193
Smith, Basil A., 910
Smith, Colin L., 810
Smith, E. A., 22
Smith, F. Barry, 657
Smith, H. Maynard, 140
Smith, Lacey Baldwin 225, 227
Smith, Paul, 720
Smith, Paul H., 545
Smith, R., 14
Smith, R. A., 42
Smout, T. C., 1250, 1272–3
Snow, W. G. Sinclair, 1271
Soden, G. T., 314
Solt, Leo F., 379
Southgate, Donald, 675
Southgate, W. M., 239
Sparrow, John, 1060
Speck, W. S., 409
Spencer, Frank, 527
Spinner, Thomas J., 690
Sprigge, Timothy L. S., 46
Spring, David, 858
Spilman, Anne, 37
Squibb, G. C., 1085
Stanlis, Peter J., 1142

Stansky, Peter, 730
Stearns, Raymond P., 380
Steele, E. D., 1329
Steele, Ian K., 417
Steiner, Zara, 768, 778, 800
Stephens, W. B., 458
Stevas, Norman St John, 1175
Stevens, John, 299
Stevens, Robert, 1086
Steward, A. C. Q., 666
Stokes, Eric T., 822, 1158, 1165
Stone, Lawrence, 170, 259, 261, 278, 280, 331, 1046
Storey, Graham, 1078
Storey, Robin L., 146
Stoye, John W., 465
Straka, Gerald M., 425
Strathmann, E. A., 167
Strauch, Rudi, 982
Strider, Robert E. L., 322
Stromberg, Roland H., 569
Strong, Roy, 290
Stuart Jones, E. A., 1308
Sturgis, James L., 679
Supple, Barry E., 444
Surtz, Edward, 73, 228
Sutherland, Lucy S., 42, 483
Swain, Joseph Ward, 1195
Swift, David, E., 610
Sykes, Norman, 420, 426
Sylvester, Richard S., 73, 75

Tate, W. E., 90
Tawney, Richard H., 259, 320
Taylor, Alan J. P., 135, 807, 813, 918, 993
Taylor, Arthur J., 583, 869
Taylor, Audrey M., 881
Taylor, E. G. R., 302
Terenzio, P. C., 808
Thirsk, Joan, 99, 262, 269–70, 364
Thomas, J. Alun, 705, 710
Thomas, Peter G. D., 487
Thomas, R. C., 361

Thompson, A. F., 738
Thompson, Edward P., 586
Thompson, F. M. L., 856-7, 1036
Thompson, Henry P., 122
Thompson, Paul, 749
Thorne, S. E., 189
Thornley, David A., 1330
Thornton, A. P., 437, 1164
Tibawi, A. L., 839
Titmuss, Richard M., 1017
Tjernakel, Neelak S., 215
Torrance, J. R., 763
Trebilcock, Clive, 879
Trevor-Roper, Hugh R., 130, 259, 349, 357, 1270
Trimble, William R., 251
Tsuzuki, Chushichi, 745
Tucker, Albert V., 772
Tucker, G. S. L., 95
Tucker, Melvin J., 162
Turberville, A. S., 504
Turnbull, H. W., 39
Tveite, Sven, 449

Uhl, Othmar, 812
Ullman, Richard H., 973
Underdown, D. E., 350, 362, 373
Upton, A. F., 322

Valentine, Alan, 489-90
Van der Poel, Jean, 51
Vann, Richard T., 427
Vaizey, John, 1351
Vidler, Alec, 912
Vincent, John L., 707, 726
Vincent, W. A. L., 1044

Wadsworth, A. P., 605
Wagner, Anthony R., 89
Walcott, Robert, 403
Walder, D., 974
Walker, Mary Antonia, 979
Wallace, John M., 1112
Walmsley, Robert, 639

Walsh, J. D., 132
Walzer, Michael, 372
Ward, Alan J., 1341
Ward, John T., 645, 674, 861
Ward, S. P. G., 539
Ward, W. E. F., 782
Ward, W. R., 558-9, 1062
Warrener, Howard, 1118
Waters, D. W., 286
Watkins, John W. N., 1120
Watson, Andrew G., 1067
Watson, J. Steven, 23, 474
Watt, D. C., 138
Waverley, Viscount, 693
Webb, Henry J., 176
Webb, Robert K., 82, 1053, 1174
Weber, Theo, 996
Webster, Charles K., 787, 1005
Wedgwood, C. Veronica, 319, 339
Wernham, R. Bruce, 171, 174
Western J. R., 534
Westfall, Richard S., 1213
Weston, Corinne Comstock, 418
Wheeler-Bennett, John W., 936, 980
White, Dean G., 1294
White, James F., 1243
White, Reginald J., 475, 639
Whiteman, Anne, 422
Whitteridge, Gweneth, 1221
Whitworth, Reginald H., 537
Whyte, John H., 1324, 1326
Wikland, Erik, 300
Wiles, R. M., 1068, 1073
Wilkes, John, 485
Wilkins, Burleigh Taylor, 1145
Willan, T. S., 67, 273, 594
Williams, C. H., 22, 125
Williams, David, 111, 653
Williams, Desmond, 1345
Williams, E. Neville, 24
Williams, Glanmor, 255
Williams, Glyndwr, 350
Williams, J. E., 585

Williams, L. J., 873
Williams, Neville J., 157, 168
Williams, Orlo C., 84
Williams, Penry H., 145, 191
Williams, W. Ogwen, 31
Williamson, James A., 143, 281, 284, 550
Willson, David H., 312
Willson, F. M. G., 767, 958
Wilson, Charles H., 438, 448, 1022
Wilson, Ronald E., 1023
Wilson, Trevor, 924
Windsor, Duke of, 937
Winkler, Henry R., 971, 976
Winstanley, D. W., 1061
Winter, James, 706
Witcombe, D. T., 387
Wolffe, Bertram P., 186
Woodfill, Walter L., 299
Woodham-Smith, Cecil, 1342
Woods, John A., 42
Woodward, E. Llewellyn, 35, 983

Woolrych, Austin H., 366
Wormald, Brian H. G., 343
Wormuth, Francis D., 308
Wright, C. E., 60
Wright, L. C., 1285
Wright, Maurice W., 766
Wright, R., 998
Wright, Ruth C., 60
Wrigley, C. C., 1014
Wrigley, E. A., 120, 601

Yale, D. E. C., 1084
Yolton, John W., 1132-3
Youings, Joyce, 30, 191, 266
Young, G. M., 22
Young, Kenneth, 696
Young, D. Murray, 769
Youngson, A. J., 1289
Yule, George, 373

Zagorin, Perez, 259, 311, 378
Zeeveld, W., Gordon, 204
Ziegler, Philip, 497

(B) SUBJECTS

Aberdeen, George Gordon, earl of, 654

Acton, John Dahlberg, Lord, 49, 1161–2, 1206

Addington, Henry, Earl Sidmouth, 497

Administration, general, 183–9, 193, 336, 414, 416, 562–3, 751–6, 767, 958, 1306, 1314; *and see* Board of Trade, Cabinet, Civil Service, Colonial Office, Council, Finance, Local government, Mint, Parish, Police, Post Office, Treasury

Africa, 806–7, 823, 824–9, 831–5; *and see* Royal Africa Company

Agriculture, 98–101, 107, 262–4, 269–70, 588–92, 856, 859–61, 895, 1277, 1280; Board of, 561

Alanbrook, Viscount, 995

Andrewes, Lancelot, 240

Antwerp, 272

Army, 175–7, 332, 433, 534–9, 772, 844; *and see* War

Art, 289–92, 1178

Ascham, Roger, 295

Ashmole, Elias, 55

Australia, 819, 1287

Bacon, Francis, 1028

Bagehot, Walter, 1175

Bainbridge, Christopher, 172

Baldwin, Stanley, 943–4

Bale, John, 1183

Balfour, A. J., 696, 836

Baltic 525, 789

Bancroft, Richard, 77

Banking, *see* Capital

Banks, Sir John, 451

Barrow, Henry, 77

Baxter, Richard, 383

Belfast, 1064

Bennet, Thomas, 57

Bentham, Jeremy, 46, 755, 1151–1152, 1191

Bentinck, Lord William, 533

Bevan, Aneurin, 950

Bevin, Ernest, 949

Birmingham, 117, 727

Blackstone, William, 1071, 1095

Board of Trade, 417, 771

Bolingbroke, Henry St John, Viscount, 1135

Books, *see* Printing

Boyle, Robert, 1217

Bradlaugh, Charles, 661

Bright, John, 677–9, 729

Bristol, 71

Britain, Battle of, 996–8

Brooke, Robert Grenville, Lord, 322

Brougham, Henry, 671

Browne, Robert, 77

232

Brunel, I. K., 867
Bucer, Martin, 216
Burghley, William Cecil, Lord, 164–5
Burke, Edmund, 42–3, 1139–49
Butt, Isaac, 1330

Cabinet, 413, 557, 959–63
Cambridge, 241, 1055, 1058–9, 1061, 1070, 1243
Canning, George, 670
Capital, 451, 574–6, 610, 880–2
Cartwright, Thomas, 77
Cecil, Lord Robert, 972; for other Cecils *see* Burghley, Salisbury
Chadwick, Sir Edwin, 759
Chamberlain, Joseph, 50, 684–6, 729, 1334
Chamberlain, Neville, 945
Chanak, 974
Chancery, 192, 1084
Channel Islands, 181
Charles I, 1269, 1301
Charles II, 365, 387
Chartism, 648–50, 773, 1285
Chatham, William Pitt, earl of, 514
Cherwell, Viscount, 956–7
Chillingworth, William, 1239
Chilston, Viscount, 688
China, 630, 803, 885, 978
Christian Socialism, 746, 911–13, 1245
Church, R. W., 910
Church of England, 208, 212–14, 222, 224–6, 229–34, 239–41, 244, 254, 293, 334, 420–5, 463, 564–5, 567–71, 896–905, 908–913, 1049–51, 1239–44; *and see* Puritanism, Reformation
Churchill, Lord Randolph, 689, 722
Churchill, Winston S., 838, 940–942

Civil Service, 336, 523–4, 558, 762–6, 964–6
Clarendon, Edward Hyde, earl of, 343
Clements, Henry, 57
Cobbett, William, 1173
Cobden, Richard, 677
Coinage, 257–8, 276, 454
Colonial Office, 769
Coleridge, S. T., 1192
Commons, house of, *see* Parliament
Corn laws, 651–2, 859–61
Cornwall, 580
Council, 27, 190–1, 1086
Courtaulds (business), 1022
Cranfield, Lionel earl of Middlesex, 320
Cranmer, Thomas, 237
Crawshay (business), 873
Crewe, Lord, 698
Cripps, Sir Stafford, 948
Crompton, Henry, 426
Cromwell, Oliver, 355–7, 360–1
Cromwell, Thomas, 163, 205
Crossfield (business), 874
Crowley (business), 607
Curzon, George Nathaniel, marquess of, 837

Danby, Thomas Osborne, earl of, 389
Darby (business), 606
Darien, 1276
Darwin, Charles, 1232–4
Dashwood, Sir Francis, 491
Derby, Edward Stanley, 14th earl of, 683
D'Ewes, Sir Simonds, 1067
Digby, Sir Kenelm, 1212
Dillon, John, 1339
Diplomacy, 34, 110, 171, 361, 428–9, 432, 522–32, 768, 777–779, 814, 969–72, 976–82; *and see* under particular countries

Disraeli, Benjamin, 658, 681–2, 714, 720
Dissent, 116, 568, 906–7, 1035, 1305
Dowding, Hugh, Lord, 998
Drake, Sir Francis, 284

East India Company, 443, 483, 615
Eastland Company, 445
Economic policy, 95–7, 278–9, 611, 622, 862, 1166–7, 1315
Edinburgh, 1063, 1289
Education, 295, 1039–64, 1168, 1170, 1203, 1281–4
Edward VI, 147, 1294
Elections, *see* Parliament
Elgin, 9th earl of, 838
Eliot, Sir John, 315, 324
Elizabeth I, 148–9, 157–61, 164, 230, 290, 1293
Elyot, Sir Thomas, 294
Empire, 5, 274, 282–5, 273, 548–549, 551, 553, 555–6, 795, 815–39, 846, 1163–5, 1329
Enclosures, 270, 440, 600
Engels, Friedrich, 748
Estienne, Robert, 287
Evelyn, John, 61
Exeter, 116, 182, 458
Exploration, 281–4, 550

Fabians, 744
Fenians, 1328
Ferguson, Adam, 1278
Field, John, 243
Filmer, Sir Robert, 1108–9
Finance, 184–9, 321, 351, 412, 441, 453, 558–60, 1016
Fisher, John, 228
Fisher, John, Lord, 984
Forbes, Patrick, 1271
Fox, Charles James, 495, 515
Foxe, John, 298

France, 793–4, 1001, 1007, 1308
Franklin, Benjamin, 1225

Gallipoli, 987
Garvin, J. L., 694
General Strike, 931
Gentry, *see* Landownership
George I, 478, 525, 562
George III, 44, 474–5, 481, 486, 510, 513
George IV, 45
George V, 935
George VI, 936
Germaine, Lord George, 489
Germany, 788–9, 809, 1005, 1200–1, 1208–9; *and see* Prussia
Gibbon, Edward, 1194–7
Gladstone, W. E., 48, 64–5, 658, 660, 714, 728, 793, 831, 901
Glasgow, 1063
Goderich, Frederick Robinson, Viscount, 673
Goodman, Godfrey, 314
Gordon Riots, 479
Gorham, G. C., 909
Gorst, J. E., 721
Goschen, G. J., 690
Graham, Sir John, 674
Granville, G. Leveson-Gower, earl of, 48
Great Depression, 877
Green, T. H., 1158
Greenwood, John, 77
Grote, George, 1198–9
Guinness, 1351
Gurney, J. J., 610

Haldane, R. B., 693
Hale, Sir Matthew, 1096
Halifax, Edward Wood, earl of, 945
Halley, Edmond, 1219
Harrington, James, 1115
Harley, Robert, earl of Oxford, 406–9

Harrison, Sir George, 763
Harrison, Robert, 77
Harvey, William, 1220-1
Hastings, Warren, 552
Hatton, Sir Christopher, 166
Hawke, Admiral Edward, 542
Hawkins, John, 284
Henderson, Sir Neville, 982
Henry VII, 146, 150
Henry, VIII 151-3, 215, 227, 290, 1290
Henslowe, Philip, 54
Herschel, William, 1228
Hobbes, Thomas, 1113, 1116-1123, 1216
Holmes, Sir Robert, 430
Home Rule, 728, 1330-1, 1334
Hooke, Robert, 1218
Hooker, Richard, 1104-6
Hopton, Sir Ralph, 363
Humanism, 294-5, 1099-1103, 1166-7
Hume, David, 1136-8
Hunne, Richard, 223
Huntingdon, Henry Hastings, earl of, 200
Huskisson, William, 640
Hyndman, H. M., 745

Imperialism, *see* Empire
Industrial Revolution, 572-87, 848-9
Industry, 104-6, 602-9, 869-79, 1022-3, 1351
Ingram, Sir Arthur, 322
Investment, *see* Capital
Italy, 784-5, 789, 1002, 1009, 1011

James I (Great Britain), 312, 324
James II (Great Britain), 309, 392
James IV (Scotland), 37, 1258
James V (Scotland), 37, 1259

Japan, 800, 804, 978, 1003
Jeffreys, George, 1096
Jellicoe, J. K., Lord, 953
Jenner, Edward, 1230
Jewel, John, 239
Jews, 115, 499, 1036
Jowett, Benjamin, 917
Joye, George, 235
Judges, *see* Law courts

Kennett, White, 426
Kent, 353, 456, 1024
Keynes, J. M., 955
Kingship, 324-5, 327
Kipling, Rudyard, 1177
Knatchbull, Sir Edward, 59
Knox, John, 1261, 1263

Labour, 452, 586-7, 892-5; Party, *see* Parties; *see also* General Strike, Trades Unions
Lancashire, 218, 1024
Landownership, 259-61, 364, 439, 442, 457, 593, 857-61, 1312
Lansbury, George, 946
Latimer, Hugh, 235
Latin America, 780, 783, 802
Law, 194-6, 304, 330, 341, 461-2, 1079-81, 1083-4, 1087-1095
Law, Andrew Bonar, 695
Law courts, 191-2, 415, 1082, 1085-6, 1096-7
Leicester, 624
Leicester, Robert Dudley, earl of, 288
Lewis's (business), 888
Ligonier, John, Earl, 537
Lilburne, John, 369
Lincolnshire, 219, 589
Literacy, 1045-6, 1053-4
Liverpool, 886
Lloyd, William, 426
Lloyd George, David, 922, 938

Local government, 31, 191, 193, 773–6
Locke, John, 1113, 1124–33, 1170
London, 14, 70, 267, 344, 467–8, 472, 749, 1024, 1038
Lords, house of, *see* Parliament
Lothian, Philip Kerr, Lord, 951
Ludlow, J. M., 746
Lugard, Lord, 829
Luxemburg, 792

Machiavelli, Niccolò, 1110
Maitland, F. W., 52, 1205
Maitland, John, of Thirlstane, 1266
Malmesbury, James Harris, earl of, 529
Malthus, Thomas, 864
Manchester, 501, 862, 884
Manning, Henry, 899, 914
Marlborough, John Churchill, duke of, 40
Martineau, Harriet, 1174
Marvell, Andrew, 1112
Marx, Karl, 747
Maurice, F. D., 911–12
Medicine, 1031–2
Methodism, 566
Middlesex, earl of, *see* Cranfield
Milner, Alfred, Viscount, 694, 1165
Mill, James, 1153
Mill, John Stuart, 1154–7
Mint, 87
Monasteries, 30, 217–19, 265–6
Moore, Sir John, 539
Moray, James Stewart, earl of, 1266
Mordaunt, John, Viscount, 38
More, Sir Thomas, 36, 73, 154, 1102–3, 1235
Morley, John, 692
Morton, James Douglas, earl of, 1266

Mundella, A. J., 868
Munich, 980–1
Music, 299

Navy, 91–3, 367, 430–1, 541, 563, 782, 840–2, 845, 934, 984, 1006; *and see* War
Nelson, Horatio, 542
Netherlands, 40, 360, 526, 827
Newcastle-upon-Tyne, 354
Newman, J. H., 47, 910
Newspapers, 1072–5
Newton, Sir Isaac, 39, 1189, 1223–7
Nicholas, Sir Edward, 318
Norfolk, Thomas Howard, 2nd duke of, 162; Thomas Howard, 4th duke of, 168
North, Frederick, Lord, 481, 490, 514–15
Northcliffe, Alfred Harmsworth, Lord, 954
Northumberland, Henry Percy, 9th earl of, 69
Nottingham, 855
Nottingham, Charles Howard, earl of, 331; Heneage Finch, 1st earl of, 1084; Daniel Finch, 2nd earl of, 410

Oastler, Richard, 671
O'Connell, Daniel, 1321–2
Owen, Robert, 634
Oxford, 1055, 1060, 1062, 1071
Oxford, earl of, *see* Harley

Paine, Tom, 1149
Pallavicino, Sir Horatio, 171
Palmerston, Henry Temple, Viscount, 675, 713, 787–9
Parish, 90
Parliament, 32, 83, 201, 203, 326, 357–8, 503, 710, 968; Commons, house of 17, 59, 84–5, 202, 224, 326, 328–9, 333,

345–50, 387, 503, 506–7, 699, 701, 703; Elections, 310, 331, 704–5, 707–9, 715–16, 925, 1319, 1332; Lords, house of 203, 386, 418, 504–5, 665, 929, 1086, 1327; *and see* Parties, Reform

Parnell, Charles Stuart, 662, 1331, 1334

Parties, 403, 405, 509, 700, 702, 711–14, 967; Communist, 927–928; Conservative, 664, 717–724, 729, 925, 1337; Independent Labour, 743, 926; Irish, 750, 1321, 1324; Labour, 734–6, 749, 931, 933, 975–6, 1048; Liberal, 663, 726–33, 749, 923–4; Whig, 391, 482, 516–18, 725

Peel, Sir Robert, 672, 712, 718–719, 1317, 1327

Pelham, Henry, 485, 511

Penn, William, 398

Penry, John, 247

Percival, Spencer, 498

Perkins, William, 1238

Persia, 808

Peter, Hugh, 380

Peterloo, 639

Petre, Sir William, 199

Philpotts, Henry, 909

Pitt, William, the younger, 496; for Pitt the elder *see* Chatham

Place, Francis, 642

Pole, Reginald, 248

Police, 773, 775

Population, 70, 109, 120, 280, 455, 595–600, 864, 1344–8

Post Office, 88, 571

Preston, John, 317

Priestley, Joseph, 1229

Prince Consort, 676

Printing, 119, 287–8, 500, 503, 554, 669, 694, 1065–77, 1316

Proclamations, 29

Prussia, 527, 793

Puritanism, 77, 232, 234, 242–7, 316–17, 334–5, 340–1, 344, 370–85, 460, 1222, 1237–8, 1270, 1300

Pym, John, 347

Quakers, 382, 427, 568

Raleigh, Sir Walter, 167, 284, 296

Rathbone (business), 886

Reform, parliamentary, 519–21, 657–9, 706; social, 278–9, 440, 460, 582–3, 863–6, 868, 930, 991, 1017, 1024–31, 1037, 1166–7, 1169, 1286

Reformation, 140, 209–11, 220–1, 227, 236, 238, 255

Rennie, John, 610

Republicanism, 1111–12

Reuter's, 1078

Richardson, Samuel, 1069

Richmond, Charles Lennox, duke of, 492

Ridley, Nicholas, 237

Rockingham, Charles, marquess of, 488

Roman catholicism, 112, 169, 232, 248–53, 335, 641, 914–16, 1043, 1300, 1318–20, 1325–6

Rosebery, earl of, 689

Rowntree, Seebohm, 868

Royal Africa Company, 447

Royal Society, 1214–15

Rugg, Thomas, 56

Russia, 525, 786, 807, 809, 973, 975

Russia Company, 273

Sadler, Sir Ralph, 197

St John, Henry, *see* Bolingbroke; Oliver, 348

Salisbury, Robert Cecil, 2nd earl of, 331; Robert Cecil 3rd

marquess of, 691, 797, 805, 828, 1160
Schnadhorst, Francis, 727
Science, 286, 302, 340, 621, 628–9, 1172, 1210–34
Seeley, Sir John, 1204
Shaftesbury, Anthony, 1st earl of, 390
Sharp, John, 426
Sheffield Smelting Company, 1023
Shelburne, William Petty, earl of, 493
Shipping, 277, 450, 887
Sicily, 533
Sidmouth, *see* Addington
Simon, Sir John, 760
Slave Trade, 616, 782, 841
Smith, Adam, 1028, 1278
Smith, Sir Thomas, 198
Smith, W. H., 687
Smuts, Jan, 51, 952
Southampton, 271
Spence, Joseph, 62
Stafford, 352
Stanmore, Arthur Hamilton, Lord, 830
Starkey, Thomas, 1101
Stephen, James, 1328
Stephen, Leslie, 1176
Stephenson, George, 867
Stout, William, 58
Strachan, William, 1069
Strafford, Thomas Wentworth, earl of, 319, 1297–8
Stukeley, William, 1190
Suffolk, 353
Sunderland, Robert Spencer, earl of, 393
Swift, Jonathan, 1304
Switzerland, 524, 791, 812

Tenison, Thomas, 426
Theatre, 300–1
Tocqueville, Alexis de, 1157

Townsend, Charles, 487
Trade, 18, 67, 71, 102–3, 271–6, 282, 320, 443–9, 612–20, 853–854, 883–90, 1272, 1303; *and see* Shipping, Slave trade
Trades Unions, 737–42, 931
Transport, 12, 114, 594, 601, 610, 646, 754
Travers, William, 243
Treasury, 86, 411, 556, 766, 770
Trent, vale of, 624
Trevelyan, Sir Charles, 764
Turkey, 34, 525, 810
Tyndale, William, 1183

Ulster, 666, 1336
Unilever (business), 1022
United States, 110, 480, 530, 543, 554, 781, 811, 852, 1341
Universities, 1055–64

Vaux family, 252
Vergil, Polydore, 72, 1181
Victoria, Queen, 901

Wake, William, 426
Wakefield, Edward Gibbon, 818
Wales, 10, 31, 111, 255, 459, 580, 653, 668, 873, 905, 1255
Walpole, Horace, 41
Walpole, Sir Robert, 484, 505
Wanley, Humfrey, 60
War, 174, 178–80, 283–4, 536, 538–40, 544–7, 551, 619, 983–1017
Webb, Beatrice, 66, 697
Wellington, Arthur Wellesley, 1st duke of, 539
Wesley, John, 1242
Wharton, Philip, Lord, 397
Whitgift, John, 240
Whythorne, Thomas, 53

Wilberforce, William, 898–9
Wildman, John, 436
Wilkes, John, 479, 520
William III, 309, 394–6, 1302

Windsor, Edward, duke of, 937
Winthrop, John, 1238
Wolsey, Thomas, 75, 172
Wyvill, Christopher, 520

WITHDRAWAL

55097